Drake
Cumberland Foreside

P9-DIA-217

Garden Flowers
in Color

A spring garden path bordered with flowering bulbs and early perennials

GARDEN FLOWERS IN COLOR

BY

DANIEL J. FOLEY

Author, *Vegetable Gardening in Color*
Annuals for Your Garden
Co-author, *Garden Bulbs in Color*

NEW YORK
THE MACMILLAN COMPANY
1948

COPYRIGHT, 1943, BY
J. HORACE McFARLAND COMPANY

All rights reserved—no part of this book may be reproduced in
any form without permission in writing from the publisher, except
by a reviewer who wishes to quote brief passages in connection
with a review written for inclusion in magazine or newspaper.

Fifth Printing 1948

❀

PRINTED IN THE UNITED STATES OF AMERICA

Completely produced by
J. HORACE McFARLAND COMPANY
MOUNT PLEASANT PRESS
HARRISBURG, PA.

INTRODUCTION

EVERY flower shown in color in this book has been successfully grown in some garden in eastern America and can
be grown as well or better in other gardens. Before it was
granted a place in this cyclopedia of garden possibilities, every
subject, whether an annual or a perennial, a shrub, a rose, or a
tree, was first challenged as to its true usefulness in the American
garden world. If it met the author's high standard in this
particular, its availability in general horticultural commerce
was then considered, as well as its garden habit, and what insects, diseases, and climatic conditions affect it adversely. If
the findings were favorable, it was admitted.

Not every subject included scored one hundred per cent in
this rigorous method of selection, but it is believed that the
general average is so high that the reader who is willing to be
guided in the designing of garden improvements by what is
herein presented, will be definitely helped.

The illustrations, for the most part, are from photographs in
color taken in a notable garden in central Pennsylvania, the
Breeze Hill Garden in Harrisburg. Into this garden for thirty

years, I have been gathering many species and varieties of plants which seem to offer real advantages to the aspiring gardener and which also serve as subjects for garden pictures. The material covers more than 350 genera and approximately 1,300 species, not including the more than 800 species and varieties of roses which a quarter-century's relation to the American Rose Society has made possible. Breeze Hill includes the carefully labeled specimens which have given point to many of Mr. Foley's selections.

However, this work is most distinctly not a mere cyclopedic putting together of plant pictures. It very definitely endeavors to inform the beginner how he may grow both rare and familiar garden flowers.

Not only have care and maintenance been in the author's mind, but also simple instructions on garden planning. As bugs and bothers are always with us, their control has been thoughtfully considered.

J. Horace McFarland

Harrisburg, Pa.
July 23, 1943

CONTENTS

GARDEN FLOWERS IN COLOR

In our enthusiasm to grow plants and to plan colorful beds and borders we must not overlook the importance of a well-kept lawn. Great stretches of velvety green grass are needed to make a setting for bright-colored blooms and to tie together the various parts of the garden. Well-prepared soil containing some organic matter to keep the roots moist is every bit as necessary as the best seed that can be obtained. Summer care, which includes watering, cutting, and weeding, must not be neglected. Many home gardeners cut their grass too close in summer; the usual result is a crop of the much-detested annual crab grass.

GARDEN FLOWERS IN COLOR

Color in the Garden

In the pages of a book like this, which is intended to be somewhat encyclopedic in scope, there is little room for the expression of personal likes and dislikes. Hence a chapter on color in the garden can merely introduce the amateur gardener to the limitless possibilities of creating living pictures with plants. In his book "The Study of Color," the distinguished artist Michel Jacobs states, "Color is only a ray of light reflected back to our eyes." But no two people see color alike, and each one of us has his own idea of what is a red rose or what color is blue. Some people are color-blind, and as far as they are concerned there is not a great deal that can be said about color.

However, color in its various forms is known to have remarkable psychological effects on people. For example, an over-abundance of red is known to excite a feeling of ill-will among both men and animals. On the other hand, there are many people who like any color, "so long as it's red." Blue is noted for its soothing, tranquil effect, but too much of it in house or garden often has a depressing effect. Pure yellow and its light tints are much to be desired for their delicacy and ethereal beauty. White flowers (all too little appreciated in gardens, especially by beginners) give us a source of light which serves to separate and intensify the brilliant colors and even the pastel shades.

To guide us in selecting harmonious colors, there are several well-known color charts, among them the famous Ridgway chart, which has long been a standard color reference in the United States. Unfortunately it is now out of print, and available copies are expensive. Most recent of all is the two-volume chart of the Royal Horticultural Society. In addition, there are numerous less-complicated charts and wheels which are often used by amateur gardeners in working out color schemes for their gardens and more particularly in creating pleasing combinations for flower arrangements.

In selecting varieties of flowers for the home garden, most amateurs are guided primarily by their own tastes. The so-called clashing colors that are sometimes seen in gardens are disturbing to color-sensitive people. As a result, we often hear the statement made that one should never grow magenta phlox or any other magenta flowers. However, great masses of magenta flowers used with white are often very pleasing. It is only when this so-called magenta color appears with violet, red, and orange that it is particularly distasteful, or again with

A rose garden brings delight for many months

GARDEN FLOWERS IN COLOR

certain shades of blue. Beginners often make mistakes in trying to plant elaborate color arrangements in gardens, but experience in working with plants, whether to achieve pleasing color combinations, a well-planned border, or merely a good garden, is the best teacher.

Seedsmen and nurserymen list many desirable varieties of annuals, perennials, flowering bulbs, shrubs, trees, and vines, and for the most part few undesirable colors are offered. In recent years plant hybridizers have introduced numerous improved forms of plants, with the result that the poor kinds are rapidly being weeded out. Every experienced gardener knows, and most amateurs soon learn, that plants of good quality, correctly named, cost little more than do those offered on bargain counters; but the little extra cost is indeed worthwhile.

ONE-COLOR GARDENS

Gardens planted with flowers of one color have provided a delightful hobby for many amateurs who have the space and time to devote to such specialties. We sometimes read interesting stories of blue, or red, or white, or gray, or even green gardens. It is only when great quantities of flowers of one color are assembled that we realize the amazing variations in nature of the tints and shades of the basic colors. To the uninitiated the very idea of a green garden may have little or no appeal, and yet green is the dominant color in the landscape during the growing season. A green garden composed of ground covers, trees, and evergreens of various types and kinds is restful and surprisingly varied, especially where there is a change of light and shade provided by well-spaced trees. Something too should be said about shadows, which are rich in purple tones and often change the appearance of blooms and foliage. Shade is an important factor in the garden. In the pages that follow, special mention is made of the wide variety of plants that flourish in shady places.

PLANTING COLOR PICTURES IN THE GARDEN

There are several ways in which a beginner can attempt to plan a colorful garden. Perhaps the best thing to do is to spend considerable time studying well-planned gardens before you attempt an adventure of your own. Many home-owners have achieved amazing results in comparatively small areas by carefully selecting plants which are attractive the year round. Experienced gardeners know that a colorful garden depends not so much upon a great variety of plants as upon the proper selection and placing of color masses. In days gone by, the notion of a garden was to have plants of as many species and varieties as you could cram into a given space. To the enthusiastic horticulturist

Hardy phlox and hemerocallis provide dominant color in summer gardens

such a garden may be the realization of a dream, but the color effects are usually spotty and confusing.

Having studied well-planned gardens, the next job is to become acquainted with plants, their habit of growth, their soil preferences, their general cultural requirements, their hardiness, and their ability to stand up under extreme weather conditions. Many charming plans for gardens have been created, but not all of them are easy to work out under all climatic conditions; for example, the particular shade of blue selected may be some rare gentian which could not possibly live through an eastern summer. In making a perennial border or an annual garden it is best to work with plants that are known to be hardy and adaptable. As you acquire skill and experience, you can add choicer plants, but it is a great mistake to order all the unusual novelties and the rare plants until you have grown the more familiar kinds. Most amateur gardeners find that more than half the fun of gardening comes from learning to know the individual requirements of particular plants. Color combinations are easy to plan.

Foxgloves, Canterbury bells, and sweet william make a pleasing combination

GARDEN FLOWERS IN COLOR

COLOR IN THE SPRING GARDEN

A drift of twenty-five or more yellow crocuses planted near a Mugho pine or any other dwarf evergreen will provide a satisfying mass of color in the early spring garden. An effect like this can often be achieved near a low-growing evergreen in the foundation planting where it can be enjoyed from a window.

Groups of five or more white tulips planted near a deep pink tree peony make an unforgettable picture. Drifts of blue pansies or forget-me-nots in the foreground provide the final flourish.

Tulips are usually dominant flowers in late spring gardens. When they are planted in groups in perennial borders they can be combined effectively with great clumps of bleeding-heart, *Dicentra spectabilis*. When pink and white tulips are used, the blue-flowering forms of Dutch iris add to the combination. Pink and white English daisies or pansies in pastel shades can be used for an edging.

Often an early-flowering tree is the center of attention in the spring garden. Large informal masses of narcissus are particularly delightful at the base of *Magnolia Soulangeana*. Tulips in front of specimen lilacs or a large plant of *Rosa Hugonis* make a pleasant mass of color.

In iris-time when the Germanica iris is in flower, we think of peonies and Oriental poppies. Since all bloom at the same time and an amazing number of varieties are available, this group of plants offers a challenge to many home gardeners.

ROSE-TIME IN THE GARDEN

When roses are planted in informal groups or close to the house, it is best to select three or more plants of one variety instead of one each of several varieties. This type of grouping is done primarily to obtain a mass of color, which is never so pleasing when varieties of different heights are used as when all of one kind are grouped together. Climbing roses trained on trellises, posts, or arbors are often planted in conjunction with bush kinds, and many beautiful effects can be achieved even in modest gardens. Clumps of delphiniums planted near climbing roses are always attractive.

EARLY SUMMER BORDERS

We are all familiar with the gaily colored borders in English gardens. Sometimes they are difficult to achieve because they require considerable care and an early start the previous year in order to obtain plants of blooming size. This is particularly true with the dominant groups of plants used in early summer borders, which include Canterbury bells, foxglove, sweet william, and delphinium, but they

Hardy chrysanthemums produce an abundance of bloom in autumn

GARDEN FLOWERS IN COLOR

15

are worth an effort. In planning a border where perennials are to be used, care must be taken to group the various kinds of plants in order to avoid a tiered or monotonous effect.

COLOR IN LATE SUMMER

At this time of year we are dependent for color mostly on the annuals and such perennials as hardy phlox, hemerocallis, and some lesser-grown kinds which ought to be more widely planted. Mention should be made, too, of the summer-flowering bulbs such as ismene, the lovely white *Hyacinthus candicans*, the calla lilies, the gladiolus, and montbretias. All of these summer-flowering bulbs are of easy culture and are particularly attractive in their season. In addition to providing great masses of color, all are suitable cut flowers. Special attention should be paid to lilies. The goldband lily and *Lilium Henryi* bloom with the platycodons. The plantain-lily, sometimes called the August lily, is a source of fragrant, white, trumpet-shaped blooms.

AUTUMN IN THE GARDEN

The smell of burning leaves, the fragrance of ripe apples, and the great heads of the purple asters are reminiscent of autumn. Flowers are on the wane at this time of year, but we can always depend upon the French and African marigolds and those choicest of all fall-flowering perennials, the Japanese anemones. The hardy chrysanthemums, available in numerous colors and forms, are the mainstay of the autumn garden. There is also the abundant color provided by the berried shrubs, some of which have brilliantly tinted foliage as well. Most familiar of all the shrubs are the flowering dogwoods, the many viburnums, the numerous forms of euonymus, and in mild climates the showy scarlet firethorn. A wide variety of flowering and berried shrubs are now being featured by leading nurserymen.

COLOR IN THE WINTER GARDEN

In winter we must rely upon a variety of green tones provided by the broad-leaved and coniferous evergreens, the colorful twig growth of familiar shrubs, and such fruits as the birds leave on trees and shrubs. Two plants not mentioned elsewhere in this book deserve a word here because of their distinctive beauty. The first is the Christmas-rose, *Helleborus niger*, a late-blooming perennial which sends forth its first flowers in November but usually can be depended upon to bloom at Christmas-time, and even later. (In severe climates it can be carried over in a coldframe.) The other is a curious winter-flowering shrub —the witch-hazel, with fanciful yellow blooms in cold January.

America's Favorite
Garden Flowers

ABELIA

This glossy-leaved shrub often grows 6 feet or more if not kept within bounds by pruning shears. Some gardeners use it in their foundation plantings; others shear it as a formal accent plant or as a hedge. It can be kept as dwarf as a foot in height, or allowed to make a tall green fence.

Although Abelia is a native of Mexico, it can be grown over a large part of the country, and has become one of the most desirable of all summer-flowering shrubs. Throughout the warm months appear loose clusters of bell-shaped white flowers, flushed pink, with reddish sepals surrounding each bloom. In autumn the rich foliage turns lustrous bronze.

An easy-to-grow shrub, *Abelia grandiflora* will flourish in full sun or partial shade where the soil is well drained. Another point in its favor is that it is seldom attacked by insects. An evergreen in mild climates and reported hardy as far north as the Great Lakes, it sometimes dies back during severe winters. Since flowers are produced on new wood, it can be pruned severely without harming the plant.

AGERATUM

Sometimes called Floss-flower, this tender annual with its clusters of fluffy, tassel-like blooms stands high on the list of garden flowers. For edging beds and borders or for window boxes, the dwarf blue *Ageratum Houstonianum* in any of its varieties can be used for a continuous display of color from early summer until frost. Both tall and dwarf kinds are listed in seed catalogs. The 18-inch sorts are delightful cut flowers; dwarf kinds vary from 4 to 9 inches. Several shades of blue, white, silvery gray, and pink are included in the extensive color range of this annual, but the blue forms are most popular. In the fall just before frost you can pot plants of the dwarf varieties and take them indoors for several weeks' additional blooming. In late winter, flowering plants for window gardens can be purchased from florists.

The seed of Ageratum is very fine and needs only a light covering. It can be started indoors in a flower pot or outside in a hotbed or cold-frame, and the seedlings transplanted as soon as they are large enough to handle. In regions where the garden season is long, the seed can be started in the open ground, but not until all danger of frost has passed. Space the small kinds 6 to 8 inches apart and allow 10 to 12 inches between the tall-growing varieties. Plants grown from cuttings of the dwarf varieties will produce specimens of uniform height for edging. Ageratum does best in rich soil that holds moisture well, but is not desirable for hot dry places because the plants are so shallow-rooted that they wilt easily.

GARDEN FLOWERS IN COLOR

FLOWERING ALMOND

If your garden is small and there is room for only a few shrubs, don't overlook the pink Flowering Almond. The graceful branches of this old-fashioned shrub are admirable as cut flowers and lend themselves well to line arrangements. The Flowering Almond, which is related to the peach and the cherry, usually grows only 4 to 6 feet high, but sometimes reaches the proportions of a small tree. Both pink and white forms are listed by nurserymen but the pink kind, under the name *Prunus glandulosa* or *P. triloba*, is the more popular. It makes a colorful display in early spring, with its tiny double flowers borne in profusion all along the branches at the time its leaves are opening.

An underplanting of English daisies, pansies, forget-me-nots, early tulips in pastel shades, white-flowering narcissus, or blue phlox with a pink Flowering Almond as the center of interest makes an unforgettable garden picture. In the shrub border this charming, showy plant belongs in the foreground because its flower-studded branches are borne close to the earth.

Full sun and well-drained garden soil are its simple requirements. The Flowering Almond can be pruned heavily immediately after flowering to assume a symmetrical form if you want it for formal use. Sometimes the plants are attacked by borers; this trouble is easily determined by a wilting of the foliage. Examine the stems carefully to locate the opening made by the borer; then poke a wire into the opening and push it as far as you can to eliminate the pest. Plants in full foliage have often been saved by this simple treatment. Cut back the damaged branches and follow with a thorough watering. Plants can be set out in early spring or late fall; they have been found hardy over practically the whole country. No fruit or nuts are produced by this ornamental shrub, although it is related to the true almond.

ALTHEA

The Shrub-althea, or Rose-of-Sharon, is a large shrub or small tree which may vary in height from 4 to 12 feet. A word about plant names is in point here, because the common name of this shrub, Althea, is also the botanical name of the Hollyhock, to which it is related. Many nursery catalogs list this plant as *Hibiscus syriacus*, its scientific name. Often associated with old-time gardens, it is decorative in large shrub borders or as a specimen; its flowering season extends from July to September. All too often in unkept gardens we see specimens of an ugly magenta form, but there are many fine hybrids with both single and double flowers in pure white, pink, rose, and red tones.

A vigorous grower, Althea will thrive in any well-drained soil, but grows best in full sun. It is easily pruned and often requires cutting back because of its unusually rapid growth. One objection to this shrub on the part of many gardeners, especially those with limited space, is the fact that it sets seed in great quantities and can become something of a weed if not kept under control. Removing the dead flowers is the solution.

ALYSSUM

Madwort is the common name of Alyssum, because in bygone days it was believed that an infusion made from certain forms would overcome anger. Both perennial and annual kinds are widely grown. Of the perennial types, *Alyssum saxatile*, known as Golden-tuft or Basket-of-gold because of its bright yellow masses of bloom, is often seen in spring rock and wall gardens. Several pale yellow forms are also available from most nurserymen.

The annual kinds, like the compact lavender form shown here, and the dwarf white one known as Little Gem, are ideal for edgings and borders. The annual Sweet Alyssum is no longer listed by botanists under the scientific name Alyssum, but rather as *Lobularia maritima*.

Alyssum is of the simplest culture. The perennial species can be started from seed in a coldframe or from cuttings rooted in sand and peat. Seed of both perennial and annual forms can be sown thinly in the open ground as early as the soil can be prepared. For border effects the annual seedlings should be thinned or transplanted to stand 4 to 6 inches apart, but the perennial sorts need at least a foot or more between plants. Full sun and ordinary soil fill its needs. In midsummer the plants often become ragged in appearance but they can be revived by shearing to encourage new growth.

Annual Alyssum, Lavender Queen

ANCHUSA

This vigorous-growing perennial, sometimes called Alkanet or Bug-loss, is characterized by its intense blue flowers. The commonest kinds in gardens are *Anchusa azurea*, which reaches 4 to 5 feet in height, and the low-growing *A. capensis*, a biennial form grown in many home gardens as an annual. Curiously enough, the most popular species, *A. myosotidiflora*, is now classified by botanists under the name of *Brunnera macrophylla*. Call it what you will, it is one of the hardiest of hardy perennials, making a first-rate ground-cover plant in sun or shade, and is often used to good advantage under apple and other fruit trees in the garden. The clusters of large forget-me-not-blue flowers shown here are borne in early spring. For striking color effects, *A. myosotidiflora* can be interplanted with daffodils, since both bloom at the same time. When full grown the plant assumes a somewhat coarse appearance, with large heart-shaped leaves on 15-inch stems.

Plants can be set out in the spring or fall in full sun or partial shade, spacing them at least a foot apart. Gardeners who need quantities of it can grow it from seed. Established plants self-sow readily and the tiny seedlings can be transplanted to other parts of the garden.

Anchusa myosotidiflora (Brunnera)

GARDEN FLOWERS IN COLOR

Anemone coronaria

ANEMONE

Commonly called Windflowers, some Anemones are indigenous to various parts of our own country and others are found in Europe and Asia. Pages could be devoted to stories about their native haunts and their historical associations. Perhaps the most picturesque of all is the lovely *Anemone coronaria*, known as St. Brigid's Anemone, which Biblical scholars tell us is the true Lily-of-the-field. In early spring rock gardens the Pasque Flower, *A. Pulsatilla*, is a choice favorite, and during the summer months many of the native species bloom in wild gardens. Autumn brings us the stately Japanese kinds.

Everyone who has seen the brilliant red, white, and blue blooms of *A. coronaria* at flower shows and in florist shops is anxious to enjoy them in the home garden. Unfortunately, the plants are extremely tender and must be heavily mulched over winter north of Washington, D. C. A well-drained location in sandy loam should be chosen if possible, and the tubers set 3 inches deep and 5 inches apart. Plantings of six or more will provide colorful bloom in May or June. In addition to the brilliance of the blooms, there is the added beauty of the curled parsley-like foliage.

In the spring garden there ought to be a shady corner for the little-known *A. apennina*, principally because of its delightful light blue, daisy-shaped flowers. This little bulbous plant appearing in late April seems to resent disturbance.

The blooms of Anemone hupehensis are similar to the Japanese kinds

A. Pulsatilla (sometimes listed as Pulsatilla) provides a double show of beauty, for it displays light purple, pink, or white chalice-shaped flowers in late April, followed by tasseled seed pods. These sun-loving plants, 6 inches high, have attractive foliage resembling carrot tops.

For shady spots in late spring and early summer there is the Snow-drop Anemone, *A. sylvestris*, with its shallow white, cupped flowers on stems a foot or more in height.

In September the Japanese Anemones bloom in all their exquisite array. Well-established plants grow 3 feet or more in height, producing double and semi-double flowers on long slender stems. The color range, in addition to white, includes a wide variety of pink and red tones. The low-growing *A. hupehensis*, averaging 15 to 18 inches in height, usually flowers before the taller Japanese kinds.

All the Anemones require a well-drained soil; loam rich in humus suits most of the species. *A. apennina* and *A. sylvestris* grow well in partial shade, but *A. Pulsatilla* seems to prefer rocky soil and full sun. The Japanese hybrids do well in rich loam with partial shade and protection from wind. Many of the Anemones will seldom need to be divided. Spring kinds are best moved after blooming and the autumn-flowering varieties should be moved in early spring.

ARMERIA

Sea-pink and Thrift are two familiar names for this group of plants, formerly known as Armeria and now classified as Statice. The kinds commonly listed in catalogs are hardy perennials. Of compact habit, the plants have grass-like foliage which makes an effective setting for the globular heads of bloom appearing from late spring to early summer. Some kinds like *Armeria Laucheana* seldom grow more than 6 inches tall; others attain a height of 2 feet. Several desirable strains are offered in the catalogs of our leading nurserymen.

In the rock garden or the foreground of a perennial border, the plants make an attractive display. Since they are quick to multiply, some gardeners like to use the more compact forms for edgings. Armeria can be expected to grow well in full sun in any well-drained soil; the clumps should be divided every two or three years in order to keep the plants thrifty. Otherwise the centers of the clumps decay, forming misshapen plants of ungainly habit.

Hybrid New England Aster

ASTER

Before plant names were systematized many species of hardy Asters flourished unnoticed in our own country, in Europe, and in Asia. About the time that young Linnaeus, the famous Swedish botanist, was beginning his great work of classifying plants, a Jesuit missionary discovered in China a delightful annual that we have come to know as the China Aster (listed botanically as Callistephus). Its common name sometimes causes confusion when you are referring to the Aster genus, which includes many worthwhile spring and fall-blooming types, most of which are long-lived hardy perennials.

In late May and early June the dainty *Aster alpinus* appears, with variations from rich violet to white available in the named varieties. The plants usually grow 6 to 9 inches high. Somewhat taller and later is *A. subcaeruleus*, with its large single light blue flowers. Of hybrid origin is the new favorite *A. Frikarti*, with large violet-blue flowers accentuated with bright yellow centers. The form Wonder of Staefa blooms over a long period from early midsummer through late autumn. The plants average 2 feet in height, with a tendency to spread.

The fall-blooming hardy Asters or Michaelmas Daisies are usually considered in three distinct groups. The Novi-Belgi, or New York Asters, 3 to 6 feet tall, are distinguished by their bushy growth and their long branching sprays of white, blue, purple, pink, or red bloom.

Similar in bloom but differing slightly in foliage are the Novae-Angliae or New England Asters, with flowers in great terminal clusters. For large shrub borders and for background effects in perennial gardens these tall hardy Asters are ideal. The plants can be kept compact by pinching the top of each stem, an operation which may well be done several times during the growing season. By dividing the plants every two years they can be kept in vigorous condition.

Additional color in autumn gardens is provided by the new dwarf Asters, which are rarely more than a foot in height. They are very compact in habit, especially free flowering, and may be used for edging.

Asters are among the hardiest of perennials, growing well in almost any well-drained area in full sun. The spring-flowering varieties need to be divided every two or three years after they have bloomed. Fall-flowering kinds are best divided in early spring.

The annual China Asters, in a multitude of forms, have long been favorites in the home garden, where they provide a colorful display over a long period and are among the most adaptable of flowers for cutting. Wilt-resistant strains are now offered by all reliable seedsmen.

Aster Frikarti   New York Aster

GARDEN FLOWERS IN COLOR

Improved Crego strain of China Aster

GARDEN FLOWERS IN COLOR

Dwarf fall-blooming hardy Aster

Seed catalogs divide Asters into several distinct types on the basis of their flower structure, their habit of growth, and their period of bloom. Giant California, reaching 3 feet in height, has large blooms with curled and interlaced petals. Then there are the Peony-flowered Asters, the Beauty Asters, as well as such early types as the Comet, Early Express or Early Wonder, Astermum, Ostrich Feather, and Giant Comet. Especially favored are the Improved Crego varieties. Some seedsmen offer strains of Queen of the Market, Royal, Invincible, American Branching or Vick's Branching, King, and Aurora varieties with quilled petals. The Pompon types which resemble button chrysanthemums are also worthy of mention, and so too are the several types of single Asters. Especially distinctive in this group are the California Sunshine hybrids with richly crested centers.

Seed of China Aster may be sown indoors or in a coldframe for early bloom, or it may be planted in the open ground. Asters grow best in rich sandy loam. In transplanting the seedlings to the garden, bear in mind the mature height of particular varieties and allow at least half that space between individual plants. By purchasing seed of wilt-resistant varieties you can be reasonably assured of success. Wherever diseased plants are discovered, they should be removed and burned at once. Root aphids, which may attack the roots of young plants, may be controlled by digging tobacco dust into the soil.

ASTILBE

Familiarly known in old-time gardens as Spirea, *Astilbe japonica* with its glossy foliage and white blooms was often used to border garden walks. The name Spirea is used to refer to those plants known scientifically as Astilbe, Aruncus, Ulmaria, and Filipendula, as well as to the many shrubby forms of the true genus Spirea. All the Astilbes are long-lived hardy perennials, varying in height from 2 to 5 feet. In addition to the common white form, there are numerous hybrids in tones of pale pink, crimson, reddish purple, and salmon; perhaps the most vivid of all is the lovely hybrid Fanal shown on this page.

The feathery flower spikes hold up well in the garden, and the plants make a sturdy mass of clean and attractive foliage. They are effective accents in shrub or perennial plantings in either full sun or part shade.

Rich moist soil suits Astilbe best. Hot dry locations should be avoided since the plants need quantities of water. It is an easy matter to keep the clumps in your garden thrifty by dividing them every three years; set the plants out in either spring or fall.

GARDEN FLOWERS IN COLOR

Ghent Hybrid Azalea

AZALEA

Azaleas have few rivals in the plant world. When we consider that the flowers vary in color from the most brilliant red to palest yellow and white, with lavender and purple shades also included, we can hardly complain if there is no true blue variety. Those who vacation in the South each year are familiar with the great Azalea gardens in Florida and Alabama, in Charleston, and in the famous Middleton and Magnolia Gardens. Throughout the East and especially in the Middle Atlantic States, both wild and cultivated Azaleas flourish.

In classifying plants, botanists have grouped Azaleas with rhododendrons, but for convenience they are discussed separately in this book. There are two broad groups: the evergreen forms and those that lose their leaves, usually listed in catalogs as deciduous Azaleas.

Because they are a part of our natural landscape the native Azaleas deserve consideration first. The Pinxterbloom Azalea, *A. nudiflora*, with pink blooms in April and May, depending on the locality, is usually found along streams and grows 6 feet tall or more. Very similar and even more fragrant is *A. nudiflora rosea*. Undoubtedly the most spectacular cf all our native Azaleas is *A. calendulacea*, most appropriately called Flame Azalea. The rich color range extends from pale to deepest yellow, through the gold and orange tints. Native plants reach 10 feet in height. Those who have tramped in the woods during June or July are surely familiar with the swamp honeysuckle—the Swamp Azalea, *A. viscosa*. The pale pinkish white flowers on plants 4 to 7 feet high, are among the most sweetly fragrant of all early summer-flowering shrubs. Then there is *A. arborescens*, the Sweet Azalea, with pale pink or white flowers borne on most vigorous plants. Known for its delightful fragrance, this shrub also provides colorful autumn foliage. One of the first to bloom in spring is the Pink-shell Azalea, *A. Vaseyi*, with clusters of soft pink fading to white.

The Oriental Azaleas which shed their leaves at the close of each season are a fascinating group. *A. altaclarensis*, the Altaclaire Azalea, is a plant of great beauty with large heads of deep orange bloom changing to a warm yellow. Notable for its delicate range of color,

An attractive planting of Azalea Kaempferi in full bloom

GARDEN FLOWERS IN COLOR

Evergreen Azaleas flourish in the lower South

from pale yellow to golden salmon, is the Chinese Azalea, *A. mollis*, best planted in part shade to retain the brilliance of its coloring.

In May the Royal Azalea, *A. Schlippenbachi*, produces pale pink flowers sometimes 3 inches across. Although very hardy, this plant is sometimes difficult to establish in the garden. If a partially shaded location is provided, the foliage will not burn in summer; in autumn it turns crimson and gold. *A. yodogawa* produces a large bushy plant which is semi-evergreen in mild climates. The double purplish blooms are attractive, but the color is a bit difficult to combine with others and is best placed by itself in the garden or associated with some white-flowering form. *A. poukhanensis* has large single flowers with conspicuous spots and is in the same color range.

Bouquet de Flore - pink-white 12" ⎫ Cherry Hill
Raphael de Smet - double-soft pink 12" ⎭

The famous Ghent hybrids, also called Pontica and Rustica hybrids, are among the choicest deciduous Azaleas for the Northeast. Curiously enough, they are not satisfactory in the lower South where the Indian Azaleas and other evergreen kinds flourish. There are many named varieties from 4 to 6 feet high or more which bloom in May, varying from palest yellow to vermilion.

The hardy evergreen Azaleas are among the most colorful of flowering shrubs, and many of them assume rich reddish and bronze tints in the fall. The following list includes some of the outstanding ones.

Many fascinating stories could be told about the introduction of the Indian Azaleas or so-called Indica hybrids, which were developed in Europe from several Asiatic kinds and brought to this country more than a century ago. The numerous varieties that have been developed are the dominant kinds grown in the gardens of the lower South. A few are hardy over a wide latitude, even in the colder regions of the eastern United States. One of the most desirable is *A. ledifolia alba*, which will attain a height of 5 feet and develop a plant as wide. The single pure white blooms are unusually large and are borne freely. Also attractive is the form known as *A. ledifolia rosea magnifica*, producing white flowers with carmine blotches and markings in the throat.

The showy blooms of an Azalea mollis hybrid

GARDEN FLOWERS IN COLOR

35

Azalea mollis hybrids planted with Scilla campanulata

The famous Kurume Azaleas were introduced to America by the late Dr. E. H. Wilson of the Arnold Arboretum. Most of these richly colored hybrids average 2½ to 3 feet in height and width, although a few eventually grow as tall as 6 feet. There are many named varieties, with both single and double flowers; the plants are slow, compact growers that bloom profusely.

Among the more familiar forms are *A. amoena*, reaching a height of 6 feet, with double rosy purple blooms in May. A difficult color in the garden, it must be used with discretion. *A. Benigiri* is a fiery red hybrid. One of the most popular of all the evergreen Azaleas is *A. Hinodegiri*, with scarlet-crimson blooms in such profusion as to conceal the foliage. A clear light pink variety blooming about the same time is *A. Hinomoyo*. The brilliant blooms of all such plants need masses of white to help accentuate the colors and to separate clashing hues.

Because of its late flowering habit and its orange-red blooms, as well as its low growth, *A. macrantha* is a very desirable addition to any Azalea collection. Hybrids of this form recently developed help materially to prolong the season of bloom. Another outstanding Azalea is *A. Maxwelli*, valued for its extreme hardiness and its deep rose coloring. A delightful companion for this Azalea is the new white form.

Practically all of the evergreen Azaleas assume a broad spreading habit, but *A. Kaempferi* is broadly columnar in form and makes delightful accents in a shrub border. The salmon-red blooms will retain their color much longer if the plants are grown in part shade. *A. rosaeflora* (*balsaminaeflora*) is a pygmy member of the family, so to speak, seldom reaching more than 10 inches in height. It forms a low

A colorful border of evergreen Azaleas

GARDEN FLOWERS IN COLOR

compact mass of evergreen foliage with double salmon-pink rosettes of bloom. This very attractive dwarf shrub needs a sheltered location.

There are several important factors to be considered in growing Azaleas successfully. Avoid windswept areas and sloping exposures, especially for the evergreen kinds. Soil that retains moisture well and keeps the roots cool is ideal. The competition offered by surface tree roots will quickly rob them of the plant food they need. Azaleas need a sour or acid soil, but neutral or sweet soils can be made acid by incorporating peat moss, pine needles, and oak-leaf mold, which also promote the growth of fine roots. Aluminum sulphate can also be used to create an acid reaction. The usual recommendation is a half-pound for each square yard of soil. Scatter it on the ground and water with a fine spray.

In areas where winters are severe, the ideal time to plant Azaleas is in early spring. Plants set out in late summer should be mulched and given protection during freezing weather. Protection may be in the form of evergreen boughs or a framework covered with burlap. In setting out Azalea plants, dig a hole larger than is needed for the individual ball of earth. Add a mixture of peat and soil and set the plants at the same distance at which they grew in the nursery; cultivation of any kind is injurious to the roots.

A large-flowered evergreen Azalea

GARDEN FLOWERS IN COLOR

BACHELORS-BUTTON

The familiar Bachelors-button, *Centaurea Cyanus*, is also known as Cornflower and Blue-bottle, and in addition there are several related species that are favorites for the home garden. For instance, the Basket-flower, *C. americana*, growing wild in the desert sands of our southern states, bears large shaggy pink blossoms on stiff 3-foot stems. Another is the fluffy Sweet Sultan, which is discussed on page 256.

The Bachelors-button, one of the commonest flowers grown in American gardens, is a hardy annual which self-sows readily, sometimes to the point of becoming a pest. In addition to several rich blue shades there are white, ruby-red, and rose forms of equal beauty. Tall-growing kinds often reach 3 feet in height but in recent years dwarf varieties averaging a foot tall have been introduced.

Full sun and ordinary soil are the requirements for Bachelors-button. For best results and early bloom, the seed can be sown in the open garden in late fall. The young seedlings are not always easy to transplant; when moving them, be sure to leave as much soil as possible with the roots and set them 10 to 12 inches apart. The blooming season can be prolonged by keeping the dead flowers picked off. In spring, seed can be sown as soon as the soil is prepared. For a continuous supply of cut flowers throughout the season, several sowings can be made at intervals of two weeks.

Balloon-flower

BALLOON FLOWER

Blue Platycodon combined with *Lilium Henryi* makes a delightful combination in July and August. Plants of *Platycodon grandiflorum* average 2½ to 3 feet in height, with clusters of single blooms in light blue, violet, white, and lavender-pink. Tall double forms and dwarf kinds are likewise interesting.

Full sun or partial shade suits Platycodon. It is slow to appear in the spring and care must be taken not to dig it out by mistake. Seed planted in May or June will produce plants of blooming size the next year.

BALSAM

When in full bloom, this old-fashioned annual, which has been cultivated in gardens for generations, has the appearance of a miniature flowering tree. Offered as *Impatiens Balsamina*, it is sometimes called Touch-me-not because the ripe seed pods snap open when touched, scattering the tiny round seeds in all directions. There are varieties 2 feet tall, as well as a dwarf bush type.

Seed of this tender annual must not be planted in the open ground until all danger of frost has passed. For an early start, it may be sown indoors, or in a hotbed or coldframe. Set the plants 12 to 15 inches apart in full sun. Transplanting them several times makes them very compact.

BEAUTY-BUSH

Many fascinating plants have been brought to us from China, the mother of gardens. Among them is the Beauty-bush, *Kolkwitzia amabilis*. This vase-shaped shrub, reaching 10 feet in height and as much in diameter, is a rapid grower. The mildly fragrant, bell-shaped pink flowers, with conspicuous yellow throats, are borne in clusters on gracefully arching stems during May and June. The Beauty-bush makes a striking specimen plant, or it can be used in a shrub border. After the flowers pass, silky seed pods appear, prolonging the attractiveness of this admirable shrub.

Beauty-bush is extremely hardy and apparently resistant to insects and diseases. Ordinary soil suits it, and full sun. Because of its vigorous and rapid growth it may require severe pruning after its bloom period to keep it within bounds. Sometimes young plants take several years to become established before they produce a great amount of bloom, but they are worth waiting for.

GARDEN   FLOWERS   IN   COLOR

BEGONIA

Begonia gigantea

For the most part we think of Begonias as decorative house plants; however, there are several species and hybrids that adorn summer gardens. Among them is the hardy *Begonia Evansiana*, which flourishes in part shade and produces pink blooms in early autumn on 2-foot stems. The tender bedding kinds of free-flowering habit with colorful pink, red, and white blooms are often planted in public parks. Perhaps the most fascinating of all for their perfection of form and richness of color are the garden tuberous-rooted Begonias classified as *B. tuberhybrida*. The original forms of these plants were collected in shady subtropical ravines and moist woods. Canny gardeners have found them highly satisfactory for planting on the north side of a building or wall, as well as in shady nooks and under deep-rooted trees.

Many kinds of Tuberous-rooted Begonias are available. *B. gigantea* has large single flowers; *B. narcissiflora* produces large narcissus-type trumpets. A form with petals deeply cut and pleasingly waved and frilled is called *B. crispa*. In this class the Duplex type, with four smaller petals arranged within the larger set, has occurred. The crested type known as Cristata is distinctive. Camelliaeflora is identical in form with the lovely camellias of the South, but has a wider color range. *B. fimbriata plena* is the name of a double fringed form which reminds one of a carnation. There is even a hollyhock type listed as *B. Martiana*, with small single flowers of mallow-pink. Clusters of small flowers characterize the Multiflora type which is ideal for bedding or window boxes, and several named varieties of this excellent form are in the trade. *B. Lloydi*, commonly called the Hanging-basket Begonia, is popular for pots or window boxes, because of its loose drooping habit.

Six inches of rich soil, composed of equal parts of soil, leaf-mold or peat moss, and old stable manure or bonemeal, will provide an ideal growing medium. The succulent stems of the plants indicate the need for plenty of water. Begonias profit by occasional applications of liquid manure as the buds begin to form.

Tubers are best started in a greenhouse in pots or flats. If a green-

Begonia fimbriata plena

needed in dry weather. Occasional sprinkling of the foliage with a fine spray benefits the plants.

In late autumn, lift the tubers after their foliage has been nipped by frost. Do not remove the soil from the roots until they are thoroughly dry. Then store them over winter in a temperature of about 50 degrees in dry peat moss or sand for use the following year.

house is not available, place the tubers in a flat of moist sand and peat; cover to a depth of a half-inch. Cover the flat with burlap and set in a warm place until growth starts. When the shoots have grown an inch or two, transplant the tubers into pots and place them in a warm room or outdoors in a coldframe. Avoid sudden temperature changes or too much direct sunlight. When all danger of frost is past, the started tubers can be set out, an inch deep. Water the roots thoroughly at least once a week, and as

Begonia Camelliaeflora

GARDEN FLOWERS IN COLOR

Bleeding-heart, Dicentra spectabilis

BLEEDING-HEART

The old-fashioned Bleeding-heart, *Dicentra spectabilis*, is one of the important hardy perennials for the spring garden. Mature specimens grow 2 feet tall and often as broad, producing graceful stems of warm pink, heart-shaped bloom from April to June, depending upon the locality. Since the foliage dies back in summer, care must be taken to mark the location of the plants.

Another related species of Dicentra is Dutchmans-breeches, *D. Cucullaria*, one of our little-appreciated native plants growing a foot tall. Its drooping clusters of dainty creamy white flowers tipped with yellow appear in April. From May through August the Plumy Bleeding-heart, *D. eximia*, averaging 15 inches in height. makes a colorful display as a ground cover in partly shaded places, or in the rock garden. It needs only a fair amount of moisture.

Grown in full sun or partial shade, the Dicentras are of easy culture. Since they flower in spring and early summer, they should be set out in the fall; however, they can also be transplanted in early spring. Divide the clumps every three years to keep them vigorous.

GARDEN FLOWERS IN COLOR

BUTTERFLY-BUSH

Summer Lilac and Butterfly-bush are appropriate common names for the many kinds of Buddleia grown in gardens. The individual florets of the bloom spikes are similar in appearance to those of the common lilacs, and in summer the butterflies literally hover around this pleasing shrub. Although the purple-flowering species and hybrids of *Buddleia Davidi* are most familiar, nurserymen now offer varieties in lavender, pink, deep red, and pure white.

The attractive flower spikes on graceful stems have a soothing, sweet fragrance; the plant is vigorous in growth and blooms freely from July to late September. Bushes average 5 to 10 feet or more in height and are often as broad. Simple pruning and their natural habit of partial winter-killing help to restrain them.

The Buddleias are among the most useful and colorful of summer-flowering shrubs. They make a quick-growing informal hedge, or plants can be used in the shrub border or perennial planting.

Well-drained garden soil in full sun or part shade suits this plant. Ample space should be allowed for it—3 to 5 feet apart for hedge use, and 4 to 6 feet when individual specimens are desired.

Butterfly-bushes can be planted in the early spring or in the fall. In sections where the winters are severe, newly set plants can be hilled up with soil and mulched with leaves. During severe winters the plants may die back halfway or even to the ground. Prune back to live wood as soon as growth starts in the spring. Cuttings made in midsummer root easily in a mixture of sand and peat; they may be kept over the winter in a coldframe.

Also known as the "Sunne's Hearbe" and the "Sunne's Bride," the Calendula was the "Winking Mary-bud" in Shakespeare's play Cymbeline. Valued as a pot-herb, it was used also as a remedy for sore teeth and as "a comforter of the heart and spirits."

Calendula
Orange Shaggy

CALENDULA

The Common or Pot-marigold of old English gardens, *Calendula officinalis*, is a hardy annual steeped in tradition. A delightful cut flower, it is often grown by florists for winter decoration. The greatly improved double Calendulas that we grow today, averaging 18 to 24 inches in height, are a far cry from the old-time single ones. Not only have they been improved in size and color range—from pale lemon to brilliant orange—but pleasing kinds with quilled petals are now offered by seedsmen.

Among the varieties listed in catalogs are Campfire (Sensation), brilliant orange with a scarlet sheen. The rich yellow chrysanthemum-like flowers of Chrysantha or Sunshine brought this strain recognition in the All-America Selections. Then there are Orange Fantasy, with large orange blooms accentuated by mahogany centers, and Orange Shaggy, a loosely formed flower with irregularly arranged petals. Radio is distinguished for its deep yellow, quilled petals. In addition, there are several worthwhile strains and mixtures listed by most seedsmen; among them is a selection of pastel colors known as Art Shades. The wide variations found in packets of mixed seeds are always a pleasant surprise.

Few cultural directions are necessary since the seed germinates with ease in a greenhouse, in a coldframe, or in the open ground. Give the plants full sun and fertile soil, keep the seed pods pinched off, and allow a foot between plants. This annual often self-sows but in a sea-

Calendula, Chrysantha

son or two it will revert to the old single type. It grows best in cool weather; during hot spells the flowers are often inferior and the plants may be attacked by aphids. Spray with any convenient insecticide.

CALLA LILY

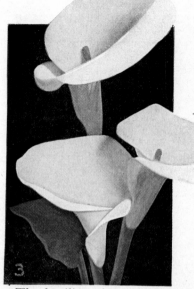

The familiar white Calla

We ordinarily think of Calla Lilies as florists' flowers, but they grow easily in gardens and bloom during the summer. Contrary to popular notions, they are not true lilies; botanists have classified them under the name of Zantedeschia. Yellow and white kinds averaging 2 to 3 feet tall, and a dainty pink form 12 to 15 inches high, are offered by seedsmen. A species listed as *Zantedeschia albo-maculata*, which is often planted in bog gardens, along streams, and in perennial borders, seems to be winter-hardy in mild climates. For showy effects, Calla Lilies should be planted in groups of five or more.

Roots can be started indoors in pots for early bloom and set out when all danger of frost has passed and the soil is warm. They can also be planted in the open ground. Rich moist soil containing an abundance of organic matter suits them, and they can be grown in sun or partial shade. When the frost has nipped the foliage in autumn, dig the roots and allow them to dry; they can be stored over winter like gladiolus in a cool dry place.

The yellow Calla

A mixture of Calliopsis

CALLIOPSIS

Calliopsis, or more correctly Coreopsis (see page 82 for perennial kinds), in its many forms is one of our most easily grown annuals. Garden enthusiasts are not always aware of the value of commonplace annuals like Calliopsis until some hybridizer puts forth an improved form. Such is the case with Calliopsis Golden Crest or Golden Crown, which received an Award of Merit from All-America Selections. It is an improved form of *Coreopsis Drummondi* producing a fair percentage of semi-double blooms. The plants are compact in form and bear large golden yellow flowers on slender stems 15 inches long. *C. tinctoria* produces clusters of flowers with rich crimson-maroon and brown markings. Many hybrid forms in shades of yellow, orange, and reddish brown, varying in height from 9 inches to 3 feet, are listed.

Few annuals are easier to grow from seed, and they self-sow readily, even to the point of becoming weeds. Ordinary garden soil and a situation in full sun are best. Plant Calliopsis in masses, scattering the seed broadcast or in straight rows in the cutting garden. For early flowers the seed can be sown in late fall (as with Bachelors-button), and for a supply of cut flowers seed can be planted in early spring and at frequent intervals during the season.

GARDEN FLOWERS IN COLOR

Few plants introduced to America have a richer historical and romantic appeal than the Camellia. Old specimens often reach a height of 20 feet or more, and sometimes young plants less than a foot tall produce blooms.

Kumasaka

Fanny Bolis

Caleb Cope

GARDEN FLOWERS IN COLOR

CAMELLIA

To gardeners in the eastern United States *Camellia japonica* is an exotic greenhouse plant with blooms favored for corsages. However, in many parts of the lower South this winter-flowering evergreen shrub, sometimes called simply Japonica, is widely grown outdoors.

Although Camellias are usually associated with azaleas, their soil requirements are not so exacting, for they can be grown in most ordinary garden soils. The plants produce their bloom from late October to May, depending upon variety and locality, in temperatures varying from 45 to 55 degrees. Along the eastern seaboard Norfolk, Virginia, seems to be their northern limit. In many parts of California and as far north as Oregon, Camellias grow abundantly. During some seasons many of the open blooms, especially the first crop, are damaged by frosts which seem to have no effect on tight buds.

Hundreds of varieties have been developed but there are many doubts as to correct names. Very often the color of the blooms varies greatly on individual plants, so that nomenclature is something of a problem. American growers are greatly indebted to the fine collections which have flourished at the famous Middleton Gardens in South Carolina for more than a hundred years. Other famous collections are to be found at the Bellingrath Gardens at Mobile, Alabama, the Magnolia Gardens on the Ashley River, and Gerbing's Azalea Gardens at Fernandina, Florida. There are many other notable Camellia gardens throughout the lower South and California.

Camellia catalogs contain descriptions of numerous varieties varying in color from white to deepest red, with many pink and variegated forms. Some are single, and others are semi-double with conspicuous clusters of yellow stamens. Among the true double kinds are flowers of rosebud and peony form, as well as the symmetric formal type.

Although Camellias have been found in a wide variety of soils, their preference is for fertile garden soil rich in organic matter. Well-decomposed stable manure is widely recommended both as a fertilizer and as a source of organic matter. The plants must have a well-drained location, and care must be taken when planting them to make sure the surface roots are level with the surrounding soil. In areas where drainage is a problem, they are generally grown in beds an inch or two higher than the adjoining level. Although the plants are usually moved in early fall, they can be transplanted at any time provided reasonable care is taken to lift them with a ball of earth. Water thoroughly after transplanting, and continue until they are well established. A mulch of peat moss, stable manure, or pine needles will help to conserve moisture.

Cup-and-saucer Canterbury Bells

CAMPANULA

Campanulas or Bellflowers, as they are appropriately called, have many uses in the garden. Some flourish in rock gardens and wall pockets; others belong in the perennial border, or in the foreground of the shrub planting. They bloom over a long period and vary in height from a few inches to 4 feet or more.

Especially adapted to wall gardens are the dwarf spreading kinds. *Campanula garganica*, from Italy, with its generous drifts of rich blue star-shaped flowers, seems to thrive best in wall crevices. *C. Portenschlagiana* (*muralis*) has tubular blossoms sometimes an inch long; like *C. garganica*, it flowers in early summer, and sometimes in autumn.

Somewhat taller are the forms of *C. carpatica*, the Carpathian Harebell. Shades of blue and white are available to provide color in the wall and rock garden during July and August. Another midsummer-blooming species is *C. rotundifolia*, the Bluebells of Scotland, which bears dainty blue flowers on fragile 15-inch stems.

In June and July when gardens are gay with sweet william, delphinium, madonna lilies, and foxglove, the showy Canterbury Bells lend a pleasing variety of color and form. The single kinds (*C. Medium*) in blue, pink, and white usually endure heavy rains more satisfactorily than the double and cup-and-saucer varieties, but all are worth growing. Since the plants average from 2 to 3 feet in height, with a tendency to send out many side shoots, they need to be staked. Unfortunately, Canterbury Bells are biennials rather than perennials, completing their life cycle in two years. This makes it necessary to start new plants from seed each year to provide a succession of bloom. Recently annual forms flowering in six months from seed were introduced to American gardens.

Many of the hardy Campanulas suitable for perennial gardens are little known, with the exception of the Peachbell, *C. persicifolia*. This sturdy perennial begins to flower in mid-June and carries on into July, supporting its large open bells on erect stems 2 to 3 feet tall. The name Peachbell refers to the clusters of peach-like foliage from which the stems rise. There are double-flowering forms in blue and white, as well as the usual single kinds. Another June-blooming species is *C. glomerata dahurica*, a compact form some 18 inches tall, with tight heads of purple bellflowers. *C. latifolia macrantha* grows 3 to 4 feet high in partly shaded places, and blooms freely during late June and July and sometimes into August. The large purple bell-like flowers are similar to those of the single Canterbury Bells, except for their loose arrangement. *C. lactiflora*, the Milky Bellflower, is easily distinguished from the

Carpathian Harebell (Campanula carpatica), Blue Carpet

GARDEN FLOWERS IN COLOR

similar-sounding *C. latifolia* by its compact clusters of shallow bell-shaped flowers on stems 2 to 3 feet tall. White, blue, and lavender forms are cultivated. They grow with ease in sun or partial shade, and bloom in early summer.

Seldom seen in small gardens is the stately *C. pyramidalis*, or Chimney Bellflower. From compact rosettes of foliage it sends up sturdy spires of distinctive star-shaped flowers in late July and August. Often the spikes tower 4 feet or more, providing the same type of accent in the August garden that foxgloves give earlier in the season. Blue and white-flowered kinds are available. Not infrequently the plants expend so much energy in producing flowers that they behave like biennials.

Campanulas have few specific requirements, thriving in ordinary soil where there is full sun or partial shade. The rock-garden kinds like *C. garganica* prefer a moist root run and seem to flourish in stony ground in the shadow of large stones. Bellflowers are easily raised from seed, which needs to be sown in late spring so that the seedlings are firmly established by early fall. With the exception of the biennial forms, new plants may be propagated by division in spring or fall.

Double Peachbell   Campanula garganica

GARDEN FLOWERS IN COLOR

Annual Globe Candytuft

CANDYTUFT

In rock and wall gardens and in perennial borders, hardy Candytuft provides masses of white in spring. Several hardy annual kinds reminiscent of Victorian gardens furnish cutting material from late spring through the summer. The perennial sorts, 8 to 10 inches tall, bloom from late April through June; the woody growth makes low spreading masses, with dark evergreen foliage. *Iberis sempervirens* is the common white kind, and several improved forms are obtainable.

Successive sowings of the hardy annual varieties can be made in the cutting garden, for they are rapid growing, with a comparatively short season of bloom. *I. amara*, the Rocket Candytuft, and *I. umbellata*, the Globe Candytuft, have produced the hybrid strains commonly grown. The Rocket form, with long white columnar flower spikes on 15-inch stems, is known as the Empress or Hyacinth-flowered type; the Globe form has flat flower heads of carmine, rose, and purple.

Full sun and rich well-drained soil suit the hardy Candytuft. Shear the plants after flowering, to encourage new growth. Established clumps can be divided after blooming or in early fall; new plants may also be started from seed sown in early June. Annual kinds can be sown outdoors in spring or fall; thin to stand 6 inches apart.

GARDEN FLOWERS IN COLOR

CANNA

Sometimes called Indian Shot because of the hard round seeds, Cannas used to be grown primarily for their showy foliage, but several French and American hybridizers improved the flowers so that now they are widely used for bedding in public parks and show places. The brilliant shades of red, pink, orange, and yellow are particularly striking when grouped in formal beds, and the large foliage in various shades of green and bronze provides an exotic effect. Like most tropical plants, Cannas are very tender and must be stored over winter like dahlias. Roots started in pots can often be obtained from florists in the spring.

Outstanding varieties are City of Portland, averaging 4 feet in height, with clear rose-pink flowers, King Humbert, a tall grower with brilliant orange-scarlet bloom and bronzy foliage, and Yellow King Humbert, a yellow form with blooms spotted orange. The salmon-pink Mrs. Alfred F. Conard and watermelon-pink Mrs. Pierre S. du Pont are popular; The President, of glowing scarlet, is a vigorous grower. Other named varieties include Mrs. Antoine Wintzer, a delightful yellow, the 6-foot Wintzer's Colossal, of bright scarlet, and Wyoming, with immense spikes of orange flowers with recurved petals.

Cannas grow best in deep, rich soil that holds moisture well. When flowers of good quality are desired, the soil should be prepared a foot or more in depth. To provide ideal drainage conditions, the bed should be crowned to a height of 4 to 6 inches above the level of the surrounding area. Set the plants 18 to 24 inches apart, according to the variety. They require an abundance of water during dry periods.

Mrs. Antoine Wintzer   Mrs. Alfred F. Conard   Wyoming

GARDEN FLOWERS IN COLOR

Cape-marigold, Dimorphotheca aurantiaca

CAPE-MARIGOLD

A hasty glance at the name Dimorphotheca gives little suggestion of the beauty of these gaily colored annual daisies from South Africa, usually called Cape-marigolds. Essentially a plant for the warm, sunny parts of the garden, the Cape-marigold is desirable for massed effects in borders, as a foreground planting for shrubs or perennials, with other annuals, or as a rock-garden plant. Other daisy-like flowers which have come to us from South Africa include the African Daisy, *Arctotis grandis* and the Transvaal Daisy, *Gerbera Jamesoni*.

The showy flowers, which tend to close at night, are borne on wiry stems a little more than a foot high. The spreading plants bloom profusely from early summer until frost cuts them down; best results are obtained where they can enjoy a long season. *Dimorphotheca aurantiaca* is brilliant orange with a dark center, and there are varieties bearing salmon and yellow flowers. The species *D. annua ringens*, of more dwarf habit, has grayish flowers with blue zonal markings.

Sow the seed where the plants are to grow, and thin them to stand 6 to 9 inches apart. In regions where the winters are mild, seed can be sown in the late fall; some kinds treated as annuals are actually perennials in warm climates. Since the plants bloom freely and are inclined to exhaust themselves, some gardeners make several sowings.

CARNATION

We call them Pinks or Carnations, but in bygone days they were known as Gillyflowers and Sops in Wine. Long cherished for their delightful spicy fragrance, garden Carnations, hybrids of *Dianthus Caryophyllus*, have been greatly improved in recent years. Many named varieties of the florist Carnations are grown in greenhouses, and in addition, there are numerous species and varieties widely used in rock gardens and perennial borders. (See Pinks, page 214, and Sweet William, page 257.) On this page we are concerned primarily with the annual and hardy perennial Carnations.

Carnations in the garden are not always satisfactory, particularly where the summers are extremely warm or damp. They prefer a cool, somewhat moist atmosphere. In rich loam they produce satisfactory results, even when planted in part shade.

Seed of both annual and perennial Carnations may be sown in a sunny window or in a hotbed during February, or later in a coldframe. Set the plants 9 to 12 inches apart in rich soil. Feed them occasionally with liquid manure, and remove all weak growth and seed pods. Small, healthy specimens of the hardy kinds usually grown in pots can be obtained from reliable nurserymen.

CASTOR-BEAN

A rather coarse-looking tropical annual, the Castor-bean (*Ricinus communis*) is hardly suitable for the small garden. As its common name suggests, it is a source of the much-detested castor-oil. While some forms are not more than 3 feet tall, others reach 12 feet or more, and in its native habitat the plant becomes a 40-foot tree. Its great palmate leaves, sometimes 3 feet across, spread over a large area. The oil is extracted from the fruit of the plant, which is comprised of three good-sized seeds within a capsule.

The Castor-bean is often planted in parks and public places, and home gardeners sometimes find it a useful plant where a quick-growing screen is desired. It makes an attractive, informal hedge and may well serve to provide temporary planting effects in newly developed areas. It grows so quickly that it helps to fill in empty places until the gardener decides what permanent planting he wants. In addition to the common kind with green foliage, there are varieties with bronzy foliage, others dark red, and one with spotted leaves.

The plants must have full sun and ample room to develop—at least 3 or 4 feet each way. Seed can be sown in the open ground after all danger of frost has passed. For an early start, plant the seed indoors or in a hotbed or coldframe.

GARDEN FLOWERS IN COLOR

CATANANCHE

The names Cupids-dart and Blue Succory are sometimes associated with this attractive summer-flowering hardy perennial. The variety *Catananche caerulea major*, illustrated on this page, is useful in the garden for its intense blue coloring, as well as indoors for its many decorative possibilities in flower arrangements. The plants average 1½ feet in height and flower freely from June to late August.

Catananche grows easily in ordinary garden soil and blooms best in full sun. Plants can be set out in early spring or in fall. Divide the clumps every two or three years.

FLOWERING CHERRY

The Flowering Cherries are among the most familiar trees in our nation's capital. Each year in April tourists from many parts of the country travel to Washington to see these spectacular trees in bloom, which were presented to the United States Government by the city of Tokyo in 1912. Most of the kinds offered by nurserymen are hybrids developed from several species, among them *Prunus serrulata*. They are offered in several forms, including broad spreading upright trees, weeping types, columnar specimens, and even dwarf varieties. Single and double forms in pink and white are grown.

Flowering Cherries flourish throughout the Eastern States with the exception of the far South and extreme North; they are also grown successfully on the Pacific coast. There are early, midseason, and late varieties, many of them bearing unpronounceable Oriental names. The late A. E. Wohlert of Narberth, Pennsylvania, developed several outstanding varieties which carry the Wohlert family name.

Full sun and ordinary well-drained garden soil suit the Flowering Cherries. They can be planted very early in spring or in the fall. Fall-planted specimens should be mulched the first winter, especially if they are in an exposed, windswept location. Most of the trees are grafted specimens, and care must be taken not to allow sucker growth to appear below the point of union. The space between trees depends upon the ultimate height of the variety.

The Flowering Cherries at Washington, D. C.

GARDEN FLOWERS IN COLOR

CHINESE LANTERN

Several common names are associated with the hardy perennial which most of us know as the Chinese Lantern-plant, *Physalis Alkekengi*. The name Physalis comes from the Greek, meaning "bladder," and the red fruits indicate its relationship to the common garden tomato. The less-familiar names Winter-cherry and Strawberry-tomato, refer to the tiny red fruit which is enclosed in the colorful seed pods. It is grown primarily for these showy orange-red pods. The stems, growing about 2 feet tall, are cut in the fall when the "lanterns" have turned color and are dried for winter decoration. In rich soil the plants may reach 3 to 4 feet in height.

The Chinese Lantern is a rapid-growing perennial which often becomes a pest because it multiplies by means of creeping underground stems. Its inconspicuous white flowers resemble those of the potato. Because of its vigorous growth it is not a desirable plant for the small garden, and most experienced gardeners are aware that places where it grows should be watched lest the plants take possession of the area at the expense of choicer perennials.

Ordinary garden soil suits this perennial; it grows best in full sun. Plants can be moved at any time, but are usually divided in early spring. To keep them from running rampant in the garden, all shoots growing out of bounds should be cut out with a sharp trowel.

The showy pods of the Chinese Lantern-plant

GARDEN FLOWERS IN COLOR

Burgundy, a double
Korean hybrid

CHRYSANTHEMUM

Delving into the flower lore of the Orient, we learn that the Chrysanthemum was cherished by the Chinese philosopher Confucius nearly 500 years before the Christian era. Many centuries later, more than forty volumes were written about this flower. Still later the plant was introduced into Japan, where it became the inspiration of a national holiday. But it was not until the close of the eighteenth century that it was taken to England, and many years passed before it was widely grown in America.

To most of us the name suggests a great variety of autumn-blooming flowers, some of which are hardy and others especially adapted to greenhouse culture. Botanists classify many familiar plants in this genus. Among them are several species of annual Chrysanthemums, Feverfew (*Chrysanthemum Parthenium*) and the familiar Ox-eye Daisy (*C. Leucanthemum*); Pyrethrum (*C. coccineum;* see page 224), the Pyrenees Daisy (*C. maximum*), and the Shasta Daisy, which is believed to be a hybrid of *C. Leucanthemum* (page 243).

Until a few years ago most of the garden varieties which were developed from the species *C. morifolium* and *C. indicum* were spoken of as forms of *C. hortorum*. Actually both the large-flowered greenhouse forms and the many garden kinds are included under this designation.

With the introduction of the famous Korean Chrysanthemums

GARDEN FLOWERS IN COLOR

(*C. coreanum*), the garden possibilities of this flower have been greatly widened. Another species, *C. arcticum*, seldom seen in its true form, was the source of the hybrid Astrid, with large single flowers of amber-pink on plants varying from 1 to 2½ feet. Other forms of this species in a wide range of color are known as Northland Daisies.

As with the hardy garden Chrysanthemums, there are among the so-called greenhouse varieties or commercial kinds many distinctive flower types, most of which are unusually large in size. In areas where the seasons are long and frosts come late, many of the exhibition varieties can be grown in sheltered places in the garden. In fact, some amateur gardeners build protecting frames which they use to cover their exhibition-flowered Chrysanthemums in late fall.

Hybridizers have been hard at work the past few years developing new types and varieties of Chrysanthemums. The aims have been not only to widen the color range and to make the plants hardier, but also to obtain varieties which flower early (late July and August). Each year many new varieties are introduced, and some of them are truly outstanding.

If we consider the characteristics of the various types listed in the nursery catalogs, the job of selecting varieties will be made that much easier. In his book "Hardy Chrysanthemums" Alex Cumming, who has contributed so much in hybridizing and developing Korean varieties, considers the following dominant types. The decorative or aster

Cushion Mums or Azaleamums

GARDEN FLOWERS IN COLOR

The new hybrid Northland Daisies

type bears large double blooms which often measure 3 or 4 inches across; a wide variety of colors is available in this group. Then there are pleasing single kinds usually with one row of petals surrounding a yellow center or disc. This group has widely attracted amateur gardeners, who enjoy the blooms for their delightful fragrance as well as their brilliant colors and their long keeping qualities. As is usual with many hybrids, there are the so-called duplex type characterized by two or more rows of petals. In recent years many attractive forms of the old pompon type, best described as button-like blooms, have been offered in catalogs. The flowers have a fine perfection of form and vary in size from a half-inch to 4 inches or more in diameter.

Considerable attention is being given Cushion Mums, also listed as Azaleamums and Magic Mums. The plants make a compact mound from 12 to 15 inches in height and often considerably wider. The double or single flowers appear in August and continue to bloom until cut down by severe frosts. A large number of hybrids varying from pure white to deepest red are offered. The plants are often used for broad borders along shrub plantings as well as in the perennial and rock garden. They are extremely hardy, multiply rapidly, and grow with amazing vigor. Truly distinctive are the fine anemone-flowering Chrysanthemums, generally with one row of ray petals accentuated by a center of quilled petals. Another addition to the Chrysanthemum group are the so-called spoon varieties, usually single in form, with long tubular petals ending in a flat spoon-like tip.

The annual Chrysanthemums, commonly known as Painted Daisies, are hybrids of *C. carinatum*, from Morocco. Conspicuous for their dark centers, the tricolored flowers are further accentuated by distinctive bands of red, yellow, or brown. The foliage is sparse and skeleton-like. *C. coronarium*, the Crown Daisy, is known for its bushy growth and its double and semi-double flowers, ranging from white to deep yellow. The Corn-marigold of English cornfields, *C. segetum*, grows 2 to 3 feet tall, with single flowers which vary in color, as do the hybrids of *C. carinatum*. For their wide color range, their free-flowering habit, and their use as cut flowers, annual Chrysanthemums are most desirable.

Chrysanthemum varieties vary greatly in their habit of growth. Some are content to produce their flowers on 15-inch stems, while others may grow to 4 feet or more in height. Careful nurture and shaping of the growing plants, together with moisture and soil conditions, largely determine their growth habit in the home garden. Because they are so important a part of the landscape they deserve a little extra care.

Full sun and rich soil are best for Chrysanthemums. They lend themselves to many parts of the garden because of their vigorous

A single Korean hybrid   Spoon Chrysanthemum

An outstanding double variety, Mrs. Pierre S. du Pont III

GARDEN FLOWERS IN COLOR

Florists' or exhibition Chrysanthemums

growth, but they resent extreme dryness; in fact, the best results are obtained when the soil is kept fairly moist. Despite their preference for moisture, it should be remembered that they require good drainage, especially in winter. To provide it, some gardeners plant Chrysanthemums in beds raised slightly above the level of the surrounding ground. Since many hybrids grow 3 feet tall or more, they need to be pinched back when 6 inches high, to produce sturdy growth. Additional pinching helps to encourage the branching habit as well as to eliminate some of the work of staking.

Chrysanthemums are easily increased by division, which is best done in early spring. Clumps should never be allowed to become woody; yearly division with some varieties is advisable. Allow at least 15 inches between plants. Well-decomposed stable manure can be dug into the ground when the plants are set out. Feedings of liquid manure or some commercial fertilizer can be applied as a side dressing at intervals during the growing season and especially when the flower buds are forming.

Seed of the hybrids is available, and seedlings are bound to provide many surprises for those who make the effort to raise their own plants. Sow seed in a hotbed, a coldframe, or in the open ground, and set the seedlings 15 inches apart.

If large quantities of special varieties are needed, cuttings from established plants can be rooted in sand and peat moss. Usually they are made from tops that were pinched back in late May or early June.

In areas where the winters are severe, many of the hybrid Chrysanthemums may need a light protective mulch of evergreen boughs, which can be put on after the ground has frozen. Choice kinds can be dug after bloom is over, and stored in a coldframe.

A Pompon hybrid
of rich coloring

A two-toned variety typical of
the brilliant-colored double kinds

Forms of annual Chrysanthemums,
which are easily grown from seed

Clara Curtis, a September-flowering variety

GARDEN FLOWERS IN COLOR

Mme. Edouard André

Belle of Woking

Clematis tangutica obtusiuscula

Clematis montana undulata

Clematis Lawsoniana

Clematis texensis, a native kind

GARDEN FLOWERS IN COLOR

70

CLEMATIS

Few climbing plants are better known than *Clematis paniculata*, but not one gardener in a hundred has ever seen some of the magnificent hybrids and little-known species which bloom in late spring and early summer. Both the large-flowered and the small-flowered species offer a new field of interest for the enthusiastic amateur. Not only are they striking in color and size, but they have a pleasing habit of growth coupled with a delicacy of form. Trellises, pergolas, arches, fences, old stumps, and the like, make desirable supports for Clematis; when grown on wires, it makes distinctive tracery on garden walls. As cut flowers in the home, many varieties can be used to advantage. Several erect-growing species for perennial borders, varying from 2 to 4 feet in height, are offered by nurserymen.

A long and impressive list of large-flowered varieties is now available. The pale mauve Belle of Woking is one of the few double-flowering forms appearing in June and July. Comtesse de Bouchaud has gracefully curved petals ranging from satiny rose to pink, from July to September. Truly distinctive is Duchess of Albany, with vigorous sprays of gorgeous pink, trumpet-like flowers borne over a long period (July to September). *C. Henryi* is known for its immense white flowers. The old velvety violet-purple *C. Jackmani* has been widely grown for a number of years; it is unusually vigorous and blooms profusely in midsummer. A striking new red form, *C. Jackmani rubra*, promises to be equally popular. Kermesina is wine-red. An extra-strong grower with large lavender-blue flowers is *C. Lawsoniana*, blooming from June to September. Mme. Baron-Veillard, with warm lilac flowers, is a beauty. Another red Clematis, the rich-textured Mme. Edouard André, is suggestive of an old Persian rug. Nelly Moser is a hybrid of *C. lanuginosa;* red bars accentuate the pale mauve and white petals. Prins Hendrik bears azure-blue flowers of immense size, with ruffled petals. Then there is Ramona, with blooms emphasized by dark anthers. Ville de Paris has red coloring on each of its soft blue petals; William Kennett is deep lavender.

Among the small-flowered varieties is *C. crispa*, the Marsh or Curly Clematis, with steel-blue, urn-shaped flowers from July to September. Another for the September garden is *C. Jouiniana*, Spingarn Variety, with large clusters of fragrant pale lavender flowers. In May and June appears *C. montana rubens*, with rosy red flowers changing to pink. The familiar *C. paniculata*, with fragrant white flowers, comes in late summer. One of the choicest of all is *C. tangutica obtusiuscula*, with small golden yellow bells on stately stems in June and occasionally through the summer. Another of the urn-shaped kinds is *C. texensis*.

A partially shaded location is ideal. When planted in full sun, the lower stems and roots should be shaded by small plants, since it is essential to keep the Clematis roots cool and moist.

Clematis can be planted in either spring or fall in a rich, well-drained garden loam of rather light texture. Sand and peat moss may be added to a heavy soil to loosen it. If your land is inclined to be acid, lime should be mixed in when planting—a handful for each plant—and if necessary it may be added occasionally thereafter, working it well into the ground without disturbing the roots. Applications of water during dry periods and the addition of well-decomposed cow manure, or other animal manure or bonemeal, will be beneficial.

In planting, set the collar of the plant at least 2 to 3 inches below the surface of the soil. Prepare a sufficiently large area to accommodate the roots easily and spread them loosely; then firm the soil well. Fasten the stems to a stake or some permanent support to avoid damaging the lower part of the main stem. It is not necessary to cultivate Clematis. Remember that spring-blooming varieties such as *C. montana rubens*, *C. montana undulata*, etc., should have dead wood cut out in early spring before growth starts; pruning is not done until fall. Varieties which produce bloom on new wood in the summer and fall should not be pruned until they have become well established; then the vines may be cut back to 3 feet to encourage new growth. However, if height is desired for some special purpose, merely remove the dead wood and thin out the stems.

A fall mulch of leaves, straw, peat, or well-rotted manure helps to prevent winterkilling; it can be dug into the soil in the spring.

Clematis Henryi is very large

Kermesina, a rich red

GARDEN FLOWERS IN COLOR

©   The new red-flowering form of Clematis Jackmani

GARDEN FLOWERS IN COLOR

CLEOME

Cleome spinosa is a big-scale annual for gardens where quick temporary effects are desired. Commonly called Spider-flower, the reference is presumably to the spider-like form of the blooms, but actually from a distance the great flower heads look more like butterflies.

A hardy annual which often self-sows in gardens even to the point of becoming a pest, it nevertheless produces a useful shrub-like plant 4 or 5 feet in height. Both white and pink forms are listed in seed catalogs. As a rule, the flowers wilt quickly when cut but their free-blooming habit and their ease of culture are desirable features.

In groups of five or more, Cleome makes a colorful mass in summer shrub borders. As a background plant in the annual garden or in combination with perennials, it is also effective. The plants are such rapid growers that they must be given ample space.

For an early start the seed can be sown in a seed-bed in late fall. In spring it may be planted in a hotbed, coldframe, or in the open ground. Seedlings transplant readily and should be set at least 18 inches apart. Full sun and ordinary soil are their simple requirements, but they usually do well in partial shade.

COBEA

Cup-and-saucer-vine and Mexican Ivy are two common names for *Cobea scandens*, which is one of our most delightful annual vines. The common name Cup-and-saucer-vine aptly describes the richly colored blooms; a white variety is also grown. Annual climbers such as this, as well as morning-glory, cypress-vine, scarlet runner, and hyacinth bean, are most useful in the home garden where quick screening effects are desired. They can be used on trellises, arbors, and pergolas, or allowed to clamber over walls.

This tropical vine is quick to find support by means of the tendrils which appear at the end of each cluster of leaves. Usually it averages 10 to 12 feet in height, but under favorable conditions it may reach 20 feet or more in a season. Essentially a tender perennial, it grows best in full sun but will tolerate light shade. The attractive flowers, greenish in the bud stage, turn bluish purple as they open. They are followed by curious plum-shaped fruits.

Seed can be started in pots indoors or in a hotbed or coldframe, and transplanted to the garden when all danger of frost has passed; or it can be sown in the open ground. Care must be taken to cover the seed very lightly, for an excess of moisture in the soil sometimes causes rotting.

GARDEN FLOWERS IN COLOR

COCKSCOMB

Greek and Latin botanical names often puzzle amateur gardeners until their meaning is discovered. The name Celosia is derived from the Greek, meaning "burned," in reference to the brilliant red blossoms. Even a fleeting glance at the crested or plumed varieties discloses their flame-like form and color. The common kinds are hybrids of *Celosia argentea* and are appropriately known as Cockscombs.

Most familiar of all is the true Cockscomb, *C. cristata*, with strangely crested flowers not unlike roosters' combs, and suggestive of the Victorian age of horse-hair and plush. These velvety-textured heads of bloom, varying in color from crimson to gold, are sometimes 8 inches or more in length and are usually 6 to 12 inches tall. The plumed Cockscombs are similar in color range, but the flowers are pyramidal in form, tapering to a point like silky feathers. Well-grown plants sometimes reach 3 feet in height. The Chinese Woolflower has many characteristics of the plumed Cockscomb, save that its flowers form rounded heads.

Sow the seed indoors, in a hotbed, coldframe, or in the open ground. Give the plants full sun and rich soil, if possible, since they respond readily to special feeding. Seedlings of *Celosia cristata* require 9 to 12 inches between plants, and those of the tall-growing species need 18 inches. Some gardeners grow all three kinds as pot plants.

Cockscomb, Celosia cristata

GARDEN FLOWERS IN COLOR

COLUMBINE

Columbines are long-time favorites that have been known and grown in the gardens of Europe for centuries, and were once highly valued for medicinal purposes. From the mountainous and rocky sections of America, Europe, and Asia, plant-hunters have collected many unusual species.

Although they grow well in full sun, Columbines are adapted to partially shaded areas in rock gardens and borders. *Aquilegia alpina*, with its short-spurred light blue flowers on 8-inch stems, belongs in the rock garden. The familiar native species of the eastern United States,

Aquilegia longissima

A. canadensis, has many garden uses; well-established clumps bloom freely and self-sow. Of hybrid origin is *A. clematiflora*, a unique form 18 to 24 inches tall, with flowers not unlike those of the large-flowered clematis hybrids. Spurs of noticeable length and a pleasing bloom combination of blue and white distinguish the Rocky Mountain Columbine, *A. caerulea* (the state flower of Colorado). Several improved forms are available, such as the variety Helenae (generally considered superior to the species *A. chrysantha*, the Golden-spurred hybrids), *A. flabellata* or the Fan Columbine, and *A. longissima*, recently rediscovered in the Southwest. For the most part the long-spurred kinds were selected from Mrs. Scott Elliott's hybrids or from Dobbie's Imperial strain. These 3-foot plants are graceful and colorful in the late spring and early summer garden.

Rich sandy loam seems to be their particular preference but Columbines establish themselves in any well-drained soil. Once they get a good start in your garden, they will pop up in many places. Sow seed in late spring or early summer, and transplant the seedlings as soon as they are large enough to handle. A light mulch will help to protect them during the first winter. Set the plants in their permanent places in the garden in early spring, leaving as much soil as possible around the roots.

Aquilegia clematiflora

CONEFLOWER

The showy purple, pink, and white Coneflowers, formerly classified as Rudbeckia, are now called Echinacea. Other familiar plants with blooms having cone-shaped centers, such as the Black-eyed Susan and several other Rudbeckias, are included here.

All of the Coneflowers can be described as coarse plants of unusual vigor, but they are especially useful for busy people who are anxious to have colorful effects in summer gardens. The old purple Coneflower *Echinacea purpurea*, a native of the Middle Atlantic States, is perhaps the least desirable from the standpoint of color, but the pink variety The King and the new White Lustre have many garden possibilities. The plants are sturdy, averaging 2½ to 3 feet in height, and bloom over a period of ten weeks or more through the summer and into the autumn. Individual flowers often last four to six weeks in the garden. Keep the dead ones picked off to encourage continuous bloom.

In small gardens there is hardly room for the Black-eyed Susan, *Rudbeckia hirta*, or for that matter its brown-eyed relative *R. triloba*, because they self-sow all too readily. Both are biennials of vigorous growth and showy, free-flowering habit. *R. hirta* ranges from 18 to 24 inches in height, bearing its gay yellow flowers singly on sturdy

Echinacea (Rudbeckia), White Lustre

GARDEN FLOWERS IN COLOR

Rudbeckia, Kelvedon Star

stems during July and August, while *R. triloba*, reaching 4 feet, produces small brown-centered flowers in large clusters over a long period in August and September. Use them in the shrub border and keep the seed pods cut off.

The Showy Coneflower, *R. speciosa* or *R. Newmani*, is a true perennial forming compact tufts of foliage from which rise 2-foot flowering stems. From late June until frost the plants bloom freely and require little care. Golden-glow, *R. laciniata hortensia*, is often considered a pest because of its ungainly habit of falling over when in flower and of attracting red lice in abundance. However, it makes a decorative mass in the background of the perennial border during July and August. The 6-foot plants need to be sprayed to check the lice.

For the annual garden there are single and semi-double forms of *R. bicolor*. One of them, Kelvedon Star shown above, is especially useful in hot dry places. Long-lasting when cut, these free-flowering plants, 2 feet or more in height, require only a minimum of care.

All the Coneflowers prefer full sun but grow well in partial shade. Ordinary soil suits them, and they endure drought satisfactorily. The biennial kinds are easily raised from seed but most gardeners rely on self-sown seedlings. With the perennial forms the usual method is root division in early spring or fall. Any of the annual kinds can be started in a coldframe or in the open ground; set them 15 inches apart.

CORAL-BELLS

It was enthusiasm for rock gardens that made us aware of the usefulness of the Heucheras. In the wild they grow on cliffs and rocky hillsides. The bronzy green foliage forms low compact tufts from which rise the graceful flower stems. Attractive in the garden, the blooms are admirable cut-flower material.

Heucheras are easily adapted to part shade, as well as to sunny places in the garden. They vary in height from 1 to 2½ feet and bloom from early June through August. The native Alum-root, *Heuchera americana*, is a worthwhile ground cover. Its compact masses of rich foliage are attractive throughout the season but the greenish white flowers are of no consequence. *H. brizoides*, believed to be a hybrid of a California species, bears bright pink bells. From the hot dry regions of Arizona and New Mexico we have the widely grown *H. sanguinea*, which winters well even in the coldest parts of New England. White, pale pink, rose, coral, and scarlet shades are among the hybrids offered. Many other horticultural forms are now mentioned in the catalogs. Typical varieties include Cascade, a dainty pink kind; Flambeau, with bright red flowers; La Perle, dark red; Pluie de Feu, fiery-colored; Rosamundi, coral. The new variety Queen of Hearts has unusually large blooms of glowing pink.

Heucheras grow more luxuriantly in rich loam, but do well under quite ordinary conditions. Good drainage is essential to prevent the crowns from decaying. The plants are easily grown from divisions best made after flowering, in late August and early September, or in early spring. Divide established plants every two or three years to keep the clumps thrifty, and be careful to keep soil firmed well near the plants, which sometimes seem to lift themselves out of the ground.

Coral-bells, Pluie de Feu

GARDEN FLOWERS IN COLOR

COREOPSIS

This Greek name means "bug-like," in reference to the form of the seeds; Tickseed is the common name. It is widely distributed along the eastern seaboard, from Ontario to Florida. Both perennial and annual kinds are grown, the latter generally listed as Calliopsis, which is discussed on page 49.

With its great yellow discs supported on long stems, this summer-blooming perennial maintains a notable display over a long period. The clumps reach a height of 2 feet and spread out considerably. A double-flowered kind is sometimes seen. Coreopsis is indispensable for its free-blooming quality and its ease of growth. Plant it in the perennial border, allowing 1½ to 2 feet between plants.

In recent years *Coreopsis lanceolata*, Mayfield Giant, has been introduced. The flowers are often 3 inches across, with a dainty fragrance in addition to a sturdy habit. Two small-flowered kinds are listed in catalogs: *C. auriculata nana*, useful in rock gardens, slightly over a foot high, and the taller-growing Golden Shower.

Few perennials are easier to grow from seed. It is better to start new plants every few years or to encourage self-sown seedlings than to divide old plants. Full sun and ordinary soil suit it.

Coreopsis, Golden Shower

Coreopsis, Mayfield Giant

Early Cosmos

COSMOS

Whether planted in rows, for background effects with other annuals, or as color masses in perennial plantings or shrub borders, forms of *Cosmos bipinnatus* dominate the scene. Few plants require as little care or self-sow as readily. Crimson, pink, and white varieties are found in both early and late-flowering kinds, which vary in height from 2½ to 6 feet or more. The double-crested forms are among the hybrids of recent years, and orange and yellow varieties have widened considerably the color range of this useful annual.

Among the early types are the Early Express and the Sensation strains. The latter is taller, with immense blooms. The late-flowering kinds often grow 6 feet or more in height and do not bloom until late fall; accordingly, in regions where frosts come early, it is wise to grow the early types. This is true also of the double-crested or anemone-flowered kinds. Several yellow and orange varieties, hybrids of *C. sulphureus*, are described on the next page.

Sow the seed in a coldframe or in the open ground, and set the plants 18 to 24 inches apart. Cosmos thrives in almost any kind of soil. It tolerates partial shade, but grows best in full sun. If the seedlings become spindly, pinch them back or transplant them.

Orange and yellow Cosmos are comparative newcomers to the garden. Unlike the pink, red, and white kinds, their foliage is somewhat coarse. Flowers are borne on long, wiry stems, which makes them ideal for cutting. Early Orange Flare illustrated here, and Yellow Klondyke, a delightful companion, average 3 feet in height. The variety Orange Ruffles, $2\frac{1}{2}$ feet tall, has semi-double blooms.

Cosmos, Early Orange Flare

FLOWERING CRAB

Along with the flowering cherries, magnolias, and dogwoods, the Flowering Crab contributes some of the most brilliant splashes of color in the spring garden. It has attractive foliage, and in autumn produces highly colored fruits as well. The Flowering Crabs, species and varieties of Malus, are generally considered small trees reaching 20 feet or more, although there are some forms that seldom exceed 6 feet in height. Both double and single-flowering kinds are sold.

Flowering Crabs are desirable garden subjects, for they are adaptable to a wide variety of soils, and will tolerate conditions which other flowering trees abhor. They stand shearing, and may be trimmed into symmetrical shapes for formal use. Plants allowed to assume their natural form can be pruned heavily after flowering without suffering any damage. They are hardy over most parts of the country.

One of the most popular varieties, and one of the earliest to bloom, is the Carmine Crab, *Malus atrosanguinea*, with single red flowers. *M. baccata* bears fragrant white blooms and yellow fruit tinted red on one side, which is considered fine material for jelly. Perhaps the most picturesque of the double-flowering forms is the Bechtel variety, with double, soft pink blooms on a medium-sized plant. *M. Eleyi* sometimes retains its red foliage color throughout the season. Fruit and blooms are likewise brilliant red in color.

M. floribunda is an early single-flowered pink variety of spreading

Malus floribunda in full bloom

habit, with yellow fruit following the bloom. The Hopa Crab, *M. Hopa*, has large red flowers and purplish red foliage. Among the dwarf forms are Parkman's Crab, *M. Halliana Parkmani*, with long-lasting pink blooms. Another of similar form seldom reaching more than 6 feet in height is the Sargent Crab, *M. Sargenti*, with white flowers followed by red fruits.

The Flowering Crabs are among the easiest flowering trees to grow. Their soil requirements are simple, and they will stand somewhat poorly drained soil. They can be planted in early spring or in the fall.

Yellow Crab-apple fruits

GARDEN FLOWERS IN COLOR

CRAPE MYRTLE

Originally introduced from China, the Crape-myrtle, *Lagerstroemia indica*, has been so widely grown throughout the South that many believe it to be a native of our Southern States. Its common name, Crape-myrtle, aptly describes the crepe-like texture of the pyramidal flower clusters, which are borne in great profusion through the summer months. These blooms provide material for really stunning table decorations, and show to best advantage when used alone.

Although not commonly seen north of Baltimore along the Atlantic seaboard, Crape-myrtle can be grown as a flowering shrub in many colder parts of the country if it is given a sheltered spot. In severe climates ambitious gardeners often protect their plants by wrapping them carefully and mulching their roots. Others treat them as a perennial, allowing them to die back to the ground each year; this is no serious drawback because the blooms are produced on the current season's growth.

Crape-myrtle is an outstanding summer-flowering shrub for several reasons. It is obtainable in white, lavender, pink, and red; perhaps the most spectacular variety of all is one with watermelon-pink flowers. The large clusters of bloom appear over a long period from early summer through September. The shapely plants respond readily to pruning. They often bloom when less than 3 feet in height, and mature specimens sometimes reach 20 feet or more. This useful plant can be grown on the lawn or can be associated with other kinds of flowering shrubs in informal hedges and borders. Full-grown plants take on the aspect of a small tree.

Crape-myrtle has few special cultural requirements. It grows easily in any well-drained garden soil and produces its most abundant bloom in full sun. However, in partial shade specimens will make a fair appearance. The beginner should be cautioned that the plants are often slow to start growth in spring. Accordingly, all pruning should be done after new growth begins; otherwise live wood may be cut off by accident.

CROCUS

Everybody knows and loves the cheery Crocuses which brave the winds and frosts of declining winter. In fact, no other early flower does more to herald the coming of spring. From the mountain regions of Europe and Asia these members of the iris family have been gathered to brighten our gardens.

The root is a corm like the gladiolus, rather than a true bulb. Deeply dug light soil and a well-drained location are the easy requirements for growing Crocuses. In the rock garden, the perennial border, or the shrub planting they are equally attractive. Sometimes they are planted in the lawn or associated with plants such as phlox, veronica, and arabis. For striking color effects, group them in clusters of a dozen.

Few people think of Crocuses as being fragrant, but E. A. Bowles, the great English authority on this group of plants, has written of the scent "consisting of a great deal of primrose with a slight touch of

Large-flowered Crocuses

GARDEN FLOWERS IN COLOR

An attractive Crocus planting

honey." Their color range varies from purest white through orange-yellow, yellow, lavender, blue, and purple. More than twenty-five species and varieties of spring-flowering Crocuses are offered.

Autumn-flowering Crocuses are all too little known in American gardens, and yet one of them, the Saffron Crocus, *C. sativus*, has been grown and cherished as a useful drug and dye for more than two thousand years. In ancient times it was sold by Phoenician merchants throughout the then-known world. The Saffron Crocus varies in color from white to lilac and has noticeable orange stigmas from which the drug is obtained. Its name should not be confused with False Saffron, *Carthamus tinctorius*, which is used in cooking.

Because they flower after the foliage has disappeared, Autumn Crocuses are used to best advantage with hosta and other foliage plants, either in the shrub border or the perennial garden. While they provide gay color in the autumn rock garden, the foliage, which is produced in spring, turns a disagreeable yellow and fades slowly.

Plant Crocus corms in the fall, 4 inches deep. Do not mow or cut the foliage in the spring until it has ripened completely. It is unnecessary to dig and store the bulbs through summer, save when the clumps become overcrowded and need dividing. Autumn-blooming kinds are usually planted in late July or August.

CYPRESS-VINE

The Cypress-vine, *Quamoclit pennata*, and the Cardinal-climber, *Q. Sloteri*, are members of the morning-glory tribe. Of rapid growth, both these annual vines have brilliantly colored flowers and dainty foliage. The Cypress-vine is noted for its crimson, star-shaped blooms which are most attractive in the early morning or after sundown. A white variety is also offered. The Cardinal-climber, on the other hand, a cross between the Cypress-vine and the Star Ipomoea, is best described as a miniature morning-glory with clusters of red flowers.

Where delicate effects of tracery are desired, against a trellis or a wall, the Cypress-vine or the Cardinal-climber will often solve the problem. The plants may reach 15 to 20 feet in a season, depending upon the locality. Blooms of the Cardinal-climber remain open all day, whereas those of the Cypress-vine are showiest in subdued light.

For an early start, seed can be sown in pots in a greenhouse or in a hotbed or coldframe, for later transfer to the garden. Or it can be planted in the open ground when frost danger has passed. As with morning-glories, the seeds have a hard coat or shell, which often causes slow germination. To hasten the process, they can be nicked with a sharp knife or soaked overnight in water before being planted. Full sun and average garden soil are their simple requirements.

GARDEN FLOWERS IN COLOR

A Decorative
Dahlia

DAHLIA

The Dahlia, which came to us from Mexico, is among our most familiar summer garden flowers. As with other plants like the rose, the peony, and the gladiolus, there is a national society devoted to the promotion of the Dahlia in America.

Numerous types have been developed. Single Dahlias are easily identified by their single row of petals, accentuated by yellow centers. The Mignon type produces single flowers on plants that seldom grow more than 18 inches tall. Very similar are the so-called Collarettes, which are single, but, as the name suggests, are marked by a row of smaller petals forming a collar between the center and the ray petals. Anemone-flowered Dahlias are distinguished by curious tubular florets in the center of the flowers, which add a rather exotic touch. The semi-double forms are known as Duplex Dahlias and tend to be confused with the true double varieties.

Peony-flowered Dahlias have several rows of petals and somewhat resemble peonies, with a row of twisted and curled petals around open centers. Among them are flowers of singular elegance and beauty. Decorative Dahlias have double blooms, symmetrical in outline, but more flat than rounded. The older, exceedingly formal and often quilled flowers are in this class. Informal Decoratives are irregular in outline.

What are known as Ball-shaped Double Dahlias are more globular than flat in form, with more or less quilled petals. The florets show a regular spiral arrangement. Closely related is the Hybrid Show or Colossal type, with florets more loosely arranged, resembling the Decorative Dahlia. A true Pompon averages about 2 inches across. Cactus Dahlias have definitely fluted petals that look not unlike a cluster of tiny glass tubes. The hybrid forms are less bizarre in outline but do suggest the curious fluted character of the type. Rapidly increasing in popularity are the Miniature Dahlias, with flowers not exceeding

Miniature Dahlias

GARDEN FLOWERS IN COLOR

Pompon Dahlia

4 inches in diameter. (Pompons are not included in this group.)

Several thousand varieties of Dahlias are available in the trade in America and Europe, with new ones being introduced each season. In the seed catalogs Pompons, together with Miniatures and Dwarf Singles or Mignons, are being featured.

The starchy tubers of the Dahlia multiply rapidly. When new kinds are offered it is not always possible to obtain enough roots, and growers sell what are known as "green plants." These are cuttings, rooted from stock plants. Dahlias are also readily raised from seed; plants will bloom the first year from seed sown in March. Several good strains are available from seedsmen.

Full sun and moist well-drained soil are desirable. In planting, set the crowns of the tubers 4 to 6 inches below the surface. A single tuber with a strong eye will produce a blooming plant the first year. If the largest flowers are desired, allow only one or two shoots to develop; when the buds form, disbud to one on each stem to produce exhibition flowers. Stake the plants securely, and give them additional feedings of liquid manure as the buds begin to form.

The tubers should be dug after the foliage has been destroyed by severe frost, and allowed to dry thoroughly in the open before being stored for the winter.

Single Dahlias

GARDEN FLOWERS IN COLOR

DAPHNE

The Daphnes are an important group of low-growing shrubs for the home garden. Some are evergreen, while others lose their leaves each autumn. In addition to attractive blooms, most of the species have the added advantage of delightful fragrance. Most familiar of all Daphnes is *D. Cneorum*, called the Garland-flower, which makes a low evergreen mass seldom more than 10 inches high and especially adapted for rock-garden use. The bright pink blooms appear with the evergreen azaleas, and the two make a pleasing companion planting in the shrub border or as a foundation group with yews. This species of Daphne often blooms again in the fall.

D. Mezereum, the February Daphne, came originally from Europe and has become naturalized in parts of the eastern United States. The lilac-purple flowers appear on 3-foot plants in April, and are followed by showy scarlet fruits in summer. There is also a white-flowering form of this deciduous species. Somewhat tender is the species *D. Genkwa*, 2½ to 3 feet tall, with pale lilac flowers appearing before the leaves unfold in spring. A recent introduction, Somerset, is a hybrid of an evergreen species. In cold climates the plants are only partially evergreen. During May and early June, spikes of heavily scented, blush-pink, star-shaped flowers appear in great abundance. The introducers recommend it as an attractive hedge plant.

D. Cneorum is sometimes difficult to get established. It prefers a sunny location in well-drained soil that is rich in organic matter. A mulch of peat helps to conserve moisture, especially during the summer months, and a light covering of evergreen boughs provides protection from winter sun and wind. For the most part, the taller Daphnes grow well in full sun or partial shade in any reasonably fertile ground.

Garland-flower, Daphne Cneorum

DELPHINIUM

A perennial garden without Delphinium would hardly be complete. Not only their stately spire-like form but the wide variations found in the blue, purple, and white flower spikes make these plants indispensable. The genus name is the Greek for "dolphin," as applied to the shape of the individual flowers. Larkspur has been the familiar name for these plants since before Shakespeare's time, but in modern usage is more often associated with the annual kinds. Many gardeners now use the name Delphinium exclusively for the perennial species and Larkspur for the annual ones. See page 152.

Hybridizers in Europe and in our own country have devoted considerable energy to the improvement of Delphiniums. As a result there are many outstanding strains and an ever-increasing number of named varieties. Until comparatively recently the light blue *Delphinium Belladonna*, the dark *D. Bellamosum*, and the typical Bee Larkspur, *D. elatum*, growing 3 to 4 feet tall (so called because the center of each flower suggests a bee sucking nectar), provided practically all the Delphinium in the June and July garden picture. With the introduction of the new hybrid strains came larger flower spikes, larger blooms —both double and single, and new color variations and combinations such as lavender, mauve, and even pink tints. Pure white varieties have been introduced, and there is a recent hybrid of deep pink.

A dwarf species, *D. grandiflorum* (*chinense*), with intense blue flowers arranged in loose panicles, is widely grown as a cut flower. The plants grow 12 to 18 inches tall and flower freely during June and July, with a recurrence of bloom in the fall if not allowed to go to seed. A white variety is available also. Though a perennial, the Chinese Delphinium can be treated as an annual if seed is sown early in the spring.

While the culture of the Delphinium is by no means difficult, some of the hybrid strains are apparently not as resistant to disease as were the old forms. They require a rich, well-drained soil and either full sun or partial shade. Since they are more subject to disease in damp weather, the plants should be set at least 1½ to 2 feet apart to allow for adequate circulation of air. Unless watched carefully, they should not be interplanted with other plants that will eventually shade or conceal them. Since extreme drought also makes them succumb to disease, they need water in dry periods. Usually the plants reach 4 to 6 feet or more in height, and require the support of stakes.

Seed should not be allowed to form unless it is being saved for a special purpose, because the energy required to produce it weakens the plants. To prevent slugs from attacking the plants in the winter, many gardeners cover the crowns with coal ashes. Crown rot, a fun-

Hybrid Delphiniums

GARDEN FLOWERS IN COLOR

gous disease, seems to be prevalent in many gardens. Unless ailing plants are worth saving it is best to destroy them and remove the soil surrounding each one to a depth of a foot. A very dilute solution of mercuric chloride poured into the soil may be used as a disinfectant. Dusting sulphur is recommended for counteracting mildew; rotenone spray, the cyclamen mite (an insect of microscopic size).

Young plants can be obtained from nurserymen but experienced gardeners often prefer to raise their Delphinium from seed. The seed can be sown as soon as the season's crop has ripened (July or early August), or in early spring. Seedlings are carried over winter in a coldframe or in a sheltered place in the garden. Established clumps can be divided in early fall or as soon as growth appears in spring. Usually Delphiniums produce two crops of flowers each season. Remove the flower spikes after blooming, but leave part of the lower stems and foliage until new growth appears at the base; then the old stems can be cut away. An application of a complete fertilizer or liquid manure and a thorough watering will help to stimulate new growth for the second crop of bloom.

A lovely hybrid of Delphinium Bellamosum

GARDEN FLOWERS IN COLOR

DEUTZIA

Deutzia is a familiar shrub on home grounds; many species are known to botanists, but only a few of them are commonly found in gardens. Perhaps the most popular are *Deutzia gracilis*, a low-growing kind, and the tall pink-flowering hybrid of *D. scabra* known as Pride of Rochester.

D. gracilis bears long slender sprays of white blooms on symmetrical, mound-shaped plants; these usually flower when the lilacs are at their height. Although the plants may grow 6 feet tall, in most gardens they range from 2 to 4 feet. Blooming somewhat later, *D. scabra*, Pride of Rochester, is a big-scale plant often reaching a height of 8 feet, with large clusters of pale pink flowers on sturdy stems. Some nurserymen offer other attractive species and hybrids with pink or white flowers; double-flowering forms are also listed.

Deutzia thrives in any well-drained garden soil and is generally hardy over a large part of the United States. Plants can be set out in early spring or fall; cuttings can easily be rooted in a mixture of sand and peat. Often young plants are irregular in growth and need to be sheared to develop symmetrical specimens.

Deutzia gracilis

GARDEN FLOWERS IN COLOR

A well-grown specimen of pink-flowering Dogwood

GARDEN FLOWERS IN COLOR

DOGWOOD

From Maine to Florida on the Atlantic coast and extending far inland over a large part of the country, the white-flowering Dogwood, *Cornus florida*, is a favorite small tree reaching 30 feet in height. The pink-flowering form, *C. florida rubra*, discovered near Valley Forge more than fifty years ago, is widely planted in home gardens and public parks.

The genus Cornus also includes many fine shrubby plants, such as the Tatarian Dogwood *C. alba*, the Silky Dogwood *C. Amomum*, the Bloodtwig Dogwood *C. sanguinea*, and the Red-osier Dogwood *C. stolonifera*. All of these are noted for their colorful twig growth, their good foliage, and their flat panicles of flowers followed by showy fruits. Other species of Dogwood worth mentioning are the Kousa Dogwood *C. Kousa*, which flowers somewhat later than the familiar *C. florida*. Earliest of all to bloom is the Cornelian-cherry *C. mas*, which reaches 20 feet in height. The flowers usually come before the maples show signs of life. In contrast to the various shrub and tree forms is the dainty Bunchberry *C. canadensis*, which seldom reaches more than 9 inches in height. The white flowers, which appear in early spring, are followed by bright red fruits.

Of all the Dogwoods, *C. florida* and its pink-flowering form are the most widely planted. In addition to its showy bloom and the picturesque horizontal growth of its branches, the Flowering Dogwood has attractive foliage which colors brilliantly in the autumn; the trees are further ornamented by striking red fruits which the birds devour as soon as they are ripe. As a specimen on the lawn or as a part of the shrub border the Flowering Dogwood can be used to advantage in gardens large and small.

The Flowering Dogwood grows well in any well-drained garden soil, in full sun or partial shade. Plants can be set out in early spring or in the fall. Most nurserymen supply them balled in burlap; this makes the task of moving specimens relatively easy. The trunks of newly set trees are often wrapped with burlap for several feet up from the ground, as a protection against borers and rodents. The Flowering Dogwood seldom requires pruning except to improve its form.

DORONICUM

Leopards-bane is the common name of this group of perennials, all of which produce large yellow daisy-like blooms in spring. Several species varying in height from 1 to 4 feet are offered by nurserymen. All are worthwhile, but oftentimes the plants die out during dry summer weather. Where the Doronicums can be grown successfully, they are among the most attractive of early-flowering hardy perennials.

Doronicum Clusi, usually less than 2 feet in height, produces its showy blooms singly on long stems. *D. cordifolium*, less than a foot tall, has glossy leaves and somewhat smaller flowers than most kinds. Among the taller sorts are *D. Pardalianches* and *D. plantagineum*, with immense blooms on stems often 3 feet in height. The medium-sized *D. caucasicum*, averaging 2 feet, combines effectively with lavender and white tulips and other spring-flowering bulbs.

The Doronicums can be grown in any well-drained soil in full sun or part shade, but they are more permanent in heavy soils that are retentive of moisture. Since they bloom in early spring, the plants are best set out in the fall or immediately after flowering. Allow 8 to 10 inches between them. Some forms die back after flowering, and care must be taken to mark their place in the border. They need to be watered in dry weather. Divide established plants every two or three years to keep them in thriving condition. The Doronicums are easily raised from seed sown in early spring.

ELEPHANTS-EAR

The Elephants-ear, *Colocasia esculenta*, with immense tuberous roots of a starchy nature, is a plant of high economic value as a source of food in the Pacific islands, where it is sometimes called Taro, Eddo, or Dasheen. This big-scale tender bedding plant is hardly suitable for small gardens, but is often seen in public parks and show places. Where quick screens are desired, it can be planted to conceal unsightly areas.

Because the leaves are similar in shape to the Caladiums, this plant is often considered a species of that genus. Fancy-leaved Caladiums are more refined in form and have brilliantly colored foliage. In the South they are very popular summer bedding plants, and the bizarre and sometimes dainty coloring of their exotic leaves makes them unusually attractive. They are decorative as pot plants in and about the house and are often used as bedding plants. Partial shade and moisture are their chief requirements. Started indoors in flats of sphagnum moss in a temperature of 75 degrees, they need to be potted as soon as sprouts develop. For best results do not give them too much space for root-development. Frequent applications of liquid manure will benefit them materially.

The Elephants-ear can be started indoors in pots, or the large tubers can be planted in the open ground after all danger of frost is past. Set them at least 8 inches deep; large roots may need deeper planting.

Elephants-ear, Colocasia esculenta

GARDEN FLOWERS IN COLOR

ENGLISH DAISY

The English Daisy, *Bellis perennis*, figured in a curious episode more than five hundred years ago, when a great argument arose among the aristocratic women of Europe as to the merits of various flowers. Some of the ladies at court maintained that the rose was the most beautiful flower, while others claimed that the English Daisy should hold first rank, but try as they would, they could not persuade old Geoffrey Chaucer, the poet, to take sides.

Several varieties with immense flowers of dark red, pink, and pure white, as well as a form with quilled petals, are offered by seedsmen, but there are those who still prefer the small-flowered kinds. Actually, the English Daisy is a perennial, but it is usually treated as a biennial. For borders or for irregular masses, few spring-flowering plants are more adaptable in the garden. As an underplanting with spring-flowering shrubs and flowering bulbs, as well as in formal beds, it makes a colorful display.

Since the English Daisy is ordinarily treated as a biennial, seed is sown in late July or early August. When the tiny plants are large enough to handle, they are set 3 inches apart in a coldframe or in raised beds which can be heavily mulched with straw, marsh hay, or cran mulch after the ground has frozen. The plants are set in their

permanent places in early spring, preferably in moist, well-drained garden soil. Allow 6 inches between them. In the hot days of early summer the plants often wilt, because they are extremely shallow-rooted. By keeping the dead flowers picked off, continuous bloom can be had from early spring until July; in areas where the summers are cool, a longer blooming season can be counted upon. Very often the plants self-sow, and sometimes seedlings appear the following year. Occasional feedings with liquid manure will help to stimulate growth of the plants and keep the blooms large in size.

GARDEN FLOWERS IN COLOR

ENKIANTHUS

Unlike the rhododendron and the azalea members of the great heath family, the dainty Enkianthus is little known to gardeners. Although it sheds its leaves in late autumn, this acid-soil shrub is a delightful plant for many parts of the home grounds. In its native habitat in Japan it assumes the habit of a small tree, reaching 20 feet in height. For the most part, plants seldom grow more than 6 to 8 feet in the eastern United States.

Enkianthus campanulatus is the species most commonly grown. The plants are columnar in form, and the blooms are borne in drooping clusters on long slender stems in late spring; the pleasing foliage assumes vivid colors in the autumn. Because of its columnar growth this shrub makes a fine accent plant with azaleas, rhododendrons, and other ericaceous plants. It can also be used to advantage with flowering shrubs and evergreens in a foundation planting. It is clean in its habit of growth, is seldom attacked by insects and diseases, and requires little care. Enkianthus is one of those worthwhile shrubs that ought to be more widely planted, despite its difficult name.

Enkianthus can be planted in spring or fall. Most nurserymen supply plants with a generous ball of earth so that it is an easy matter to set out the plants. Add several shovelfuls of peat moss to the soil mixture to provide a good growing medium for fibrous roots. It can be grown in full sun or partial shade, and can be expected to flourish wherever rhododendrons, azaleas, and other acid-soil plants grow.

GARDEN FLOWERS IN COLOR

EPIMEDIUM

The common name Bishops-hat, sometimes associated with Epimedium, brings to mind the curious biretta-shaped flowers which appear in April. A careful examination of an individual flower reveals an exquisitely modeled skull-cap, surmounted by a square petal formation—a truly remarkable miniature of the familiar ecclesiastical headdress. Barrenwort is another common name of this hardy perennial.

White, yellow, rose, red, brownish red, and even violet tones are found in the flowers of the many hybrids which have been developed from Japanese and Persian species. Perhaps more significant than the flowers is the remarkable foliage of the various species. Notably oval in form, the leaves show rich red and bronze tones when they unfold, and retain some of this coloring through the season even into the winter months. Epimedium is a highly desirable ground cover, increasing rapidly in moist soil. In rock and wall gardens its flowers and foliage show to good advantage.

Grow Epimedium in sunny or shady areas and give it rich loam, or plant it in the rock garden. The plants can be set out in spring or fall, and when established, should be divided every three years. This hardy perennial grows luxuriantly in moist soil.

Epimedium growing with white trillium

GARDEN FLOWERS IN COLOR

EUONYMUS

Euonymus radicans

There are innumerable forms of Euonymus; some are shrubs, others assume the form of small trees, and still others are trailing evergreen shrubs which take on some of the habits of vines. Most Euonymus are distinguished for their colorful fruits, which are borne in the autumn, and some have the added advantage of evergreen foliage. Many of the kinds that shed their leaves are brilliantly colored in the fall. There are few gardens where some form of Euonymus cannot be grown successfully.

Euonymus alatus, sometimes called the Winged Euonymus because of the corky wings which are produced along the stems, makes an attractive large-scale shrub 8 feet or more in height and often as broad. The form *compactus* is usually desired for the small garden because of its lower height. The plant makes a pleasing appearance throughout the season and is especially colorful in the fall with its conspicuous fruits and foliage. Other shrubby or tree-like forms include *E. atropurpureus*, sometimes called Wahoo or Burning-bush, reaching 25 feet in height; *E. Bungeanus*, with showy yellowish fruits; *E. europaeus*, also a big-scale plant, and the evergreen *E. japonicus* and its various forms. A partially evergreen kind, *E. patens*, has attractive large light green leaves and pinkish fruits in the fall.

Among the trailing or climbing sorts are the evergreen *E. radicans*, known as Wintercreeper, and its many varieties, commonly grown on walls and banks. The showy reddish fruits of several forms are colorful in autumn. A tiny-leaved form known as *E. radicans minimus* (*E. kewensis*) makes a delicate tracery around the bases of sun dials, in rock gardens, or on low walls.

The shrub and tree-like forms of Euonymus can be grown successfully in full sun or in partial shade. Plants can be set out in spring or fall; many nurserymen offer pot plants of the trailing kinds. The soil requirements of Euonymus are simple and they require little care, except the use of pruning shears to keep them in bounds. The evergreen climbing or trailing kinds thrive in well-drained garden soil in full sun. They are easily propagated from the stems that trail along the ground; these take root readily. Unfortunately, where the summers are hot and dry, they are often subject to scale.

GARDEN FLOWERS IN COLOR

EUPATORIUM

Mist-flower, Eupatorium coelestinum

Both the name Eupatorium and the common names of several of the species remind us of the medicinal value of this group of plants commemorating an ancient king of Pontus, who is supposed to have used some species for healing purposes. The widely distributed Joe-pye Weed of our swamps, *Eupatorium purpureum*, took its name from some Indian herb doctor. Boneset and Thoroughwort have had familiar household associations since the early settlers came to our country.

With the exception of the White Snakeroot, *E. urticaefolium* (or *ageratoides*), and Mist-flower, *E. coelestinum* (sometimes called Conoclinium), the Eupatoriums belong in the wild garden. Like many native plants, they are not adequately appreciated by gardeners. A clump or two of Boneset, *E. perfoliatum*, associated with cardinal-flower and *Iris Pseudacorus*, is an effective combination for the edge of a small pool.

The White Snakeroot with its loose heads of fluffy, white, ageratum-like flowers on 3 to 4-foot stems, brings light to dark shady nooks in August and September. In late summer and early autumn the Mist-flower provides a long period of soft blue color in the garden. The attractive flower heads have prompted the common name of Hardy Ageratum. Eighteen inches seems to be the maximum height of this plant, which grows with equanimity in sun or shade. The Mist-flower combines delightfully with *Begonia Evansiana*, and both thrive under similar conditions. It makes an excellent ground cover among shrubs.

Ordinary soil suits these plants, and moisture is an advantage. Full sun, partial shade, or even fairly dense shade will not hinder their growth. They are easily increased by root division, which can be done in spring or fall. This group of perennials increases rapidly, sometimes to the point of becoming a nuisance. In the small garden they can be kept in check by resetting every other year.

GARDEN FLOWERS IN COLOR

EVENING-PRIMROSE

The Evening-primrose, classified by botanists as Œnothera, has long been a garden favorite. Many of the species, some of which are called Sundrops, grow wild in various parts of the United States and several have been used by scientists to prove theories of plant breeding. Most of them are hardy perennials.

The sturdy *Œnothera biennis*, varying from 2 to 6 feet in height, is a familiar weed primarily suited to the wild garden. Perhaps the form most commonly seen in gardens is *Œ. fruticosa Youngi*, with its great clusters of bright lemon-yellow, saucer-like flowers on compact plants 18 to 24 inches tall. The improved variety Illumination is illustrated on this page. The Missouri Sundrop, *Œ. missouriensis*, is semi-prostrate in form and less than a foot in height. Although the great cup-shaped, greenish yellow blooms measuring several inches in diameter endure for only a single day, they leave behind them a curiously twisted mass of petals. A dainty pink-flowering species, *Œ. speciosa*, grows about 15 inches tall.

Evening-primroses grow best in ordinary soil and full sun. To check their rampant growth reset them every other year in early spring or fall. Root division is the easiest method of propagation.

Evening-primrose, Illumination

GARDEN FLOWERS IN COLOR

EVERLASTING

Although the common name Everlasting is primarily associated with the annual Acroclinium (more correctly Helipterum), numerous annuals are cultivated for their straw-like blooms which are dried for winter bouquets. Some gardeners use the word Everlasting or Strawflower in referring to these plants; among the commonest are Ammobium, Gomphrena, Helichrysum, Statice (Limonium), and Xeranthemum. (The Strawflower, Helichrysum, is discussed on page 251.) All are of easy culture and can be grown in a wide variety of soils.

The Everlasting known as Acroclinium (*Helipterum roseum*) is an attractive annual with rose-pink flowers on 15-inch stems. Arrangements of the fresh blooms in varying stages of development make unusual flower combinations.

Sow the seed in full sun and set the plants 4 to 6 inches apart. This annual is best grown in rows in the cutting garden, where sowings made at intervals of two weeks will provide an abundance of flowers. For drying, the blooms should be cut before they are fully open, then the foliage removed and the stems hung up to dry in a dark place with the flower heads down.

FLAX

The Flax of commerce, *Linum usitatissimum*, has no decorative value in gardens but several perennial and annual species of this genus have attractive flowers.

Among the hardy forms is the dainty Golden Flax, *L. flavum*, with glaucous foliage and bright yellow flowers on 12 to 15-inch stems in June; it makes a charming rock-garden subject. *L. perenne* is the familiar garden form, but it is rapidly being replaced by *L. narbonense*, which produces large, brilliant blue flowers in great profusion. Both species vary from 18 to 24 inches in height. The scarlet Flax, *L. grandiflorum*, is an annual kind 15 inches tall with conspicuous blooms resembling those of *L. narbonense* in form.

Both perennial and annual kinds of Flax are easily grown from seed in full sun and ordinary soil; in fact, established plants self-sow readily. The annual kinds can be sown in early spring.

Linum narbonense

GARDEN FLOWERS IN COLOR

Forget-me-nots show best in masses

FORGET-ME-NOT

The familiar Forget-me-nots seen in spring gardens are species and hybrids of the genus Myosotis. Most of the kinds commonly grown are hardy annuals or biennials. This plant self-sows readily and often spreads rapidly in gardens where moisture conditions are favorable.

Blue, pink, and white forms of Forget-me-nots are available from seedsmen. They produce blooms in early spring, flowering best during cool weather. The bloom period can be greatly extended if the plants are not allowed to go to seed. Catalogs list forms of *Myosotis alpestris* (*sylvatica*) in several shades of blue. These delightful spring-flowering plants are compact, varying from 6 to 10 inches tall. The everblooming Forget-me-not, *M. palustris semperflorens*, is a tall sort a foot or more in height, with large clear blue flowers.

Sow the seed in midsummer and set the plants 3 to 4 inches apart in coldframes or in beds raised above the level of the soil. A covering of hay or straw or any other available material will provide protection through the winter months. Mulches of this sort are never applied until the ground has frozen hard. Very often plants that self-sow come through the winters satisfactorily without any protection.

FORSYTHIA

One of our most familiar early spring-flowering shrubs is the charming Forsythia, often called Golden-bells. Several species and hybrids are offered by nurserymen. Where plants of weeping habit are needed, *Forsythia suspensa* is ideal; it is a vigorous, rampant grower and makes an attractive, loosely formed plant. The variety *Fortunei* is noted for its upright habit and its arching branches. *F. intermedia* produces unusually large, pure yellow blooms on upright-growing plants reaching 8 feet in height. Where a pale yellow kind is desired, the hybrid *primulina* will fill the need. *F. ovata* makes a compact plant seldom more than 5 feet tall, and blooms a week earlier.

Few shrubs are of easier culture; they can be planted in spring or fall. The most important thing to remember about Forsythia is that the plants should not be sheared into ugly symmetrical forms but rather should be allowed to assume their natural habit of growth. Plants are best pruned immediately after flowering because bloom is produced on the previous year's growth.

The showy yellow Forsythia is a harbinger of spring

GARDEN FLOWERS IN COLOR

FOUR-O'CLOCK

~ The Four-o'Clock, *Mirabilis Jalapa*, is an old-time favorite that has been somewhat neglected in recent years. This tropical plant, some-times called Marvel-of-Peru, is treated as an annual throughout the colder parts of the United States, but it is really a perennial with large fleshy roots. The plant grows 3 feet or more in height and often as wide, forming a large shrub-like mass. The delightfully fragrant blooms appear in late afternoon and remain open until the sun strikes them the following morning. For quick growing effects, especially for hedges or temporary foundation plantings, the Four-o'Clock is most desirable. Usually the seed is offered in a mixture of colors, including red, yellow, white, and variegated forms.

Seed may be sown in the open ground as soon as danger of frost is past. The Four-o'Clock does best in full sun and is not particular as to soil. Allow 15 to 18 inches between plants. Home gardeners dig the roots in fall and store them over winter as one would dahlias, but it is an easy matter to start new plants each year from seed.

FOXGLOVE

The Common Foxglove, *Digitalis purpurea*, is a familiar biennial in early summer gardens. The plants grow from 3 to 6 feet tall, with blooms varying in color from white to deep rose and salmon. Rose shades are dominant in the Giant Shirley strains and salmon in the Lutzi hybrids. Two yellow species, *D. ambigua* (*grandiflora*), 3 feet in height, and *D. lanata*, about 2 feet tall, are true hardy perennials.

Experienced gardeners speak of Foxgloves as biennials rather than true perennials. That is, under ordinary conditions, they bloom the second year from seed, and then die. Sow the seed preferably in June or early July so that the plants may become well established before frost. Foxgloves require a well-drained location. Some gardeners transplant them into beds or coldframes to carry them over winter; others set the plants in their permanent places in autumn and protect them with marsh hay, evergreen boughs, or strawberry baskets.

Hybrids of Digitalis purpurea

GARDEN FLOWERS IN COLOR

Crown Imperial, Fritillaria imperialis

FRITILLARIA ·

There are many kinds of Fritillarias, but perhaps the best known of all is the showy Crown Imperial, *Fritillaria imperialis*. The oddly checkered petals of *F. meleagris*, known as the Guinea-hen Flower or the Checkered-lily, probably suggested to botanists the generic name Fritillaria, meaning "dicebox." Most species are more curious than beautiful, and many people object to their unpleasant odor.

The Crown Imperial grows 2 to 4 feet tall, producing large clusters of bell-shaped flowers in crown-like form during April and May; orange and red varieties are preferred. The Guinea-hen Flower, although less showy, is on the whole easy to grow and finds itself at home in a rock garden. Several distinct varieties averaging a foot in height send forth bell-shaped flowers in April and May. Little known in the East are the California species, *F. recurva*, *F. lanceolata*, and *F. pudica*.

The Crown Imperial demands deep rich soil; the bulbs are set 6 inches deep in the fall. They seem to resent the encroachment of other plant roots and often send out weak growth with only a few flowers. Bulbs must be planted as soon as received, and the foliage allowed to die down naturally after bloom is over. The Guinea-hen Flower prefers a light moist soil. Apparently the California species prefer semi-arid conditions with perfect drainage in dry summer weather.

GARDEN FLOWERS IN COLOR

FUCHSIA

Few gardeners realize that the lovely potted plants of Fuchsias seen in florist shops during the late winter and early spring are actually tropical shrubs. Some kinds are seldom more than a foot in height, but there are others that reach 40 feet or more in their natural habitat, New Zealand. For the most part, the Fuchsias grown in gardens in the colder parts of the United States are treated as tender plants which are set out after all danger of frost has passed. In recent years nurserymen have featured the new hardy kind, *Fuchsia magellanica*, and several hybrid forms. Of a somewhat trailing habit, it is sometimes used on walls and is particularly pleasing in gardens, where the plants may reach 2 feet or more in height.

Fuchsias grow well in partial shade and require rich moist soil. Plants of the hardy kinds may be set out in spring or fall. Most growers recommend a protective mulch for the hardy Fuchsia planted north of Philadelphia. The many tender kinds grown in summer gardens can be carried over winter in a greenhouse, or the roots can be hung up to dry in a frostproof cellar. Some gardeners cut back the tender kinds and put them in boxes of soil over winter.

Fuchsia magellanica

FUNKIA

Funkia, also known as Plantain-lily, is a hardy perennial listed botanically as Hosta. For broad masses in partial shade, these plants make excellent ground covers.

Hosta caerulea is vigorous in its growth, with large dark green leaves. The sturdy flower spikes, sometimes 2 to 3 feet tall, support large purple blooms during July and August. The Narrow-leaved Plantain-lily, *H. japonica* (sometimes listed as *H. lancifolia* or *lanceolata*), is commonly grown. It is easily recognized by its unusually narrow leaves and its lilac-blue flower spikes, averaging 2 feet, in July and August. The variegated forms, broadly marked with creamy white, have been used so much for border effects that long rows of them are tiresome to look at. The Fragrant Plantain-lily, *H. plantaginea*, is an August-blooming species—hence the name August Lily. Its bright green foliage grows in dense clusters from 1 to 1½ feet tall.

Plantain-lilies are ideal for shady areas but will grow well in full sun. Rich, well-drained loam is their only requirement. The plants may be raised from seed or propagated by root division.

Hosta caerulea

GARDEN FLOWERS IN COLOR

Perennial Gaillardia and Gypsophila

GAILLARDIA

Gaillardia, familiarly known as Blanket-flower, reminds us of the brilliant color contrasts characteristic of the hand-woven materials made by Indian tribes in the Southwest. These showy flowers are native to various parts of the United States, and in recent years both annual and perennial kinds have been greatly improved.

Scorching summer heat has little or no effect on the Gaillardias, for they bloom persistently if the seed pods are removed. With stems seldom more than 2 feet tall, the flowers average 2 to 4 inches in diameter. Many shades of red, orange, yellow, and brown of varying intensities are characteristic of the perennial species, *Gaillardia aristata*.

There are several named varieties in separate colors. Burgundy is described as wine-red. All too often Gaillardias grow rankly and flop over other plants, but this characteristic has been reduced in the hybrid Goblin, which grows only 12 to 15 inches tall, and bears bright yellow flowers, zoned with red. Mr. Sherbrook is a large soft yellow kind. Ruby derives its name from the unique red tone of the blooms. Sun God Improved has bright yellow flowers of immense size. In addition to other named varieties there are several excellent strains available. The Gaillardias are most effective in sizable masses, and bloom from June until frost. They are admirable cut flowers, and the curious curved stems often add grace to an arrangement.

G. pulchella is the source of many of the annual hybrids. These range in color from the rich red of Indian Chief to the yellowish or white blossom of The Bride, and include many showy combinations in both single and double forms.

Gaillardias are easily raised from seed, or they may be propagated by root division. Set them in full sun, preferably in light loam, and allow a foot between plants. When grown in the shade the plants are usually loose and spreading in growth. For continuous bloom keep the seed pods picked off. Seed of the annual kinds can be sown in a hot-bed, a coldframe, or in the open ground.

The annual Gaillardia, Indian Chief

GARDEN FLOWERS IN COLOR

GENTIAN

To many gardeners the Gentians offer a challenge, since numerous species are difficult to grow. It is because of the extraordinary blue coloring of the flowers that they are so much admired. Many English gardeners make a real cult of raising them.

During the warm days of late spring, the rare Trumpet Gentian of the Alps, *Gentiana acaulis*, or Stemless Gentian, as it is called, sends forth its sapphire trumpets, which sel-

Gentiana acaulis

dom rise more than 4 inches from the ground. Perhaps the easiest species for the beginner is the Bottle Gentian or Closed Gentian, *G. Andrewsi*, a native of the eastern United States. The plants grow 15 to 18 inches tall, each stem supporting a cluster of fair-sized bullet-like blue flowers. This species is easily naturalized in wild gardens.

Truly an aristocrat among native plants is the rare Fringed Gentian, *G. crinita*. This difficult biennial is almost impossible to transplant from the wild—perhaps fortunately so. It is among the less common of our native plants, and should not be picked in the wild. Hardly a plant for beginners, it rewards the skilled gardener. Those who are anxious to grow it should buy potted plants from a reputable nursery.

From northern Asia comes the early summer-blooming *G. septemfida*. The bluish gray trumpets, borne singly and in clusters, are usually more than an inch long and nearly as wide. Two species of recent introduction that have proved amazingly hardy deserve mention here. *G. hascombensis* bears attractive bright blue flowers speckled white at the base, on 6-inch stems. Somewhat similar is *G. Przewalski*, with clusters of blooms on stems about 1 foot tall. Both bloom during July and August.

Only experienced gardeners attempt to grow Gentians from seed. All others buy plants at nurseries, and then attempt to find suitable places for them. Moist soil, containing some sand and peat or leafmold, is necessary to retain the moisture which these plants require. A partly shaded location is desirable where the summers are warm.

GERANIUM

Few plant names are more familiar than Geranium, but the florists' plants we commonly call Geraniums are botanically known as Pelargoniums. More accurately the genus name Geranium is associated with a group of annual and perennial plants some of which are native to the United States. In these paragraphs we are primarily concerned with the common florists' Geranium, *Pelargonium hortorum*. Mention should also be made of the many delightful fragrant-leaved species and hybrids, as well as the decorative Martha Washington kinds.

Varying shades of pink and red and white are found in the Common or Fish Geranium. Some have variegated foliage; others are noted for their dark zonal markings on the leaves, and still others have plain green foliage. Essentially plants for winter window gardens and outdoor window boxes, Geraniums are sometimes used in formal beds.

Plants are readily obtainable from florists and can be set out when frost danger has passed. Geraniums do best in full sun and ordinary garden soil. Where there is an over-abundance of plant food in the soil, the plants are inclined to produce more foliage than flowers. If Geraniums are desired for indoor use, cuttings can be made in late summer and rooted in a partially shaded place. They can then be potted and taken indoors before heavy frosts arrive.

GARDEN FLOWERS IN COLOR

GEUM

Several species of Geum or Avens, as it is commonly called, are native to America but the showiest kinds, developed from *Geum chiloense*, are those cultivated in gardens. From late May through early summer they are at their best, and to be most effective they should be planted in groups of three or more. Numerous hybrids have been introduced in recent years, varying in height from 1 to 2 feet. The bright blooms appear on graceful sturdy stems well above compact masses of foliage which are attractive all season. Although the Geums are spoken of as hardy perennials, they do not always winter well in cold climates.

G. Borisi is of dwarf habit, with orange-scarlet blooms. Perhaps the two most familiar forms are the scarlet Mrs. Bradshaw and the warm golden yellow Lady Stratheden. Many catalogs list Princess Juliana, with warm yellow-red flowers, Fire Opal, described as orange-scarlet, and Red Wing, a brilliant strawberry-red.

Full sun and well-drained garden soil, as well as an abundance of moisture during blooming time, are the requirements of Geum. Plants can be set out in spring or fall, allowing 10 to 12 inches between them. With fall planting, it is good practice to provide a winter mulch of evergreen boughs or some light material.

Geum hybrids

GARDEN FLOWERS IN COLOR

GLADIOLUS

More than a hundred and fifty species of Gladiolus are known, but few of them are of garden interest, except as they have been used in hybridizing to produce the many varieties commercially grown today. Several thousand are listed by the American Gladiolus Society.

Collectors of this flower speak of three classes: the exhibition type, the large decorative, and the small decorative kinds. Colors ranging from the deepest purple to the softest pink are to be found in the varieties available. In recent years, the Primulinus types have become increasingly popular. They are sometimes spoken of as Waterfall Gladiolus because they were first collected fifty years ago near Victoria Falls in the tropical forests of Africa. Their delicate flowers, predominantly in pastel shades, are gracefully poised on slender stems.

The Gladiolus are among our most popular summer flowers, largely because of their rich and varied colors, their distinction as cut flowers, and the ease with which they may be grown almost anywhere. The bulbs, or corms, are comparatively inexpensive, and the cut flowers ship well. For cutting purposes they are best grown in rows; several plantings will provide bloom from early July until frost. In the garden they are very pleasing when massed in groups in the shrub border or

GARDEN FLOWERS IN COLOR

among perennials. If they are planted deep they will seldom need staking, though the large-flowered varieties may require support.

The corms are planted 3 to 6 inches deep, according to their size and the texture of the soil. Rich, well-drained loam, occasional applications of fertilizer, and generous amounts of water will produce results that will abundantly repay the gardener.

The corms should be dug in the late fall after a killing frost. It is best to cut the tops close to the ground before digging. Since Gladiolus are most easily propagated by the little cormels which are attached to the corms, care is necessary in handling them, if one wishes to propagate a given variety. After the lifted bulbs have been dried and the soil has been shaken off, separate the newly developed corms from the remains of the old ones, which may then be discarded. Store the newly formed corms in a frostproof cellar.

In recent years Gladiolus growers have found thrips a problem, for they feed on the foliage, flowers, and corms, and do great damage. It has been found that they are harbored over winter in the corm. The simplest all-round treatment is an application of naphthalene flakes. A dose of one ounce to each hundred corms is scattered among them at the beginning of storage, to remain only four weeks, after which the disinfectant may be removed.

GARDEN FLOWERS IN COLOR

During the summer months the Gladiolus is a source of cut flowers for both the home gardener and the florist. Although the individual spikes are rather stiff, they can be effectively combined with other flowers to make striking arrangements in large containers.

GARDEN FLOWERS IN COLOR

GLORY-OF-THE-SNOW

Few plants have been more appropriately named than Chionodoxa, which is Greek for "Glory-of-the-Snow." Introduced to American gardens from the mountains of Crete less than a hundred years ago, *Chionodoxa Luciliae* bears intense blue, star-shaped flowers. It blooms with the first warm days of spring and shows to best advantage in the rock garden or in combination with other spring-flowering bulbs. The most striking effects are accomplished when it is planted in broad masses. Once established in the garden, it will multiply year after year and seldom require resetting. Planted in the foreground near forsythia or the star magnolia, and combined with masses of the early-flowering *Tulipa Kaufmanniana*, it makes a truly charming picture. A white and a pale pink form are also offered by seedsmen. The species *C. sardensis* sends forth its blue flowers somewhat earlier than the more familiar kind.

Like other spring-flowering bulbs, Chionodoxas are planted in the fall. Set the bulbs 3 inches deep and about the same distance apart. They grow well in most well-drained garden soils and can be set out in full sun or partial shade. A top dressing of stable manure applied in late fall will aid materially in keeping the bulbs thrifty.

GORDONIA

One of the choicest of American shrubs is the lovely *Gordonia alata-maha*, often listed and referred to as Franklinia or the Franklin Tree. It was discovered along the Alatamaha River in Georgia by William Bartram, son of the famous Philadelphia Bartrams, who named it in honor of Benjamin Franklin. However, the tree had previously been named Gordonia, and that is now the name accepted by botanists. Cultivated specimens are the only ones now known to exist, for since Bartram transplanted to his Philadelphia garden the tree he discovered, no further wild ones seem to have been found.

This attractive small tree begins to bloom when plants are 3 to 4 feet high, and mature specimens 30 feet tall are known. Gordonia has several desirable features. It produces its large pure white flowers from August into September. In autumn the foliage assumes brilliant colors.

Plants do best in acid soil, in full sun, especially near pools, lakes, or streams, for in its native habitat Gordonia was found in moist places. Along the eastern seaboard it has proved hardy in the New York area, and it has been grown successfully in and around Boston.

GOURDS

From the standpoint of utility, Gourds have been grown for generations, but in recent years their decorative value has also been appreciated. They belong to the Cucurbitaceae family which includes cucumbers, melons, pumpkins, and squashes, and the name Gourd is applied to their durable fruits.

Growing Gourds offers many surprises because of the unique forms of the fruits and flowers. Beginners usually buy seed in mixed packets, but collectors aim to grow the many species of several genera. These trailing plants scramble easily over old fences or along the ground. Some gardeners grow them on wire fences. For many years Gourds have fascinated Dr. L. H. Bailey, and his book "The Garden of Gourds" records the interesting story of this extraordinary family.

Plant the seed in hills 4 to 6 feet apart, like squash or melons, using several seeds in each hill. Gourds thrive best in a warm, sunny location, and the seed should not be planted until all danger of frost is past. Sometimes the vines are eaten by squash bugs, cucumber beetles, and other chewing insects which can be repelled with any convenient insecticide. Do not harvest the fruits until they are ripe and the colors are fully developed. Set them in a warm, dry place and remove all soil from the hard shells. Some gardeners polish them with floor wax and others shellac the hard surfaces. Those not satisfied with the natural colors paint them.

A representative collection of Gourds

GARDEN FLOWERS IN COLOR

The common Grape-hyacinth

GRAPE-HYACINTH

The Grape-hyacinth, *Muscari botryoides*, is one of the daintiest of our early spring bulbs, with delicate 8 to 12-inch spires of blue and white flowers. It makes a delightful combination when planted in masses with yellow or white trumpet daffodils.

Many species of Muscari are available, but most of them are little known. A tassel-flowered kind known as *M. comosum*, and its variety *monstrosum* or *plumosum*, are curiously feathered types. *M. botryoides* (the Latin for "bunch of grapes") is the common Grape-hyacinth. The variety Heavenly Blue has larger flowers and grows with more vigor than the common Grape-hyacinth. Many catalogs list *M. armeniacum*, with larger flower spikes than *M. botryoides*.

The bulbs are planted in the fall, from October until the ground freezes. Set them in groups, 2 or 3 inches deep, in full sun or partial shade. The bulbs often produce foliage in the fall.

HAWTHORN

The Hawthorns are small spiny trees which deserve more attention in the home garden. In addition to pleasing foliage and showy blooms, they bear colorful fruits which are tempting to birds. Some are broad-spreading and shrub-like in form, while others have the aspect of a small tree. They can be used as specimens on the lawn or as striking accent plants in shrub borders. Hedges of Hawthorn are both charming and useful on the home grounds, since the spines on the stems make them impenetrable.

Many species and forms are listed by nurserymen. *Crataegus coccinea*, the Thicket Hawthorn, produces its white flowers in early spring, followed by large scarlet fruits. Then there is the familiar *C. Crusgalli*, the Cockspur Thorn, which bears attractive bloom and dull red fruit; its spines are several inches long. Most commonly seen in gardens are the forms of *C. Oxyacantha*, the familiar Hawthorn of the English countryside. Double-flowering forms in white and pink, on plants averaging 12 to 15 feet in height, are also offered by many nurserymen. Perhaps the most generally used of all the Hawthorns is Paul's Scarlet, with brilliant double scarlet flowers in May.

Hawthorns grow best in rich garden soil and produce most abundant bloom in full sun. They are extremely hardy plants of easy culture, requiring little care, and can be planted either in early spring or in the fall. They often need to be pruned for appearance.

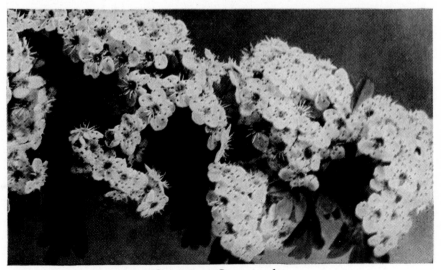

Crataegus Oxyacantha

GARDEN FLOWERS IN COLOR

HEATHER

The common Heather found in gardens is *Calluna vulgaris*. Many forms of this evergreen shrub are offered by nurseries. Pink, white, and crimson varieties which bloom through the summer months, as well as some with variegated foliage and others of compact habit, are available. The common Heather makes a good ground cover in sunny areas, and individual plants are often used in rock gardens because of the evergreen character of the foliage. Some kinds are seldom more than 6 inches in height, while others may grow a foot or more. The genus Erica, known as Heath, is sometimes confused by gardeners with Calluna.

Heather is best planted in sunny locations where there is an abundance of organic matter in the soil. Many garden soils need the addition of peat to make an ideal growing medium, for like all members of the Heath family, Calluna needs acid soil. Plants can be set out in spring or fall.

Various forms of Calluna vulgaris

GARDEN FLOWERS IN COLOR

HELIOPSIS

Among the hardiest of hardy perennials, the genus Heliopsis, especially in its improved forms, is widely planted in hardy borders. Both the single and double forms closely resemble sunflowers. Several species are native of hot dry places in many parts of the United States. The plants and the blooms are somewhat coarse in appearance but they are particularly desirable for showy effects. They flower freely during the summer and early fall, and require little care.

Two species, *Heliopsis helianthoides*, often called the False Sunflower, and *H. scabra*, the Orange Sunflower, are the source of many hybrid forms offered by nurserymen. Several shades of yellow and orange are available. Perhaps the most familiar hybrid is the orange-yellow form listed as *H. incomparabilis*, pictured above, with plants varying in height from 3 to 4 feet.

Heliopsis can be set out in spring or fall in ordinary soil. Since they are ideal for hot dry places, they should be planted in full sun. Established plants need to be divided every three years. By removing the dead flowers the blooming season of this sturdy perennial can be extended. As with other members of the sunflower family, aphids have a special fondness for the hairy stems, but this objectionable feature can be overcome by spraying with a nicotine compound.

HELIOTROPE

Like mignonette and lemon verbena, the Common Heliotrope—
Heliotropium arborescens to botanists—is one of those old-fashioned tender plants which were widely grown in the days of our grandmothers.
It is cherished not only for the rich color of the blooms but for their
delightful fragrance. An extremely tender perennial, it flourishes best
during warm weather and needs rich soil.

Many improved forms about 2 feet tall are available from florists,
varying in color from white to deep violet. They are sometimes grown
in formal beds and public parks. Heliotrope can be used to advantage
in both perennial and annual gardens.

Plants obtainable from florists can be set out after all danger of
frost has passed. Ambitious gardeners sometimes start plants from
seed which is sown indoors in February. The seedlings are transplanted as soon as they are large enough to handle. For the best results, provide a sunny location and rich garden loam. If plants are desired for the window garden, cuttings can be made in late summer.
Some gardeners prefer to dig old plants in the fall and store them in a
frostproof cellar over winter.

An improved form of Common Heliotrope

GARDEN FLOWERS IN COLOR

Hemerocallis, Patricia

HEMEROCALLIS

The modern hybrid Day-lilies are a far cry from the old-fashioned yellow and orange kinds, often called Lemon Lilies, that grew in the gardens of our grandmothers. In addition to a wider color range, varying from palest yellow to dark red and including pastel tints and bicolor forms, the new Day-lilies have been improved in size and in height, and some are delightfully fragrant. The season of bloom of the hybrid forms has been so greatly extended that the Hemerocallis can be considered the hardy perennial mainstay of the summer garden. By careful selection it is possible to have them in bloom from May until September. What is more, they are among the most adaptable of hardy perennials for the shrub border and the perennial garden. The gracefully arching foliage is attractive at all times and provides an effective background for low-growing perennials. Amazingly free flowering in habit, they are drought resistant and are seldom attacked by insects or diseases.

The name Hemerocallis, meaning "beautiful for a day," explains the common name Day-lily, which is sometimes applied to the plantain-lilies or hostas as well. Despite the fact that individual blooms

Hemerocallis, August Pioneer

last but a day, the many-branched flower stems bear quantities of buds which provide new blooms each day over a long period. This distinctive feature and the fact that they shed their dead blooms quickly, makes the Hemerocallis a desirable cut flower for indoor decoration.

A number of species and several hundred named varieties and strains are available from nurserymen. The most familiar species is *Hemerocallis aurantiaca*, which produces its burnt-orange blooms in June and July. Another tall kind is *H. citrina*, with lemon-yellow flowers. *H. flava*, the common lemon Day-lily, blooms in late May and June. The popular old orange species, *H. fulva*, often reaches 5 feet and is seen as a garden escape along country roadsides in midsummer. Among the dwarf kinds are *H. Dumortieri*, *H. Middendorffi*, and *H. minor;* these seldom grow more than 1½ feet tall and are particularly useful in foregrounds of borders.

Undoubtedly the finest of the hybrid Day-lilies are the originations of Dr. A. B. Stout, of the New York Botanical Garden. Some bear blooms of tremendous size measuring 5 inches across, while others 2 to 3 inches in diameter are carried in heavy branched sprays. They vary in height from 2 to 4 feet and more. To attempt to offer a selected list of named varieties would be difficult, because most amateurs who have specialized in Day-lilies have their own particular favorites. A representative collection is one that includes varieties offering a wide color range and a succession of bloom. Two varieties found in almost every nursery catalog are Hyperion and Ophir. Hyperion produces delightfully fragrant, citron-yellow blooms on 3½-foot stems during July and August. Ophir, blooming about the same time, has golden yellow flowers of immense size on stems 4 to 5 feet tall.

Few perennials are more adaptable and permanent throughout the entire United States. The Day-lily will grow well in full sun or partial shade, and ordinary garden soil suits it. Plants can be set out in spring or fall; allow 2 to 3 feet each way between them. Be careful not to set the plants too deep; the "bleach" mark on the foliage indicates the proper depth. Established clumps need to be divided after three to four years. An occasional top dressing of well-decomposed stable manure improves the quality of the bloom.

Hemerocallis Hybrids, Serenade and Boutonniere

GARDEN FLOWERS IN COLOR

HIBISCUS

Hibiscus Rosa-sinensis

Like the tree peony, the chrysanthemum, the lotus, and other favorite Oriental plants, the Hibiscus was highly cherished in old Chinese gardens. The name Hibiscus is confusing to many amateurs, since it includes both herbaceous and shrubby forms, some of which are widely known under other names. The familiar shrub Rose-of-Sharon, discussed on page 21, is classified as *Hibiscus syriacus*, and okra or gumbo, a popular vegetable in the South, is a related species. Musk-mallow, *H. Abelmoschus*, usually grown as an annual, is valued for its seeds, which have a musky odor and are sometimes used in making perfume. Other showy members of the great mallow family include the Hollyhock, *Althea rosea* (see page 138), and the delightful annual *Lavatera trimestris* (see page 155). All are characterized by large showy blooms, attractive foliage, and unusually vigorous growth.

We are concerned here with two distinct forms, the hybrids of *H. Moscheutos*, the Common Rose-mallow, and *H. Rosa-sinensis*, the Rose-of-China. The Common Rose-mallow, a hardy perennial, often grows 6 feet or more in height, producing shrub-like masses of large foliage. From late July through September the spectacular trumpet-shaped blooms, often 6 inches in diameter, are borne in great abundance. White, pink, and red kinds are available. This vigorous plant is particularly pleasing in the shrub border or as a background in a large perennial garden. The Rose-of-China, *H. Rosa-sinensis*, a native of tropical Asia, is often seen in the far South and along the west coast. For the most part it is treated as a greenhouse subject in the eastern United States.

The Rose-mallows may be grown from seed or from division of established plants. Since the plant blooms late in the season, it is best to divide or set out roots in early spring. Rich moist soil and full sun suits them best. When grown in partial shade they need to be staked.

HOLLY

To most home gardeners the name Holly suggests the common American Holly, *Ilex opaca*, which is used for Christmas decorations. It makes an attractive lawn specimen or it can be used in foundation plantings and shrub borders.

There are numerous other species that are widely adapted to American gardens. Some such as *I. cornuta*, the Chinese Holly, and the round-leaved form *I. cornuta Burfordi*, *I. Aquifolium*, the

Ilex cornuta Burfordi

English Holly, and *I. Cassine*, the Dahoon Holly, are essentially plants for southern gardens. Although specimens of these kinds are found as far north as Philadelphia, they are not reliably hardy in the eastern United States. The black-berried Japanese Holly, *I. crenata*, makes a good hedge; it is an ideal substitute for boxwood. Numerous forms, including one with curiously curved glossy leaves, are offered by nurserymen. The Inkberry, *I. glabra*, with smooth evergreen foliage and blue-black fruits, can be used to advantage in foundation plantings. The

American Holly

deciduous Winterberry, *I. verticillata*, makes a splendid shrub with red fruits in late fall.

All the Hollies seem to prefer an acid soil rich in organic matter. They can be set out in early spring or in early fall. If plants are moved in the fall, a generous mulch of peat moss is good insurance. It is essential that both staminate and pistillate, or male and female, forms be planted to obtain fruit. Evergreen forms are often cut back severely after planting.

HOLLYHOCK

Although often spoken of as perennials, Hollyhocks are not long-lived and many gardeners treat them as biennials. However, if the flower stalks are cut back after bloom-time, the plants will often live over and blossom the following year. Both double and single forms of *Althea rosea* are commonly grown. An annual kind introduced in recent years produces bloom in five months from seed. Hollyhocks are most easily grown from seed sown in late June or early July. Seedlings should be transplanted just as soon as they are large enough to handle, for tap-roots make large plants difficult to move.

HONEYSUCKLE

The name Honeysuckle is generally associated with the Loniceras, but those familiar with our native plants sometimes use it to refer to the so-called swamp honeysuckle, *Azalea viscosa* (see page 33). There are more than 150 species and forms of this genus, including both shrubs and woody climbers. They are noted for their vigorous growth and showy flowers—many of them very fragrant—and in addition, many have attractively toned foliage and bright fruits.

Perhaps the commonest of all is *Lonicera japonica Halliana*, Hall's Honeysuckle, a partly evergreen climber often used as a ground cover. There are numerous rapid-growing shrubby forms but here we are concerned primarily with the climbing kinds. *L. Heckrotti* and its hybrids are useful climbing plants with showy flowers. *L. sempervirens*, the Trumpet or Coral Honeysuckle, bears spectacular clusters of bloom in summer. Numerous colorful hybrids are listed by nurserymen.

For the most part, Loniceras are easy to grow, vigorous in habit, and hardy over a wide area. Many of the climbing sorts are attacked by aphids that can be repelled by a nicotine spray.

A hybrid of Lonicera sempervirens

GARDEN FLOWERS IN COLOR

HYACINTH

The familiar Dutch Hyacinths are a rich source of color and fragrance in the early spring garden. All the varieties in commerce are hybrids of *Hyacinthus orientalis*, native to the warm shores of the Mediterranean.

In recent years home gardeners have been using Hyacinths for striking color masses in the foreground of shrub borders as well as in perennial plantings. The blue and white varieties make delightful combinations when planted with daffodils. Holland growers have produced many kinds with flower stalks of enormous size, which after a few years revert to slender spikes of graceful form.

Both single and double-flowered varieties are listed in catalogs. In the blue and purple shades, one finds many pleasing tones. Bismarck, Czar Peter, Forget-me-not, and Perle Brillante are among the light blues. King of the Lilacs has large spikes of true lilac color. Ivanhoe is an improvement on the deep violet-blue of King of the Blues. Dr. Lieber and Grand Maitre are best classed as deep blue tones. Queen of the Blues reminds one of the lovely porcelain-blue in chinaware.

Pink and red varieties are holding interest in current catalogs. Dame d'Honneur is vivid rosy red, and General De Wet is a delicate rose. White margins on the petals of Hjalmer Branting distinguish this rose-colored Hyacinth. La Victoire is well named, for its carmine-rose flowers are very brilliant, as are the heavy rose spikes of Marconi. Robert Stieger has been called crimson, and Roi des Belges is a most unusually dark red shade. The brilliant pink of Gertrude seems to have been improved in the variety Pink Pearl. Herald, Lady Derby, and Mont Rose are in the rosy pink class, while Gigantea, Norma, and Princess Margaret are among the best of the pastels. City of Haarlem is a pure yellow sort; Goethe, King of the Yellows, and Yellow Hammer are all worth growing. Among the desirable white kinds are Albatros (Arentine Arendsen), L'Innocence, and La Grandesse.

Set the bulbs 5 to 6 inches deep and about the same distance apart, in well-drained garden soil. While fertilizer is essential, it must not be allowed to touch the bulbs; dig it well into the subsoil. Well-decomposed stable manure or compost dug into the soil before the bulbs are planted will keep them growing. An annual top dressing of stable manure or bonemeal applied late in the fall is good garden practice.

A colorful planting of Hyacinths

GARDEN FLOWERS IN COLOR

A hybrid of Hydrangea opuloides

HYDRANGEA

Both shrubby and climbing forms of Hydrangea are widely grown in gardens throughout the country. Perhaps the two most popular kinds are the much over-planted *Hydrangea paniculata grandiflora*, or Peegee Hydrangea, and *H. hortensis (macrophylla)*, the common forcing Hydrangea of florists. Other distinct kinds are the attractive *H. petiolaris*, the climbing Hydrangea, *H. quercifolia*, the Oak-leaf Hydrangea, and the improved forms listed as the hybrids of *H. opuloides (macrophylla)*. Hydrangeas are unquestionably among the showiest of hardy shrubs for garden use. They bloom over a long period, have sturdy foliage, and are vigorous growers. The lesser-known kinds have been overlooked because the common Peegee is so widely planted.

The wild Hydrangea called *H. arborescens* is an American native from which the hybrid Grandiflora, or Hills of Snow, was developed. This improved form is widely used in gardens, especially in shady areas where it is pleasing throughout the summer. The white flowers, produced in large loose masses on long stems, make an attractive appearance over a long period. The common forcing Hydrangea is often used in foundation plantings or grown in tubs. Its glossy foliage and large heads of blue and pink flowers have been extremely popular throughout the country. Many of the plants in gardens were originally small potted specimens obtained at Easter-time and later set outdoors. The vigorous plant is hardy over a wide territory.

The climbing Hydrangea, *H. petiolaris*, is a most useful early summer-flowering vine. It has glossy foliage and large flat heads of white bloom, and clings readily to walls. Very similar and often confused with it is *Schizophragma hydrangeoides*, differing only in the form of its bloom. Another desirable species for shady areas is *H. quercifolia*, the Oak-leaf Hydrangea. The foliage resembles an enlarged oak leaf, and white blooms are borne over a long period.

Hydrangeas are shrubs of easy culture and are seldom attacked by insects or diseases. They grow best in fertile garden soil. Special mention should be made of the common forcing Hydrangea, which is hardy except in climates where the winters are extreme. Some gardeners in cold climates protect the plants with a mulch over winter. Plants grown in tubs are usually stored in a frostproof basement through the winter months and are repotted each spring in fresh soil. The coloring of the pink-flowering forms can be changed to blue by the addition of iron or alum to the soil.

Hills of Snow Hydrangea

Peegee Hydrangea

GARDEN FLOWERS IN COLOR

IRIS

Iris cristata

The Iris has been a favorite garden plant through many centuries and many civilizations. More than 150 species have been classified, not to mention the tremendous number of garden hybrids that have been introduced through the years. From a botanical standpoint, the Irises most commonly grown in American gardens fall into four groups: the bearded (erroneously called German Iris in the trade), the beardless, the bulbous, and the crested. All the types are interesting in gardens.

The tall bearded Irises, hybrids of *Iris pallida*, *I. variegata*, and other species, are popular in nearly every state in the Union. From late May through a good part of June they bloom abundantly, some on stems 4 feet high while others seldom exceed 2 feet. The upright petals of the flowers are known as standards; the lower petals have pronounced beards from which the name bearded Iris is derived. Although not so widely grown as their tall relatives, there are many intermediate forms averaging 18 to 24 inches in height. These usually link the blooming season of the tall kinds with the hybrids of the dwarf *I. pumila* which bloom in early May. Both the tall and intermediate forms are useful in shrub and perennial plantings; dwarf Irises flourish in rock gardens.

The beardless group includes many choice Irises, differing from the bearded kinds both in form and in their preference for moisture. The upper petals or standards are narrower than those of the bearded kinds, and the entire flower is more delicate in appearance. These are essentially water-loving plants for low areas and streamsides. Nevertheless many of them are easily adapted to garden culture, even in fairly dry soil. *I. sibirica* and *I. orientalis* are the sources of the white, lavender, blue, and purple varieties which resemble our wild Blue Flag, *I. versicolor*.

The 2½ to 4-foot plants make large clumps of attractive narrow foliage among which the flower stems develop. More spectacular in size are the Japanese Irises, *I. Kaempferi*, which bloom in late June and July, thus prolonging the Iris season. Their preference for moisture is well worth the effort involved to provide it, because the blooms are rich-textured, exotic, and even bizarre in their beauty. Still more bewildering are the curious Japanese names attached to many of the varieties. *I. Pseudacorus*, the Fleur de Lys of France, or the Yellow Flag, is a fascinating species in any garden. It grows vigorously and produces many distinctive yellow blooms in late May and early June.

Bulbous Irises are excellent cut flowers that combine well with many May-flowering perennials. Both the Dutch (*I. Xiphium hybridum*) and the Spanish (*I. Xiphium*) kinds are favorites with florists for forcing and are hardy out-of-doors. The English Irises (*I. xiphioides*) bloom ten

Iris Kaempferi

GARDEN FLOWERS IN COLOR

Tall Bearded Iris

days later than the kinds previously mentioned, and they, too, are most attractive in the garden.

There are two species of crested Iris worth mentioning. The first, the native *I. cristata*, blooms in early May in many rock gardens. The other species, *I. tectorum*, is the famous Roof Iris of Japan, so called because it has been grown for centuries on the roofs of Japanese homes.

Irises present few difficulties for the amateur gardener, since they grow easily in either full sun or part shade. The bearded kinds thrive in well-drained ground that is definitely on the dry side. They prefer a

A favorite form of bulbous Dutch Iris grown by florists, which flourishes in gardens even in cold climates.

GARDEN FLOWERS IN COLOR

sweet soil and respond to frequent feedings of bonemeal; many gardeners occasionally dig lime around the roots of their plants. Irises are usually planted or reset after their flowering period is over, but they may be moved in early spring also. It is perfectly natural for the rhizomes of bearded Iris to rest on the surface of the soil. When reset, they should be barely covered. They grow vigorously, and need to be divided at least every three years. The Iris borer, their worst enemy, is easily detected by the yellowed condition that appears in the center of each group of leaves in early summer. Unless the variety is especially desirable, dig up and destroy the infested rhizomes and reset the remainder of each clump.

All of the beardless kinds may be planted in low moist locations, or along streams and ponds, but they may also be grown easily in the perennial border of the average home garden. Japanese varieties need plenty of water when the buds are forming. Since all of these kinds are also vigorous in their growth, they need to be divided at least every three years.

Bulbous Irises are planted with other spring-flowering bulbs in October. Set them 4 to 5 inches deep in well-drained soil, and for striking effects plant them in groups of five or more. They send forth a slight growth of grass-like foliage in autumn.

Iris sibirica

GARDEN FLOWERS IN COLOR

ISMENE

Basket-flower and Spider-lily are common names for Ismene. This attractive member of the amaryllis family, now listed as *Hymenocallis calathina*, originated in the Andes and is a most useful summer-flowering plant. In an effort to give it rightful recognition, the American Amaryllis Society speaks of it as "Amerindian Lily." The curious lily-like blooms look as if some ambitious grower had snipped the edges with a pair of scissors in an effort to improve upon nature. The sturdy, 2-foot plants have strap-like foliage and strong flower stems. They can be planted in groups of six or more in the foreground of a perennial border or shrub planting to provide masses of color during the summer months. Summer-flowering bulbs deserve more attention from the home gardener, and Ismene is one of the truly worthwhile kinds.

Ismene grows well in most garden soils. Bulbs can be set out as soon as danger of frost has passed. Plant them 4 to 5 inches deep and allow 8 inches between them. Over a large part of the eastern United States the bulbs are not hardy, but must be lifted in late autumn and stored in a frostproof place over winter. In warm climates they are allowed to remain in the ground the year round.

IVY

Numerous variations of English Ivy, *Hedera Helix*, have been developed in recent years. Home-owners who are seeking good ground covers for shady areas are finding that large masses of the various kinds of Ivy make distinctive and unusual ground covers. Since Ivy clings readily by means of adventitious roots, it is widely used on walls to soften architectural features.

Perhaps the hardiest form available for use in the home garden is *Hedera Helix baltica*, a small-leaved kind of great vigor. For those who like out-of-the-ordinary plants there are variegated, bronzy-leaved, and curly-leaved forms.

Ivy is an ideal plant for shady places. It grows best in rich, moist soil and is easily propagated by cuttings which can be placed in water until roots form or in moist soil in a shady place. Usually the most satisfactory results are obtained when cuttings are made in late summer. Sometimes plants grown in full sun burn back and winterkill badly during severe winters, but they can be cut back to live growth.

LABURNUM

Often called the Golden-chain Tree, *Laburnum anagyroides* is among the choicest of small trees for the home garden. The showy yellow flowers, which remind one of wistaria, usually appear in May; mature plants may reach 30 feet in height. Perhaps the most common form offered by nurserymen is the hybrid *L. Vossi*, with greenish bark and long sprays of clover-like leaves. The Scotch Laburnum, *L. alpinum*, blooms in June or July. The Laburnum is a picturesque plant for the shrub border or can be used as a specimen on the lawn.

As a rule, Laburnum is not a long-lived tree. It requires a sunny location in well-prepared garden soil and may be set out in either spring or fall. Care must be taken to obtain plants with well-developed root systems from a reliable nurseryman. Sometimes the plant is difficult to move successfully.

Golden-chain Tree

GARDEN FLOWERS IN COLOR

LARKSPUR

Outstanding among tall-growing annuals are the many hybrids of *Delphinium Consolida* and *D. Ajacis*, which are usually spoken of as Annual Larkspur. The perennial species discussed on page 94 are also called Larkspur by some gardeners, but in recent years, especially since the many hybrid forms have been developed, the name Delphinium has come to be associated with the showy large-flowered hybrids. The word Delphinium is from the Greek meaning "dolphin" and refers to the shape of the individual blooms.

These excellent annuals with their quaint, spire-like forms suggesting antique candelabra, are well adapted as accent plants for large mass effects, and for middle-ground or background groups in borders. Some gardeners prefer to grow them in combination with other annuals or in rows in the cutting garden, while others allow them to self-sow yearly in the perennial border. Few annuals are more decorative for flower arrangements.

Both single and double-flowering forms are available, but most gardeners prefer the double kinds. The Giant Imperial strain produces spikes of flowers in many tints and shades on stems 3 feet or more in height. Among them are Blue Spire, Carmine King, Coral King, Exquisite, a rich pink, Gloria, deep rose, La France, salmon-pink, Lilac Spire, Sweet Lavender, and White Spire. There are also several strains of dwarf habit.

Perhaps the most vivid of the dwarf Larkspurs is the delightful *D. grandiflorum* (*chinense* or *sinense*), which is seldom more than 2 feet tall. Although a perennial, it is often grown as an annual, since the seed germinates readily. The loosely arranged panicles of brilliant blue are highly treasured for cutting, and several crops of bloom can be enjoyed if the plants are not allowed to form seed.

Since annual Larkspurs are hardy and do not transplant easily, it is best to sow the seed where they are to flower. This may be done in early spring or in the fall, particularly if one desires an early crop of flowers. To hasten the germination of the seed, wrap it in a cloth and subject it to alternate thawing and freezing for several days. Mix a little sand with the seed for more even distribution, and thin the plants to stand at least 9 inches apart. A sunny location suits them, and they prefer rich loam to stony soil because of their slender tap-roots. Start the seed of *D. grandiflorum* indoors or in a coldframe, and, as this species endures transplanting, set the plants 9 inches apart. If the soil is inclined to be strongly acid, dig in a little agricultural lime. Annual Larkspur that self-sows in gardens year after year tends to revert to the old single types.

Giant Imperial Larkspur

GARDEN FLOWERS IN COLOR

LAUREL

This native evergreen shrub has several familiar names; among them are Laurel, Mountain-laurel, and Calico-bush. The true Laurel is *Laurus nobilis*, commonly known as the Bay Tree; the Mountain-laurel with which we are concerned here is classified as *Kalmia latifolia*. The genus name is in compliment to Peter Kalm, a pupil of the renowned Linnaeus, who explored the American colonies for plants in the eighteenth century. *K. latifolia* produces large clusters of saucer-shaped, soft rose-colored blooms in late May and June on plants varying in height from 2 to 10 feet.

Mountain-laurel is a hardy, very ornamental shrub that makes a really spectacular display in the Appalachian Mountains each spring, where it grows and blooms profusely with the native azaleas and rhododendrons. Both Pennsylvania and Connecticut have chosen the Mountain-laurel as their state flower.

Another native species worth mentioning is *K. angustifolia*, Sheep-laurel, which is sometimes called Lambkill. Unlike the Mountain-laurel, its blooms are borne in lateral clusters around the stems, and it is essentially a plant for the wild garden.

Well-grown specimens of Mountain-laurel from nurseries are widely used in gardens, where their glossy foliage is attractive the year round. Laurel combines well with other plants for foundation groupings, as a specimen plant, or associated with azaleas, rhododendrons, and other flowering shrubs. The individual blooms are especially intriguing, varying from pink to white. Like most of the broad-leaved evergreens, Laurel does best in a peaty acid soil. It can be grown to advantage in full sun or partial shade, and plants may be moved in spring or fall. Flower clusters should be removed from the plants as soon as bloom is over, in order to encourage the development of new flower buds for bloom the following year.

LAVATERA

The Annual or Tree-mallow, an improved form of *Lavatera trimestris*, has never received the attention it deserves from amateurs, and yet it may well be considered the annual counterpart of the large-flowering Hibiscus often found in perennial gardens.

Masses of this sturdy, tall-growing plant (usually 3 to 4 feet high, and suggesting the name Tree-mallow) are most desirable for background effects in the annual garden, or for color splashes in the perennial border. The warm rose-colored flowers, hollyhock-like in appearance, and the rounded dull green leaves, are useful for arranging with other blooms.

Start the seed outside where the plants are to grow. Although the seedlings do not transplant readily because of their taproots, which are so characteristic of the Mallow family, it is not impossible to transplant them. Some gardeners start them indoors and pot them before setting them out. Full sun and ordinary soil are the simple requirements for growing Lavatera.

LEUCOTHOË

Like Mountain-laurel, *Leucothoë Catesbaei* is one of our native broad-leaved evergreens that deserves a place in the home garden. In addition to its glossy evergreen foliage, which is rich in red coloring when new leaves are unfolding, it produces white flowers during May in drooping clusters along the underside of its arching branches. Usually the plants average 2 to 3 feet in height, but established specimens may reach 6 feet or more. It grows wild in the Appalachian region from Virginia to Georgia and Tennessee, and is widely cultivated by nurserymen.

Because of the graceful arching growth of the stems, clumps of Leucothoë are particularly desirable with other broad-leaved and coniferous evergreens. Often plants are used in groups under flowering dogwood trees and in foundation plantings, as well as in combination with other deciduous trees. Leucothoë seems to grow best in partial shade, and presents an attractive appearance throughout the year. Sprays of the foliage are sometimes used in flower arrangements for distinctive effects.

Like other broad-leaved evergreens, Leucothoë grows best in moist acid soil that is rich in organic matter. The necessary acidity can be added to most garden soils by the use of acid leaf-mold or peat moss. New plants can be set out in spring or fall; large clumps are easily divided as the home gardener finds need for additional plants. Sometimes old wood dies back severely in winter, but it can easily be pruned as soon as growth starts in the spring. Plants grown in exposed or sunny areas are often subject to weather burn; this condition, too, is remedied by pruning.

LIATRIS

Sometimes our native plants are overlooked in favor of exotic ones, but fortunately such is not the case with *Liatris pycnostachya*, commonly known as Kansas Gayfeather or Blazing Star. This striking hardy perennial produces long sturdy spikes of rich purple bloom in late summer, averaging 3 to 5 feet. The narrow grass-like leaves add to its beauty. It is especially desirable not only because of its late bloom but also because it serves as a useful accent plant in the hardy border or the wild garden. In addition, the blooms last well when cut and combine well with other flowers where outstanding arrangements are needed.

Fairly recent introductions are the lovely hybrids of *L. scariosa* sometimes referred to as Rattlesnake Master and Blue Blazing Star. The variety September Glory sometimes reaches 6 feet, with amazingly long spikes of purple bloom. A delightful white-flowering companion is the variety White Spire. Both these hybrids are much sought after to add interest and beauty to the autumn garden. They combine well with hardy chrysanthemums, hardy asters, marigolds, *Cimicifuga racemosa simplex*, and other fall-blooming plants.

Since Liatris grows well in hot dry places and blooms in late summer, it is very useful for the home garden. The plants can be set out in early spring or fall. For best effects plant them in groups of three or more, and allow at least a foot between individual plants. Established plants can be divided every three years. Although the original species are found in poor soils, the improved forms respond readily to soils rich in available plant food.

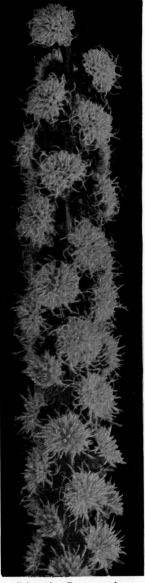

Liatris, September Glory, with its showy spires of fluffy, button-like blooms.

LILAC

The old-fashioned Common Lilac, *Syringa vulgaris*, has been grown in gardens for generations. Although cultivated for more than three hundred years, it remained unnoticed by hybridizers until a century ago when a Frenchman, Victor Lemoine, undertook the improvement of garden varieties. As a result, many outstanding kinds, commonly referred to as French Lilacs, have been introduced. Both single and double-flowering forms are available, with colors ranging from dark red-purple through many shades of blue and lilac to a pure white. In addition, hybridizers have improved the size of the individual florets and the flower clusters.

Many notable species of Lilacs are found in the great collections in public parks. Outstanding among them are the plantings at Highland Park, Rochester, New York, and the Arnold Arboretum, Boston, Massachusetts. With the exception of the Persian Lilac, *S. persica*, few of these are found in gardens, but a number are available from nurserymen who specialize in unusual plants. The 12-foot Hungarian Lilac, *S. Josikaea*, has deep purple blooms in June and large oval foliage. *S. microphylla*, a slender-branched shrub, seldom more than 5 feet tall, bears delightfully fragrant clusters of small lilac-colored bloom in May and June. Occasional flowers appear later in the season. An extra-early-blooming kind is *S. oblata* and its variety *dilatata*, which makes a display of pale lilac blossoms in late April or early May. Connoisseurs of Lilacs generally include *S. pubescens* and *S. villosa* in their collections. Home gardeners who have ample space find great pleasure in collecting species and varieties.

Lilacs can be grown in a wide variety of soils, and their requirements are simple. They do best in full sun and respond readily to applications of stable manure, which is considered more desirable for these plants than chemical fertilizers. Generous feedings of well-decomposed stable manure dug around the plants will produce satisfactory results. In areas where the soil is inclined to be acid, hydrated lime should be dug around the plants. This is easily done after the flowering period. Keep the plants growing vigorously, and remove all dead flowers, to prevent the plant from setting seed.

Lilacs are rapid growers and often reach 10 to 12 feet or more in height. Hence pruning to check the height of the plants as well as to increase production of bloom is most important. They are generally pruned during the late winter, when all weak growth is removed, and care taken to avoid cutting off the stems bearing flower buds. Since many of the French Lilacs are grafted, all suckers produced below the point of union must be removed; otherwise, the understock may outgrow the hybrid.

Several pests attack Lilacs; first among them is the oystershell scale, which is easily recognized on the stems. An oil spray applied before growth begins in the spring will destroy this pest. Several diseases are sometimes evident, too; all branches affected should be removed and burned. Mildews can be checked by spraying with sulphur.

French Hybrid Lilacs are delightful in the home garden

GARDEN FLOWERS IN COLOR

Regal Lilies and rambler roses make a pleasing combination

GARDEN FLOWERS IN COLOR

LILY

Among the loveliest but at the same time the most exasperating of flowers are the Lilies that we attempt to grow in our gardens. Of course, some hardy ones like the Regal and the Candlestick Lilies flourish with little care, but such species as the Madonna, the Auratum, and the Speciosum often try the patience of even experienced gardeners. Many theories and opinions have been presented in an effort to make Lily-growing easier, but it is now generally acknowledged that mosaic disease is at the root of most of the trouble and is by far the most serious drawback to raising Lilies successfully.

In recent years several keen scientists have gone to work on the problem. Chief among them is George L. Slate, of the New York State Agricultural Experiment Station, whose book "Lilies for American Gardens" was published by Charles Scribner's Sons, New York, in 1939. Amateur gardeners who would specialize in Lilies will find this volume of inestimable value. The best advice that can be given is to patronize reputable growers who supply disease-free bulbs in good condition. The inexpensive but shriveled and diseased bulbs often sold in department stores are worth no more than they cost, and at best are a liability.

An amazing number of Lily species have been introduced to American gardens, and many named hybrids have been developed; some require more care than others. Those discussed here are generally available and are the familiar kinds grown in the home garden.

Lilium auratum, the Goldband Lily, is undoubtedly the most spectacular of all, with its yellow bands and reddish markings on waxy white petals. Plants vary in height from 3 to 6 feet and usually bloom in July or August, though bulbs set out in spring bloom later. Few Lilies have a more penetrating fragrance; one flower will scent an entire room. Several improved forms are listed by bulb growers; among them is the variety *pictum*, with darker spots than the type. The variety *platyphyllum* is most robust, with larger blooms. Set the bulbs 9 to 12 inches deep, depending upon their size. Unfortunately this species is often infested with mosaic, and unless disease-free bulbs can be obtained home gardeners can seldom hope to be successful.

The Meadow Lily, *L. canadense*, ranges in color from light yellow to orange-red, with purplish spots on the inner side of each drooping trumpet. It is a common native 2 to 4 feet in height, usually found in moist meadows. June and July are bloom-time for this dainty Lily. The bulbs need to be set 8 inches deep.

One of the oldest Lilies in cultivation is the Madonna Lily, *L. candidum*, long cherished for its pure white, fragrant blooms. It flowers with delphiniums and roses in June and early July. Established bulbs produce six or more blooms on stems 3 to 4 feet tall. Because it sends forth a growth of foliage in early fall, the bulbs must be planted in late summer. For best results they are set 2 inches deep. (See page 164.)

Common in gardens are numerous forms of the Candlestick Lilies, which include *L. dauricum*, *L. elegans*, *L. croceum* (known as the Orangeman's Lily), and *L. umbellatum*. Mostly yellow, orange, and red, the showy blooms are held erect on stems 1 to 2 feet tall, and make a bright splash in gardens in early summer. Grown in shrub borders and perennial gardens, they require little care. Connoisseurs of Lilies

The Goldband Lily,
Lilium auratum

GARDEN FLOWERS IN COLOR

The Meadow Lily, Lilium canadense

do not favor them because they harbor the mosaic disease and evidence of its presence in these Lilies is not easily detected. They grow well in full sun, and the bulbs are set 4 to 6 inches deep.

A fairly recent introduction, *L. formosanum,* a large white nodding trumpet-shaped Lily, is greatly prized for its ease of culture, its free-flowering habit, and its sturdy stems. The delightfully fragrant blooms, often marked on the outer side with purple, are borne in clusters. One form which varies in height from 2 to 6 feet and blooms in late summer and early fall, is known as Wilson's variety. An early summer-flowering kind seldom more than 2 feet tall is listed as Price's variety. Both forms are easily raised from seed, and bulbs of blooming size can be obtained the second year. The mature bulbs are set 8 inches deep. Since this form is often subject to disease, it is desirable to grow *L. formosanum* from seed. (See page 166.)

L. Hansoni is a gay orange-yellow Lily blooming in late May or June; it grows 2 feet or more in height and requires little or no attention. Remarkably long-lived, it is seldom subject to disease and makes an attractive appearance when planted in colonies. Set the bulbs 6 to 8

GARDEN FLOWERS IN COLOR

The Madonna Lily, Lilium candidum

inches deep and plant some low-growing perennial among them.

L. Henryi, from China, is particularly successful when interplanted with rhododendrons and azaleas. The golden orange blooms are borne in late July and August on slender arching stems 4 to 6 feet or more in height. It is a long-lived easy Lily and retains its color best in partial shade. Set the bulbs 8 to 10 inches deep. (See page 167.)

A purplish pink Lily seldom seen in modern gardens is *L. Martagon*, sometimes called the Turban or European Turks-cap Lily. The unpleasantly scented flowers appear in June; the pure white form is preferred to the type. Set the bulbs 6 inches deep in a shady location.

Sometimes called the Western Tiger Lily, *L. pardalinum* is widely distributed in moist areas along the West coast. The spotted, bright yellow and orange blooms are borne in great abundance on 4 to 6-foot stems. An improved form, *L. pardalinum giganteum*, sometimes called the Sunset Lily, is valued for its immense blooms on sturdy stems.

Although of western origin, these Lilies grow with ease in the eastern United States and make a brilliant display in June. This is a Lily for full sun; the bulbs are set 4 to 5 inches deep. (See pages 167 and 168.)

The Regal Lily, *L. regale*, is undoubtedly America's favorite, because of its beauty of form, its delightful fragrance, and its ease of culture. Introduced from western China shortly after the turn of the century by the plant explorer E. H. Wilson, the Regal Lily has been widely grown throughout the country and flourishes with amazing vigor. The plants vary in height from 2 to 6 feet and when mature will produce ten or more funnel-shaped blooms on a single stem during July. The white flowers have a canary-yellow throat with rosy purple markings on the outside. A sunny location and well-drained garden soil are the simple requirements for this Lily, which is amazingly adaptable and usually disease-free. Set the bulbs 8 inches deep. Flowering bulbs can be grown from seed in two to three years. No garden is complete without this decorative Lily. (See page 160.)

In late summer and fall the Speciosum Lilies contribute their measure of beauty to garden beds and borders. Distinctive in form, color, and fragrance, this Oriental species, like the spectacular Goldband Lily, is a favorite of gardeners everywhere. The blooms, varying from four to ten in number, are borne on sturdy stems 2½ to 4 feet tall. The typical form is white with pink shading and crimson spots. A pure white variety of exquisite beauty is offered by seedsmen. Several crimson varieties listed as *magnificum*, *Melpomene*, and *rubrum* are

The Candlestick Lily, Lilium dauricum

GARDEN FLOWERS IN COLOR

Lilium formosanum

noted for their brilliance. If disease-free bulbs are obtained from reliable growers, the home gardener is usually assured of success with this fine Lily. A well-drained site in full sun or light shade suits it. The bulbs are planted 6 to 8 inches deep. (See page 169.)

Known as the American Turks-cap Lily, *L. superbum* is one of our native plants distributed along the eastern seaboard. A truly striking Lily with great spikes of orange flowers on stems 6 to 8 feet tall, it blooms during July and August and grows abundantly among such acid-soil plants as azaleas, rhododendrons, and other favorites. Full sun or partial shade and a moist soil rich in organic matter are its requirements. Set the bulbs 6 to 8 inches deep.

Choice and dainty describes the lovely Coral Lily, *L. tenuifolium*, now classified as *L. pumilum*. (See page 170.) Slender, graceful stems less than 2 feet tall support the delicately fragrant, coral-red blooms, which appear in June. Often planted in rock gardens, it is also effective in groups in the hardy border. A delightful yellow-flowered form, Golden Gleam, is favored by many home gardeners. This Lily grows readily in sunny locations but often is not long-lived. The bulbs are planted 5 inches deep; quantities of them can readily be raised from seed.

Although somewhat common, the Tiger Lily, *L. tigrinum*, has a place in gardens because of its brilliant color in late summer. This vigorous Lily grows readily in a wide variety of soils, and has become a garden escape in many parts of New England. The large showy recurved orange blooms with dark spots are borne on sturdy stems 4 feet or more in height. The variety *splendens* is larger and brighter. Unfortunately this Lily is susceptible to mosaic, and care must be taken to obtain clean bulbs. The tiny bulbils which form in the axils of the leaves germinate readily. The Tiger Lily grows well in full sun or light shade. Cover the bulbs with 6 inches of soil.

Sound, plump, disease-free bulbs with live roots are essential for success with Lilies. If the bulbs cannot be planted as soon as received, they should be potted at once or packed in moist sand until they can be set out. Lily bulbs are offered in spring and fall, but early fall is generally the best time to plant them because then they have an opportunity to become established before spring growth starts. Very often spring-planted bulbs give a poor performance the first year. Oftentimes bulbs arrive in the late fall or early winter after the earth has frozen. Advance preparations made by mulching the ground where the bulbs are to be set is good practice, or they can be potted and carried over winter in a coldframe. Some gardeners move Lilies in spring after growth has started, but care must be taken to move as much soil as possible with the plants. The proper planting depth varies according to the species and the size of the bulb, but a common

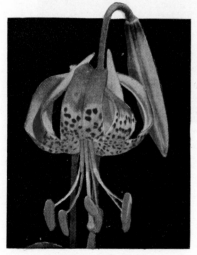
Lilium pardalinum

Lilium Henryi

GARDEN FLOWERS IN COLOR

The Sunset Lily, Lilium pardalinum giganteum

rule is to set them approximately three times their own depth.

Most Lilies can be expected to grow satisfactorily in any well-drained garden soil that produces good vegetable root crops. Extremely light soils may be improved by adding compost in the form of leaf-mold or peat moss. Some experienced growers use well-decomposed stable manure with great success, but it must be thoroughly decomposed. Some of our native species of Lilies grow in low moist areas, but the bulbs are always found in well-drained locations. An open but protected spot is especially desirable. Light shade is preferable to full sun; a ground cover that provides shade around the roots and conserves soil moisture is ideal.

In planting Lilies, provide holes large enough to accommodate the bulbs and roots without crowding. Allow at least a foot between tall-growing kinds, and 6 to 8 inches for the smaller ones. Some gardeners set the bulbs on their sides and surround them with sand to insure protection against excess moisture. The location of all bulbs should be marked and a mulch provided after the ground freezes.

A summer mulch of peat moss helps to conserve moisture and keep down weeds, and a mulch of coarse material over winter is good garden insurance. When Lilies are cut, care must be taken to leave enough of the foliage and stems for the normal growth of the bulb. The plants should not be allowed to form seed.

A consideration of Lily diseases is of vital importance because they determine success or failure. The serious Lily mosaic disease is caused by a virus in the plant, but curiously enough it is not transmitted

The Speciosum Lily, Lilium speciosum Melpomene

GARDEN FLOWERS IN COLOR

through seeds. It is easily recognized by light and dark mottling on the leaves, which are sometimes twisted and distorted; some plants lose their lower leaves and have a stunted appearance. The disease is transmitted by the melon aphis. Perhaps the easiest way to check it is to grow Lilies from seed. Infected plants should be dug and destroyed as soon as the disease is discovered.

Another disease common to Lilies is botrytis blight, caused by a fungus. It is easily detected by round or oval spots on the leaves, which appear during damp weather; as the weather gets warmer, these spots dry out. Frequent spraying with Bordeaux mixture will check this trouble, and destroying all affected parts of the plants helps materially to keep the disease from spreading. Several other diseases are sometimes troublesome but the two mentioned here are the worst.

The Coral Lily, Lilium tenuifolium (pumilum)

GARDEN FLOWERS IN COLOR

LILY-OF-THE-VALLEY

The Lily-of-the-valley, *Convallaria majalis*, has been cultivated in gardens for centuries. It was a particular favorite in medieval times, as evidenced by its frequent appearance in the tapestries and illuminated manuscripts of the period. The sweet fragrance and delicate form of this garden treasure delighted the Elizabethans, and its popularity continues to be widespread. The roots were formerly sold in apothecary shops for heart ailments. "Valley Lilies," as the florists call them, are always in demand for use in wedding bouquets or in old-time garlands. Several improved forms of this hardy perennial, including a pale pink-flowered variety, are offered by nurserymen.

Lilies-of-the-valley are easily grown indoors in bowls for winter decoration. For best results secure roots, or pips as they are known in the trade, that have been held in cold storage. Plant them in loam, sand, or sphagnum moss, and keep them in a dark place for about two weeks. As the pips sprout, give them more light. In the average home they will flower four weeks from planting.

As a ground cover in shady places, and especially under trees, the Lily-of-the-valley does well. Although it endures considerable neglect, it thrives best in rich soil, and ought to be divided when the roots become overcrowded. Occasional feedings of decomposed stable manure applied in late fall help to keep the plants vigorous. Roots can be set out in spring or fall.

GARDEN FLOWERS IN COLOR

171

Annual Lobelia

LOBELIA

The annual Lobelia which sends forth myriads of miniature blue flowers in midsummer, and the brilliant Cardinal-flower native to streamsides throughout the eastern United States, are the outstanding members of this genus. Of the annual forms, hybrids of *Lobelia Erinus*, Cambridge Blue is noted for its brilliance, and Crystal Palace for its deep blue flowers and rich dark foliage. The annual Lobelias, averaging 4 to 6 inches in height, are ideally suited for edging beds and borders, and combine well with other tender plants for window and porch boxes. Both compact, bushy forms and trailing kinds are listed by seedsmen.

The Cardinal-flower, *L. cardinalis*, is a hardy perennial for moist places in sun or partial shade. It can be grown in hardy borders provided the soil is rich in organic matter and retentive of moisture. Plants can be set out in spring or fall.

The seed is usually planted indoors or in a hotbed or coldframe six to eight weeks before the plants are to be set out. It is hardly advisable to sow the seed in the open ground unless one lives in an area where the spring season comes early. Plants can be obtained from florists, to be set out in sun or light shade when all danger of frost is past.

GARDEN FLOWERS IN COLOR

172

LOOSESTRIFE

Some European plants have so readily adapted themselves to American conditions that we speak of them as natives. Such is the case with the Purple Loosestrife, *Lythrum Salicaria*, which has become widely naturalized along streams and the banks of ponds and other low moist places. To a limited extent the species *L. virgatum*, with somewhat smaller flowers, has also become a wilding. The name Lythrum, of Greek origin, meaning "blood," is probably a reference to the styptic qualities of some species, or an allusion to the brilliant coloring of some of the flowers. A hardy perennial, it tends to self-sow readily when once established in the garden.

Loosestrife adapts itself to ordinary treatment in perennial and shrub plantings. During July and August, the Purple Loosestrife is at its height, producing long spikes of colorful bloom on stems 3 to 4 feet tall. *L. Salicaria* is a warm purple tone, and the form *L. roseum superbum* may be described as rose-purple. The variety listed as The Beacon is an improved form of clear rosy red.

Full sun and ordinary garden soil will satisfy this plant. Loosestrife can be planted near water or in a moist place or in the perennial or shrub planting, since it easily adapts itself. The plants can be set out in spring or fall; established plants need to be divided every three years. By keeping the dead blooms picked off, the flowering season can be prolonged.

Lythrum, The Beacon

GARDEN FLOWERS IN COLOR

Hybrids of Lupinus polyphyllus

LUPINE

These stately plants are prized by amateur and professional gardeners alike, but often they are difficult to grow in areas where the summers are hot and dry. Three distinct types of Lupines are cultivated. The Tree Lupine, *Lupinus arboreus*, a native of California, is seldom seen in the eastern United States, but the annual kinds, hybrids of *L. Hartwegi*, are offered by most seedsmen, and the perennial hybrids of *L. polyphyllus* are widely cultivated.

The white, blue, purple, and pink varieties of *L. Hartwegi* reach 2 to 3 feet in height. In May and June *L. polyphyllus* produces showy spikes of bloom ranging from blues to pale buff and apricot.

Where early summer heat is excessive, Lupines often die out because of drought or the ravages of insects and fungous diseases. Sow the seed in early spring to obtain good-sized plants before midsummer. Seed often fails to germinate because gardeners neglect to "chip" its hard coat. Rich, well-drained loam and a sunny position suit Lupines. Annual kinds are sown outdoors, and thinned 9 to 12 inches apart.

LYCHNIS

Old-fashioned hardy perennials like Mullein-pink, Jerusalem Cross, and German Catchfly flourished in the nineteenth century, and still have a place in modern gardens. These Lychnis species bloom during June and July. *Lychnis chalcedonica*, the Maltese or Jerusalem Cross, produces large rounded heads of scarlet flowers on 2 to 3-foot plants; it needs to be used with discretion because of its brilliance. The clusters of deep pink to crimson blooms of the Mullein-pink, *L. Coronaria* (often listed as *Agrostemma Coronaria*), are supported on sturdy stems above the distinct woolly gray foliage. Sometimes this plant blooms so freely that it completes its cycle in two years like a true biennial, but it self-sows readily. Well-developed plants average 2½ feet in height. *L. Viscaria*, the German Catchfly, bears panicles of red or purple bloom with sticky patches on their underside. Several outstanding garden forms about 15 inches tall are included in this species.

The variety *splendens* has showy single pink flowers, and *L. Viscaria splendens flore-pleno* is the familiar double form with rosy purple flowers that are fine for cutting.

Hybridizers have produced several named kinds, resulting from a cross between two species. *L. Arkwrighti*, a compact form averaging 12 inches, sends forth its scarlet and vermilion blooms in midsummer. *L. Haageana* grows about the same height, but blooms somewhat earlier.

The various species and hybrids of Lychnis may be grown in ordinary soil in partial shade as well as in full sun. The plants are started from seed or increased by division. They can be set out in spring or fall. Allow 8 to 15 inches of space between them, depending upon the height of the species grown.

Lychnis Viscaria splendens flore-pleno

GARDEN FLOWERS IN COLOR

The Starry Magnolia, Magnolia stellata

MAGNOLIA

Braving the cold winds of early spring, the Magnolias bloom abundantly for several weeks. The familiar broad spreading kinds like *Magnolia Soulangeana* assume the form of a small tree, while others such as the dainty Starry Magnolia, *M. stellata*, are usually more shrubby. Some bear their blooms before the foliage develops, and others like *M. grandiflora* have glossy evergreen foliage of leathery texture.

As specimens on the lawn or in combination with flowering shrubs and trees, Magnolias are attractive throughout the year. They are picturesque in their habit of growth, and flourish with little care. Oftentimes in gardens where space is limited there is need for a small tree to provide shade or a point of interest. *M. Soulangeana* or any of its improved forms can be depended upon to fill such a need.

The earliest to bloom of all the Magnolias is the Starry Magnolia, *M. stellata*. It is free branching in habit, and mature plants often reach 12 feet or more in height and width. In early spring while frosts still threaten, the large star-like white flowers unfold in great profusion. The 3-inch blooms have a waxy texture and pleasant fragrance but are often damaged by heavy frosts, especially in localities where spring comes late. A pink-flowering form is offered by some nurserymen.

M. Soulangeana, sometimes called the Saucer Magnolia, is widely planted over a large part of the country. In its native habitat the plant assumes the habit of a tree 20 feet or more in height, and often nearly as broad. During April and May, depending upon the climate, this attractive Magnolia makes an elaborate display. The large, cup-shaped, fragrant flowers are a combination of white with pink and purplish coloring on the outer side of the petals; often they measure 5 inches or more in diameter when fully open. Among the hybrid forms are a pure white variety and *M. Soulangeana Lennei*, which blooms later than the type, with reddish purple coloring on the outside of the petals. The variety Alexandrina is also valued for its rich color and its late flowering habit, which is important in cold climates.

Two choice Magnolias seldom seen in gardens are *M. Sieboldi* (*parviflora*) and *M. glauca* (*virginiana*), the Sweet Bay which is native along the Atlantic seaboard. *M. Sieboldi* bears its fragrant, cup-shaped, white blooms during June and July on broad spreading plants. The curious center of each bloom resembles an inverted strawberry. Of columnar form is the stately Sweet Bay, *M. glauca* (*virginiana*), with glossy foliage and creamy white blooms followed by red fruits. The Bull Bay, *M. grandiflora*, of southern gardens deserves mention because of its rich foliage, showy blooms, and colorful red fruits. Other interesting native species include *M. acuminata*, the Cucumber-tree, with immense foliage and blooms, followed by conspicuous fruits, *M. macrophylla*, the Large-leaved Cucumber-tree, which produces the largest leaves and flowers of any American tree, and *M. Fraseri*.

Magnolias flourish in most well-drained soils. Careful preparation of the ground before planting is good garden practice. Most nurserymen supply balled and burlapped plants that can be moved easily in spring or fall. Little pruning is necessary except to improve the form of the plants; well-decomposed stable manure will help to keep them vigorous. Allow space for the plants to develop their natural form.

An improved form of
Magnolia Soulangeana

GARDEN FLOWERS IN COLOR

Marigold,
Yellow Supreme

Marigold, Harmony

MARIGOLD

The African and French Marigolds, hybrids of the genus Tagetes, that bloom so abundantly from midsummer to frost, are of Mexican origin. Probably the story recorded by John Gerard in 1597 accounts for the name "African" Marigold, for he told of its introduction to England by Charles V after the battle of Tunis. The French types were first introduced into the gardens of France. The name Marigold, originally attached to *Calendula officinalis* in honor of the Virgin Mary, has been commonly associated with several yellow flowers.

With their wide variations in height, color, and form it is possible to use these "hard-luck" annuals in many parts of the garden. The African varieties, for background planting, average 2½ to 4 feet or more in height; the French forms, for the middle ground, grow from 9 inches to 2½ feet; the dwarf *Tagetes signata pumila*, for edging purposes or pot culture, grows 9 to 12 inches tall.

For gardeners whose leisure time is limited, the various kinds of Marigolds are especially valuable. They are seldom attacked by insects or diseases, and thrive with little care. Because of their long-keeping qualities, they are very desirable for indoor decoration. Marigolds combine well with chrysanthemums, hardy asters, the eupatoriums, cimicifuga, and other fall-blooming hardy perennials. These showy

Marigold, Little Giants

annuals can be used to advantage in the foreground of shrub borders.

Marigolds, like zinnias, have attracted the attention of the hybridizers, with the result that we now have odorless kinds among the African types, one of which is known as Crown of Gold. The center petals of the orange flowers are curled and twisted, forming a high crown, surrounded by a row of flat, somewhat drooping guard-petals. Then there are the Dixie or chrysanthemum-flowered hybrids with well-formed flowers, curiously incurved and quilled; these are available in orange, gold, and yellow shades. Dixie Sunshine, a yellow chrysanthemum-flowered type of distinct pyramidal habit, requires a long period of growth before flowering, and is best adapted to gardens of the South and Southwest. Guinea Gold well describes the gleaming orange-gold blooms of an excellent variety with looser and flatter form than older types. Yellow Supreme is in many respects the yellow counterpart of carnation-flowered Guinea Gold. Among the most recent introductions is the Mission Giant Marigold Goldsmith, growing 2 feet tall or more, with warm golden yellow flowers. A dwarf African strain called Little Giants grows about 18 inches tall.

Double and single, tall and dwarf forms are found among the French Marigolds. Among the tall varieties separate colors are available in both single and double forms. As with many annuals, the great variations in color are most easily realized by planting packets of mixed seed. Josephine, a tall single kind, is commonly grown. The velvety blooms —a combination of dark brown, red, and gold—are supported by long, slender stems.

Many named varieties appear among the dwarf French Marigolds, which average 12 to 15 inches in height. Dwarf Royal Scot is golden yellow with mahogany stripes. Harmony has a crested orange center, accentuated by maroon petals. Legion of Honor, sometimes called Little Brownie, is often less than a foot high; each yellow petal of the flower is marked with a blotch of crimson. The Marigold Spry, a delightful combination of light yellow surrounded by maroon petals, and Yellow Pigmy, with double blooms of lemon-yellow, are among the latest achievements in the compact forms of French Marigolds. Of all the dwarf Marigolds, none is more free flowering or more delightful than *T. signata pumila*. Its delicately cut foliage is hardly noticeable because of the profuse flowering habit of the yellow and orange forms.

Marigold seed may be sown in a sunny window, a hotbed, a coldframe, or in the open ground. The African and tall French varieties need ample space for development; allow 18 to 24 inches between the seedlings. Most of the dwarf French types may be set 12 to 15 inches apart, but 6 inches is enough for *T. signata pumila*. Marigolds are essentially sun-loving plants thriving in hot dry areas.

Marigold, Josephine

GARDEN FLOWERS IN COLOR

Mignonette, like a breath of fragrance from an old continental parlor, recalls the quaint gardens of the nineteenth century, in which scented flowers were more important than they are today.

MIGNONETTE

The Latin name of this North African plant, Reseda, means "I calm," an allusion to its supposed healing power for bruises. Though its fragrance is not penetrating, it is a delicate scent which adds materially to bouquets.

Several improved varieties of *Reseda odorata* are available: Goliath, a giant red-flowered kind; Machet, a dwarf variety; and Golden Queen, a yellow form, are all worth considering, as are other special strains which individual seedsmen feature. All are of subdued coloring. The plants are often loose in form and of a somewhat sprawling habit of growth.

Because plants are not easily moved, seed should be sown in the open ground and the plants thinned to a distance of 6 to 9 inches. Several sowings are necessary for a succession of bloom, and the seed is best planted in the cutting garden in beds. Mignonette grows satisfactorily in partial shade and does best in cool weather.

MOCK-ORANGE

Mock-oranges, which are species and varieties of the genus Philadelphus, are sometimes erroneously called Syringas. The name Syringa is, of course, the genus name for the lilac. Valued for its fragrant white blooms in June, the Mock-orange is so called because the fragrance of some species resembles that of the orange blossom. Some are compact growers of fountain-like form ranging from 5 to 7 feet in height; others are erect plants reaching 12 to 15 feet or more. The Mock-orange makes a decorative specimen plant, or it can be included

Common Mock-orange, Philadelphus coronarius

in the shrub border or foundation planting where space permits.

The Common Mock-orange, *Philadelphus coronarius*, often seen in gardens, is extremely fragrant. Several improved forms are available from nurserymen. As a result of hybridizing, plantsmen have developed many named varieties from the hybrid forms *P. Lemoinei* and *P. virginalis*. These are characterized by blooms of immense size and a pleasing fragrance; both double and single-flowering forms are obtainable. Among those worthy of special mention are Atlas, with immense single white blooms, and Belle Etoile, notable for its delicious fragrance and the violet marking near the stamens. Enchantment is a double-flowered form with blooms borne in clusters. The fragrance of the hybrid Innocence is comparable to that of sweet peas. Seldom more than 3½ feet tall, Girondole is notable for its dwarf habit and its double blooms. An old favorite is the lovely double hybrid Virginal, with fragrant blooms in abundant clusters. A Chinese species, *P. pekinensis*, and a hybrid form, *P. Zeyheri*, are among the kinds available from nurserymen. Both are known for their vigorous growth and their free-flowering habit. Several forms with variegated foliage are sometimes seen in gardens.

Shrubs of easy culture, the Mock-oranges can be planted in spring or fall. They grow well in full sun or light shade, are for the most part remarkably hardy, and flourish in a variety of soils. Bloom is produced on the growth of the previous season, and pruning is best done immediately after flowering has ceased. By the elimination of old wood each year, the plants can be kept healthy and more compact. Skillful use of the shears helps to keep the plant shapely.

MONARDA

Rich in historical associations, this favorite native American plant has been widely cultivated for many years. During the time of the Revolution, the residents of Oswego, New York, used the mint-scented leaves of *Monarda didyma* for making tea—hence the common name, Oswego-tea. Other familiar names are Bee-balm and Berga-mot. The plant has a special attraction for hummingbirds.

For those who object to the brilliant red coloring of the species *M. didyma*, and the variety Cambridge Scarlet, there are several kinds of more subdued shades. Salmon Queen, the white-flowered *M. didyma alba*, and Perry's Variety, an unusual purple-red kind, are also obtainable. *M. fistulosa* produces blooms in varying shades of lavender and purple. From late June through early August the Monardas pro-vide colorful flowers on 3-foot stems.

Monarda grows well in sun or shade, and can be set out in spring or fall. This long-lived hardy perennial needs to be reset every two or three years because of its vigorous, spreading habit.

Monarda didyma

GARDEN FLOWERS IN COLOR

Aconitum Napellus

MONKSHOOD

Aconitums belong with the most desirable of our perennial plants because of their varied rich blue hues, their extended season of bloom, and their adaptability to shady situations. The common name, Monkshood, refers to the shape of the flowers. In late June and early July, the spikes of *Aconitum Napellus* produce blooms on stems with an average height of 3 to 4 feet. *A. Napellus bicolor* is somewhat more compact, and is easily distinguished by its blue and white flowers. Sparks' variety, with loose-branching flower spikes, blooms in July and August.

The species *A. autumnale*, 4 to 5 feet in height, with its long spikes of dark blue flowers, blooms in September and October, as does *A. Fischeri*, the Azure Monkshood, which bears its rich flowers on compact, glossy-leaved plants 2 to 3 feet tall. Dr. Wilson brought to us from China *A. Fischeri Wilsoni*, known as the Violet Monkshood, which blooms in late autumn. The foliage is dull, and the flowers, on tall slender stems 6 feet or more in height, add a welcome note of blue to the autumn garden.

For the most part Monkshood is a background plant which enjoys some shade. Rich soil and the "hands-off" policy suit it best. Divisions of the tuberous roots can be set out in spring or fall.

MONTBRETIA

Montbretias might well be called miniature forms of *Gladiolus primulinus*. Botanically, these summer-flowering bulbs are known as Tritonias. English hybridizers have produced many interesting and striking hybrids from *Tritonia crocosmaeflora*, some of which grow 3 feet tall in rich soil.

For desirable outdoor effects, Montbretias need to be planted in the middle ground in the garden picture. The many hybrid forms have a brilliant color range varying from pale yellow to deep orange-red, and require a background of foliage, either evergreen or deciduous. Then, too, the stems are rigidly straight and need the softening influence of loose foliage as a foreground. Planted in groups of six or more, they provide dominant accents in the shrub border or with perennials. Masses of white flowers planted near them will enhance their beauty. From a decorative standpoint, the flowering spikes of Montbretias are distinctly valuable not only for their vivid coloring but also for their enduring quality as cut flowers. When grown for cutting purposes they are best planted in rows.

Set the corms at least 3 inches deep and 6 inches apart in full sun. Rich, light soil and liquid manure will produce vigorous flower spikes. Although they are quite hardy in the milder parts of the East, they are dug and stored over winter in a frostproof basement by many gardeners. Deeper planting is essential (6 to 8 inches) if the bulbs are allowed to remain in the ground over winter; mulch with coarse material.

GARDEN FLOWERS IN COLOR

Morning-glory, Heavenly Blue

GARDEN FLOWERS IN COLOR

Flowers from a mixed packet of Morning-glories

MORNING-GLORY

There is something indescribably beautiful about the large trumpet-like blooms of the Morning-glory, *Ipomoea purpurea*, borne in great profusion and usually perched high on trellises or arbors. In dull weather they remain open nearly all day, but the hot sun quickly wilts them.

The striking Early or Improved Heavenly Blue variety is preferred to the original hybrid because it flowers earlier. It combines effectively with the showy red Scarlett O'Hara and the pure white Pearly Gates. Giant Pink is another popular color. Comparatively little known are the semi-double and double rose-pink flowers of Rose Marie. The Moonflower, *I. mexicana alba*, bears its large white blooms at night.

Morning-glory seed does not always germinate easily. Some gardeners soak it overnight or longer in warm water to soften the hard shell. Others nick one end of each seed with a knife or file and place the seed on moist sand, covering it with wet burlap until germination occurs. When this method is used, transplant the tiny seedlings into small pots, and set the plants out when the ground becomes warm. The seed may be sown indoors, in a coldframe, or where the plants are to bloom. Full sun or light shade is satisfactory, but soil that is too rich causes the growth of foliage rather than flowers.

MYRTLE

Two very popular ground covers are Myrtle or *Vinca minor*, and Japanese spurge, which is listed as *Pachysandra terminalis*. Both are evergreen and can be used in sun or shade. On slopes, under trees, and in areas where grass cannot be grown successfully, these adaptable plants are extremely useful.

Myrtle is valued not only for its glossy evergreen foliage but also for its attractive blue flowers in early spring. In addition to the widely used species *V. minor*, there are several hybrids, including white and pink-flowered kinds and some with variegated foliage. Bowles' Variety has larger and more intense blue flowers.

Myrtle can be grown in a wide variety of soils. Plants can be set out at any time provided they are watered freely until established. Few hardy evergreen plants grow more rapidly. To increase them, old clumps can be divided or the creeping stems which root readily along the ground can be cut off and replanted.

Vinca minor, Bowles' Variety

GARDEN FLOWERS IN COLOR

NARCISSUS

Barri variety

Among the most permanent of all spring-flowering bulbs are the many forms of Narcissus commonly referred to as Daffodils. In recent years collectors of these flowers have associated the name Daffodil with the large-flowering trumpet forms. Another common name that is sometimes confusing is the term Jonquil. The true Jonquil is a small cluster-flowered Narcissus with rush-like foliage, listed as *Narcissus Jonquilla simplex*.

Planted in broad masses in association with shrubs or in perennial gardens, Narcissus make a colorful display in the early spring garden. Many of the small cluster-flowered kinds are attractive in rock gardens, and some amateur gardeners naturalize Narcissus in their lawns. All the Narcissus are delightful cut flowers; many people who specialize in growing these various types take pride in displaying them at spring flower shows. By selecting varieties from the various classes, it is possible to enjoy Narcissus in the home garden for a period of two months.

Because of the wide variety of species and hybrid forms, the Narcissus has been classified into eleven broad groups; this classification is used by seedsmen and bulb growers who offer the bulbs for sale. Descriptions of the numerous varieties refer to the trumpet, or central portion of the flower, and the perianth, which comprises the segments surrounding the trumpet.

The most popular of all are the Trumpet Narcissus, with large blooms in shades of yellow and white. Long shapely trumpets larger than the perianth segments are typical of this showy type, which includes an amazing number of varieties. With the exception of a few of the species, the Trumpet Narcissus are among the first to bloom. Some are moderately priced, while others are definitely for the connoisseur. The Trumpets are subdivided into three groups, which include yellow, white, and bicolor forms. (See pages 192 and 194.)

Many distinctive varieties are found among the Incomparabilis group, which comes into flower shortly after the Trumpet varieties. These intermediate forms have comparatively short trumpets which are better described as mere cups. These warmly colored chalice-like cups and the pale perianths are truly picturesque. The blooms are pleasing as cut flowers. (See page 194.)

The third division includes the so-called Barri Narcissus, named for

GARDEN FLOWERS IN COLOR

A clump of bicolor Trumpet Narcissus

the distinguished English plantsman, Peter Barr, who helped to popularize the Narcissus around the world. Small, brilliantly colored cups distinguish this group, which includes many fragrant varieties. (See pages 190 and 194.)

Of soft coloring are the Leedsi Narcissus, with white perianth segments and cups which are white and pale citron, sometimes tinged with pink or apricot. There are numerous varieties which appeal to collectors and to those who admire pastel tints. (See page 194.)

The fifth division includes the Triandrus and Triandrus hybrids, natives of the Spanish peninsula. These dwarf plants have slender rush-like foliage and small dainty blooms, borne singly or in clusters. *N. triandrus albus* is often called Angel's Tears. (See pages 194 and 195.)

Although few varieties are included in the Cyclamineus and Cyclamineus hybrid group, they are outstanding for their particularly early flowering habit and distinctive form. The variety February Gold is among the earliest of all the Narcissus to bloom, though in northern gardens it does not flower in February. (See page 195.)

GARDEN FLOWERS IN COLOR

Long cultivated in old gardens, the Jonquilla and Jonquilla hybrid Narcissus comprise a favorite group. Narrow rush-like leaves and deliciously fragrant flowers borne in clusters on long stems characterize this particular group. Both the species and several named varieties are listed by growers, including the Campernelle Jonquils, *N. odorus*.

Flowering somewhat later than the large-flowered Narcissus are the dainty Poetaz hybrids. These are hybrids of *N. Tazetta* and *N. poeticus ornatus*. The blooms, in clusters of four to eight, have light yellow cups and pale perianth segments; both single and double-flowering forms are included, and all are noted for their delightful fragrance. Some, like the Chinese Sacred-lily, Grand Soleil d'Or, and the Paper-white Narcissus, are not hardy in northern gardens but are grown indoors during the winter months. (See page 196.)

The Poet's Narcissus or Poeticus varieties came originally from southern Europe. They thrive in moist situations and are often found in partial shade. Profuse flowering in habit, they are easily recognized by their snow-white petals and their tiny flat eyes or crowns.

Campernelle Jonquil, Narcissus odorus

GARDEN FLOWERS IN COLOR

Yellow Trumpet

Leedsi variety

Incomparabilis variety

Barri variety

Leedsi variety

Triandrus variety

GARDEN FLOWERS IN COLOR

194

N. poeticus recurvus, usually referred to as Pheasant's Eye, is often naturalized in spring gardens. (See page 196.)

Some home gardeners enjoy the Double Narcissus, which include both yellow and white-flowering forms. These are often grown by florists for forcing. (See page 196.)

Many valuable species which can hardly be grouped with any of the foregoing classes are listed in catalogs, and comprise the eleventh class. Some are miniature in form, and all are interesting.

One of the most curious of all is the Hoop Petticoat, *N. Bulbocodium*, with dainty little bulging flowers on slender stems a few inches high. There are several improved forms, including one of pale yellow, a white variety from North Africa, and the showy *N. Bulbocodium conspicuus*, with uplifted golden yellow blooms on 4-inch stems. (See page 196.) These are earliest to bloom and show to best advantage in the rock garden. Another interesting species listed in catalogs is *N. juncifolius*, of miniature form, with rush-leaved foliage and tiny yellow, fragrant blooms on 4-inch stems. Often in bulb catalogs we find the Triandrus hybrids and the Cyclamineus forms listed with the species Narcissus or Daffodils. All flourish in rock gardens, seldom need to be disturbed, and can be depended upon to make a brilliant show for many years. Although not difficult to grow, many of them are seldom seen in home gardens.

A word should be said about naturalizing Narcissus, because this practice is often followed in large woodland areas where a high degree of lawn maintenance is not required. Since they bloom before most trees are in full foliage, Narcissus are often planted underneath. Little care is required once the bulbs are planted. It is important that the foliage be allowed to mature completely before being cut off.

Triandrus species   Cyclamineus variety

GARDEN FLOWERS IN COLOR

Narcissus grow easily in most well-drained garden soils. Bulbs are planted in September, the earlier the better, so that the bulbs can form roots and become established before winter sets in. Four to 5 inches is the average depth for planting and the minimum spacing between the bulbs, but they can be set an inch or two deeper in light sandy soils. Since they are usually left in the ground for several years, the soil should be carefully prepared before planting. Bonemeal can be used to advantage in improving the soil or as a top dressing each fall. As the clumps increase in size, they need to be dug and reset. This job can be done after flowering, or the bulbs can be dug in late spring and replanted in the fall. Narcissus require little care, but the foliage must be allowed to die down after the blooming period in order to provide for the proper development of the bulbs.

Poeticus type

Double type

Poetaz type

Narcissus Bulbocodium

GARDEN FLOWERS IN COLOR

Single Nasturtiums

NASTURTIUM

Nasturtiums grow with such great vigor that they are well suited for covering large areas, especially unsightly places. The trailing varieties, forms of *Tropaeolum majus*, are often trained on trellises, but they grow downward over banks and walls with greater ease. Shades of scarlet, crimson, maroon, rose, salmon, yellow, and white are sold by seedsmen. Lobb's Mixture, developed from *T. Lobbianum*, is outstanding.

The semi-double Gleam Hybrids are medium in height. Golden Gleam, Orange Gleam, Scarlet Gleam, and other shades are listed in catalogs; the Glorious Gleam Mixture includes many shades.

The dwarf or Tom Thumb Nasturtiums are as varied in their color range as are the tall single kinds. Golden Globe, Scarlet Globe, and the Globe Mixture produce their semi-double flowers freely on compact plants averaging a foot in height.

Sow the seed in the open ground as soon as the soil becomes warm. Some gardeners start it indoors in pots, and later transfer the plants to the garden. Full sun and poor soil are their meager requirements. The black lice often found on the plants may be eradicated with a nicotine or pyrethrum spray.

GARDEN FLOWERS IN COLOR

NICOTIANA

Fragrance gives a tantalizing, indefinable atmosphere to every garden, and this fact is reason enough for growing the annual Nicotiana commonly spoken of as Flowering Tobacco. Although somewhat ragged in appearance during the heat of the day, the 2-foot plants take on a stately grandeur from late afternoon (when the fragrance is emitted) until early morning. They help to make a garden a very pleasant place in the evening. If the flowers are cut when the petals are expanded, they will remain open in water.

The hybrids of *Nicotiana affinis*, and more particularly the strains with red flowers (*N. Sanderae*), can be planted with the white form, *N. sylvestris*, which often grows 3 feet tall. A compact variety known as Crimson Bedder grows 15 inches tall, and there is a delightful white form listed as Snowstorm. All bloom freely from midsummer until checked by frost.

The seed can be sown in a hotbed, a coldframe, or the open ground. Since it is extremely small, care must be taken not to plant it too deep; the usual practice requires careful preparation of the soil so that the seed can be scattered over the surface and pressed in with a board or a brick. Set the seedlings 15 to 18 inches apart in a sunny location. This annual frequently self-sows in gardens.

Flowering Tobacco in variety

GARDEN FLOWERS IN COLOR

Oxalis Bowieana

OXALIS

When hanging-pots were found in nearly every kitchen window, the winter-flowering *Oxalis variabilis* was a very popular house plant and the old-fashioned *O. Bowieana* was commonly grown in the home garden. *O. variabilis* is the tender kind often grown indoors. It makes showy color masses with its shades of deep rose, pink, white, and lavender. *O. cernua* is a bright yellow kind. In rock gardens or as an edging plant in sunny or partly shaded areas, *O. Bowieana* is particularly delightful. The brilliant pink flowers on 6-inch stems are produced from midsummer till frost, and are very showy. The clover-like foliage with reddish markings tends to close toward dark.

For window culture set at least three bulbs in a 4-inch pot, or five in the 6-inch size. Place them just below the surface of the soil, in a fairly rich potting mixture. The bulbs need a rest and should be allowed to dry off in late spring before being stored for the summer. The bulbs of *O. Bowieana* are usually set out in spring when frost danger has passed. Since they are not hardy, they need to be dug in late fall and stored over winter in a frostproof place.

PANSY

It is rather significant that the Johnny-jump-up, or Heartsease, *Viola tricolor hortensis*, parent of the modern Pansies, is being featured now in the catalogs of many American seedsmen. For more than two hundred years these sprightly-faced flowers have been bobbing up here and there in American gardens, unnoticed and neglected. Yet they have persisted, and are now introduced as Shakespeare's Pansies. And so they are, for they are similar in form and color to the Heartsease that was used in Elizabethan tussie-mussies or nosegays.

Pansies are often interplanted with spring-flowering bulbs; they also make excellent border plants or broad masses in the perennial garden. Few spring-flowering plants are more abundant in their bloom or more picturesque in the garden. The quaint markings make the individual flowers look almost like human faces. Delightful effects can be created by planting Pansies in window boxes and strawberry jars. The sweetly fragrant blooms make useful cut flowers, especially when they are picked with long stems and some foliage.

Surprising as it appears at first glance, the giant-flowered Pansies of our twentieth-century gardens have been developed from the tiny Heartsease of Shakespeare's day. Similar in form are the large-flowered violas which flower freely even in warm summer weather, in contrast to Pansies which grow best in cool temperatures. All are members of the viola tribe discussed on pages 276 to 278.

The Trimardeau strain of Pansies is known for its medium-sized flowers and extraordinary color range, including a number of separate colors. Then there are the present-day giant-flowering kinds: Roggli or Swiss Giants and their dwarf hybrids, the Maple-leaf Giants, the Non Plus Ultra Mixture, the Mastodon Pansies, the Masterpiece strain, the Orchid-flowered Pansies, and the many other special strains of the seedsmen. Named varieties in selected colors offered by the leading growers are favored by gardeners who enjoy distinctive color combinations in their gardens.

Most satisfactory results are obtained by sowing the seed in early

August for bloom the following spring. Select a partially shaded location for the seed bed, or use a coldframe. It is important to keep the seed bed moist, because the summer sun and wind tend to dry out the soil quickly. In preparing the ground for the seedlings one should remember that Pansies need a soil rich in available plant food. Use well-rotted cow manure, sheep manure, or commercial fertilizer, digging it well into the ground; allow the fertilizer to become thoroughly integrated with the soil for several weeks before planting. Drainage is equally important; if the soil is heavy, or if the area is low, raise the beds to a height of 4 inches above the surrounding level. Set the seedlings 4 to 6 inches apart and give them occasional applications of liquid manure. If plants are not carried over in a coldframe, the best winter protection is straw or hay, and it should not be put on until the ground has frozen hard. Many amateur gardeners complain that Pansies become "leggy" in late spring, and stop blooming. They fail to realize that it is essential to remove all seed pods and to cut back the straggling growth to keep the plants in a healthy condition.

Many strains of Pansies are notable for their distinctive markings

GARDEN FLOWERS IN COLOR

Penstemon, Cherry Glow

PENSTEMON

Many of the Penstemons are adapted to rock gardens, and tall-growing kinds are desirable for the perennial border. *Penstemon barbatus Torreyi*, with its long slender spikes of coral-red flowers resembling curious tubes of blown glass, blooms in June and often into August. Unfortunately the plants have a tendency to become ungainly in habit; they vary from 18 to 30 or more inches in height, and thus require staking. The dainty Pink Beauty is usually more compact in habit. Several large-flowered hybrids of Penstemon were introduced recently. Among them are Garnet and Cherry Glow, with large, rich red flowers.

A delightful prairie species with very large lavender-blue flowers in June is *P. grandiflorus*. Perhaps the most easily grown is the Foxglove Penstemon, *P. laevigatus Digitalis*. It forms attractive clumps 2 to 3 feet tall. Recommended for hot dry exposures is *P. pubescens* (*hirsutus*), with short spikes of violet to soft pink bloom on 15-inch stems.

Penstemons require a well-drained fertile soil and can be grown best in full sun or light shade. They are usually propagated by division in early spring or fall, but many species are easily raised from seed. Some of the choicer kinds are not always tolerant of eastern summers. The dwarf forms often need a protective mulch over winter.

PEONY

For more than a thousand years Peonies have been cultivated in China and Japan. Yet the Chinese kinds, both *Paeonia albiflora*, which is the source of our numerous garden varieties, and the Tree Peony, *P. suffruticosa*, were unknown to European gardens until the late eighteenth century. The European species, *P. officinalis*, the old-fashioned red "Piney," has been cultivated in many parts of the continent since the days of the Crusades. Usually its double red flowers appear ten days before the first of the Albiflora hybrids. It has long been familiar as a dooryard plant in northeastern United States, where it often provides bloom for Decoration Day.

The Tree Peony, *P. suffruticosa*, often seen in old gardens is again gaining favor. The showy flowers with ruffled petals, masses of golden stamens, and distinctive markings appear in early May before the familiar hardy herbaceous forms make their display. To be sure, they are more costly than many garden plants but they are notably long-lived, and improve with age. Plants known to be fifty years old are

Japanese Peony, Mikado

GARDEN FLOWERS IN COLOR

still thriving in old gardens. They make a low compact mound 2½ to 5 feet tall and 4 to 5 feet or more in width, with foliage that is attractive throughout the season.

The many named varieties of the Chinese or herbaceous Peonies familiar to all garden enthusiasts had their origin in *P. albiflora.* In this large group there are several outstanding types. The single varieties usually have one or two rows of petals accentuated by a great central cluster of yellow stamens. The Japanese types are similar in form but they are notable for their modified stamens which look like clusters of thinly shredded petals. Among the double varieties there are several variations of form, none of which show any trace of the true stamens that are found in the single varieties. Besides white kinds, many shades of pink and red are available in early, midseason, and late varieties.

Peonies require rich garden soil and a sunny location. Since they resent disturbance and need to be moved only when the plants show signs of deterioration in growth and bloom, it is essential to prepare the soil thoroughly. Dig deep, and use well-decomposed cow manure or some commercial fertilizer. Bonemeal is helpful, and lime is needed where the soil is known to be acid.

In planting, set the roots so that the eyes are 2 inches below the surface of the ground. Peony specialists seem to agree that too deep planting is often the cause of lack of flowers. September and October are the two best months for setting out Peonies. Fungous diseases are much more detrimental to them than are insects. To counteract crown rot, browning of the buds, and discoloration of foliage and stems, spray with Bordeaux mixture. Badly diseased plants should be destroyed.

Tree Peonies, showing semi-double and double kinds

Peony Walter Faxon is an old standby

GARDEN FLOWERS IN COLOR

PETUNIA

Petunia, Celestial Rose

In recent years American gardeners have become Petunia-conscious. New varieties are being put on the market every year, and many seed catalogs require several pages to describe them. It is significant that these popular bedding plants have been recognized with many awards in the All-America Selections. Several years ago Pennsylvania State College tested as many as 426 varieties, which had been collected from seed-houses throughout the world. As one would expect, there were many duplications because of the existing confused nomenclature. The name Petunia comes from South America, where the plant is native; it is reported to be a local name for tobacco.

Few flowers are more widely used in parks and gardens, and this familiar annual may well be called the "window-box plant of America." For masses, large or small, Petunias are most effective. Blooming with unlimited freedom, they adapt themselves to both formal and informal gardens. The flowers are produced in a great many different forms— some are single, some are ruffled, and others are double or semi-double. All tend to be bushy in form, but some are more prostrate than others (especially the Balcony varieties), and still others are decidedly compact. An infinite variety of rose and blue shades, with rich velvety tones of purple and dark reddish violet, in addition to pale yellow and pure white, are the dominant colors.

In classifying Petunias according to their habits and uses, it seems natural to consider first the common hybrid, or single bedding type. These bloom profusely, reseed themselves freely, and grow about 18 inches high. A wide range of color and the most brilliant mixtures are found in this class. Igloo is an unusual white variety with a yellowish throat. Radiance, Pink Beauty, and Topaz Rose belong in the cerise and rose-red class. The distinctive five-pointed star-shaped flowers of Hollywood Star mark a new trend in improved forms.

Medium-sized flowers on more compact and erect-growing plants, averaging 12 inches in height, are provided by the desirable bedding group listed as *Petunia compacta.* Rosy Morn, with its white throat, Rose of Heaven, Celestial Rose, Heavenly Blue, Salmon Supreme, and Cream Star are typical varieties in this most useful class. Martha Washington is even more compact and dwarf; it produces delightful lavender-pink ruffled flowers, with wine-red veins extending into a large violet throat. English Violet is deep purple-violet.

A new strain of dwarf, compact, miniature Petunias is now receiving attention. Rose, pink, white, and violet forms are obtainable. The little ball-shaped plants, 6 to 8 inches high, are admirably adapted for edging, bedding, window boxes, and pot culture. More pendulous in habit are the large-flowered Balcony Petunias, a glorified hybrid type. In addition to white, rose, crimson, and blue, there are named varieties like Black Prince, a velvety red, and Netted Blue Gem, a steel-blue tone.

The large-flowering single varieties, like the velvety Elk's Pride and Snowstorm, are plain petaled. Then there are the large-flowered single fringed sorts frequently called Fluffy Ruffles. These include the popular golden-centered rose-pink Theodosia, the dark-throated deep coppery red Romany Lass, Scarlet Beauty, Violacea, and White Beauty. Glamor is among the newer rosy salmon shades. Those with large veined throats are called Ruffled Giants. In the dwarf fringed group are many brilliantly colored varieties.

The Giants of California strain is the largest flowered of all Pe-

Petunia, English Violet   Petunia, Snowstorm

tunias. Both the tall kinds, often 18 inches high, and the dwarf ones are free flowering, with huge veined throats in heavily textured, ruffled flowers. Double and semi-double blooms in this gigantic-flowered strain may likewise be obtained in tall and dwarf plant forms, and varieties in separate colors are available. The Victorious Mixture, noted for its fine selection of choice kinds, is listed by many seedsmen. A word of caution is advisable here: the seed of these giant double Petunias is very expensive, and strains of any value cannot be purchased cheaply.

Petunias are tender perennials but are usually treated as hardy garden annuals. Sow the seed indoors in a light soil mixture in pots or flats during February or early March, or in a hotbed or coldframe. Mix the tiny seed with sand; press it into the soil with a board or a brick. Transplant the seedlings as soon as they are large enough to handle. When setting them out, allow 8 to 15 inches between plants, depending upon the variety, and give them a sunny location. Seed may be sown outdoors, but high-priced seed deserves more care and protection than is possible in the open. Petunias grow best in full sun but will tolerate partial shade. Sometimes seedling plants are allowed to remain in flats or coldframes until they become spindly. To produce sturdy growth these plants can be pinched back.

Petunia, Glamor

GARDEN FLOWERS IN COLOR

Mikado, a showy variety of Phlox paniculata

PHLOX

It is difficult to conceive of a garden without hardy Phlox—both the creeping kinds for the spring garden and the showy heads of *Phlox paniculata* for midsummer and early autumn. Through the summer the annual Phlox also provides an abundance of color in the garden and a convenient source of cut-flower material. Some kinds are so low-growing as to form mats in the rock and wall garden, and others belong in the shrub or perennial border. The old Greek name meaning "flame" is appropriately applied to this genus of brilliantly colored blooms. Because of its easy botanical name, no generally used common name is applied to the group as a whole.

Although it is not ordinarily considered a native plant, the creeping evergreen *P. subulata* is widely distributed in the eastern United States. In wall and rock gardens Moss Phlox makes its splash during April and May. With the many varieties available in varying shades of pink, lavender, blue, and white, there is no need to bother with the common magenta form. Recently attention has been called to a fine early Phlox, *P. camla* or *P. camliensis*. It is taller than *P. subulata*, with upright flowering stems, and it blooms later, sometimes recurring in the fall.

For shady gardens or in combination with spring bulbs, few perennials are more desirable than *P. divaricata (canadensis)*. Laphami is an improved form, with larger blue flower heads on longer stems. Blue Phlox and Wild Sweet William are common names for this species.

P. suffruticosa Miss Lingard is commonly conceded to be one of our best white-flowering plants, with glossy foliage and large pyramidal heads of bloom.

Many pages might be devoted to descriptions of the showy varieties of summer-blooming Phlox, *P. paniculata* (sometimes erroneously called *P. decussata*). When selecting Phlox varieties one should bear in mind the variations in height that are available, as well as the extended blooming period that it is possible to have. Pleasing in fragrance and spectacular in color, the individual florets of the great flower heads are in many instances unique for the contrasting "eyes" that mark them. Few perennials offer a greater array of pink, red, lavender, purple, and

Phlox Drummondi, Gigantea Art Shades

GARDEN FLOWERS IN COLOR

An attractive planting of Phlox subulata varieties

white tints and shades than do the garden Phlox. From early summer until frost they send forth an abundance of bloom, and vary in height from 15 inches to 4 feet or more.

The Annual Phlox of gardens, *P. Drummondi*, grows 12 to 15 inches tall and is often used for borders or in broad masses with other annuals. Among the named varieties and strains listed by seedsmen are Brilliant, a rich crimson; Carmine; Chamois-Rose, a soft pink; Isabellina, light yellow; Kermesina, a scarlet-striped kind; Leopoldi, rose with a white eye; Purple King; and white. Gigantea Art Shades is an unusually large-flowered strain composed of many delightful pastel hues. A variety with star-shaped flowers in a wide color range is listed as Star of Quedlinburg, or Star Phlox. The dwarf forms of Annual Phlox make showy border plants for annual or perennial gardens and shrub borders.

These American natives are adapted to many parts of the garden.

GARDEN FLOWERS IN COLOR

They seem to have no particular preference as to soil. All of those mentioned here grow readily in full sun or partial shade with the exception of *P. divaricata* and several of the lesser-known species, which prefer some shade to prevent their roots from drying out in summer. Phlox is easily propagated by root division or by cuttings. Root division of the early-blooming varieties is best done after flowering, but plants of all species may be moved in full bloom provided they are well watered. Cuttings of the various species are easily rooted in sand. Amateurs wishing to increase plants pinch them back when they reach a height of 6 inches, and place these cuttings in sand to root.

The Paniculata varieties are most commonly subject to mildew, which can be checked by dusting the foliage with sulphur. When watering the summer-flowering Phlox, care should be taken not to wet the foliage. To eliminate the magenta colors, cut off all faded flowers to prevent the growth of seedlings. Contrary to popular opinion, *P. paniculata* varieties do not revert to the original magenta color; rather, the seedlings often germinate near or in the center of the root of the parent plant, and eventually take possession after smothering out the more desirable named variety.

Seed of Annual Phlox can be started in a hotbed, a coldframe, or in the open ground. Set the plants 9 inches apart in full sun. Remove the seed pods, and the plants will flower freely until killed by frost.

Phlox divaricata (canadensis)

GARDEN FLOWERS IN COLOR

Physostegia, Vivid

PHYSOSTEGIA

False Dragonhead and Obedience are the familiar names for Physostegia. The first common name refers to the curious open-mouthed form of the individual flowers. Obedience is an allusion to the hinge-like arrangement which connects each flower with the stem, permitting the rows of blooms to be moved about the spike.

During August and September when most perennials are out of bloom, the showy spikes of False Dragonhead make their appearance. All the botanical varieties and the horticultural hybrids originated from the species *Physostegia virginiana*. *Alba* is a most desirable white form averaging 3 feet or more in height. *P. virginiana grandiflora* has showy, bright pink flower spikes on sturdy stems 3 to 4 feet tall, while the hybrid Vivid is a compact form seldom more than 18 inches tall— one of our most useful fall-blooming perennials. Two new hybrids, Summer Glow and Rosy Spire, are outstanding for their warm rosy crimson color. Summer Glow is the taller, usually reaching 4 feet or more, while the 3-foot Rosy Spire is deeper in color. These easily grown perennials are well adapted to the perennial or shrub border.

Ordinary soil and either full sun or partial shade are suitable for Physostegias. Few plants are more easily propagated by root division in spring or early fall. In fact, it is necessary to reset them every year or two to keep them in bounds.

PINKS

A mixture of hardy Pinks

Few of our common garden flowers have as many pleasant associations as do the many kinds of garden Pinks, particularly the progenitors of the modern carnations. Known as Gillyflowers (before the name was more definitely attached to stocks) and Sops in Wine, these spicily fragrant, satiny-textured blossoms have charmed many generations of gardeners. An amazing number of species and varieties are cultivated in gardens today. (For the hardy Carnation, *Dianthus Caryophyllus*, see page 58; Sweet William, *D. barbatus*, is discussed on page 257.)

From the Allwood Nurseries in England have come the delightful Allwood hybrids. They grow in compact form, and average 12 to 15 inches in height. During June and July the plain-colored or striped blooms are at their best. From the high mountains of Switzerland and Greece comes the dainty *D. alpinus*, a rock-garden species which prefers some shade for its large, single, short-stemmed flowers. Another rock-garden kind is *D. deltoides*, the Maiden Pink, which makes a broad mass of slender 6-inch stems, each supporting clusters of tiny pink flowers about the size of a dime.

Named varieties like Beatrix, the Bristol Hybrids, Furst Bismarck, Rock Raven Red, and the delightful salmon-pink Old Spice are offered by nurserymen. Old favorites for borders or for masses in the rock garden or perennial garden are the Grass Pinks, *D. plumarius*. Their blue-green foliage makes an effective mat for the soft-textured, deliciously fragrant blooms.

Many Dianthus are easily raised from seed, but named varieties are propagated from cuttings or root division. Plants can be set out in spring or fall. They need to be divided and reset every two or three years because of their rampant growth. Full sun and gritty soil containing some lime suit them best. By keeping the seed pods picked off, the blooming season may be prolonged.

GARDEN FLOWERS IN COLOR

POPPY

Poppies are the "glamor girls" of the garden because their blooms, though spectacular, are short-lived. Some are natives of the Alps and arctic regions; others flourish in the Mediterranean area and still other kinds, notably the genus Eschscholzia, are widely distributed along the West coast of the United States. Although many Poppies are hardy perennials, not all are permanent. Such annual kinds as *Papaver Rhoeas*, the Corn Poppy, *P. somniferum*, the Opium Poppy, and *P. glaucum*, the Tulip Poppy, are widely grown in gardens.

Hybrid Oriental Poppies

GARDEN FLOWERS IN COLOR

In recent years, Iceland Poppies, *P. nudicaule*, have had their share of attention from the hybridizers. Flowers of improved size in delicate pastel shades produced on plants of compact form are available in the strains offered. The 12 to 15-inch stems are notable for their graceful form. During June and July they are at their best.

Decidedly spectacular are the showy Oriental Poppies, with their tremendous flowers and vigorous growth. They vary in height from 2 to 3½ feet or more. For those who object to the vivid red and orange shades, there are many named varieties in white, pink, and rose with contrasting markings of black, maroon, and purple. Oriental Poppies need a generous background of foliage to accentuate their coloring.

California-poppies, forms of *Eschscholzia californica*, are annuals for the hottest part of the garden and need ample space in which to display themselves to best advantage. They make bushy plants 12 to 15 inches tall, and are sometimes interplanted with narcissus and tulips to carry on a succession of bloom. A wide variety of color is available in the named varieties and strains offered by seedsmen.

P. Rhoeas, the Corn Poppy of Europe, is the source of the delightful Shirley varieties, including single and double forms. Many showy hybrids of the Opium Poppy, *P. somniferum*, are listed in seed catalogs; especially outstanding are the Carnation and Peony-flowered varieties. The Tulip Poppy, *P. glaucum*, has great scarlet cup-shaped blooms which strongly resemble tulips.

Double Annual Carnation-flowered Poppies

GARDEN FLOWERS IN COLOR

California-poppies

All Poppies thrive in well-drained soil and full sun. *P. nudicaule* is usually a short-lived perennial because of its profuse blooming habit, but it often self-sows. It is easily grown from seed sown in early summer. Since the seedlings are not easily transplanted, they need to be handled with as much soil as possible. Oriental Poppies have long tap-roots, and field-grown plants should be transplanted during their dormant period from August to October. Pot-grown plants can be set out at any time. The home gardener needs to remember that after the flowering period the foliage of the Oriental varieties turns yellow and disappears, making it necessary to mark the location of the plants with a garden stake.

Seed of the annual kinds may be sown in the fall for early flowering, followed by successive sowings for midsummer bloom. Mix the tiny seed with sand or finely sifted loam for more even distribution, and scatter it lightly. Care is needed in covering the seed, and a fine spray of water settles it. Light brushwood or chicken wire helps to keep cats and dogs from disturbing the soil until the seed has germinated. Since Poppies are not easily transplanted, the weaker seedlings should be pulled out, allowing 9 to 12 inches between plants. A sunny location produces the best results. While the largest flowers are grown on rich soil, Poppies grow well under ordinary conditions. Once established, they return each year; in fact, self-sown plants are unusually vigorous.

The bright blooms of Portulaca

PORTULACA

This Brazilian native may well be considered an easy annual for everybody's garden, since it needs only a hot sunny location and grows freely in any kind of soil. Its Latin name means "purslane" (pussley), to which it is related. Sun-rose, Sun-plant, Wax-pink, and Rose-moss are some of its many common names.

An ideal ground cover for hot dry areas, it blooms incessantly, and requires no care except weeding. Plant Portulaca where grass is difficult to grow. It has been used to advantage in driveways, between and along the sides of paved areas. Single and double-flowering kinds are obtainable in many colors. A rapid-growing annual, it can be used for edging beds and borders when spring-flowering plants like pansies and English daisies have faded. Often Portulaca is sown in beds where spring bulbs have flowered.

The tender annual Portulaca must not be planted until all danger of frost has passed. Prepare the soil before sowing, and mix the fine seed with sand for even distribution. Scatter it broadcast and press it in lightly with a board or brick. Seedlings can be transplanted at any time, even in full bloom, to fill in bare spots. Portulaca self-sows frequently in areas where the winters are mild.

PRIMROSE

There is a sort of old-time charm and fascination about Primroses. The genus name Primula, from the Latin meaning "first," refers to the earliness of the blooms—the first of the spring. Cherished by the garden-loving Anglo-Saxons, the cheerful yellow Primroses carry us back into history nearly a thousand years. From medieval records we learn that stewed roses and Primroses constituted a rare delicacy.

The English Primroses (*Primula acaulis* or *P. vulgaris*) were great favorites in Elizabethan times, and have never lost favor with garden enthusiasts. Many hybrids with remarkable color variations, including the curious double or hose-in-hose types and *P. Auricula,* are cultivated now.

P. elatior, the Oxlip of Shakespeare's day, holds its flowers well above the foliage on sturdy stems several inches tall. Then there is the Cowslip (listed as *P. veris, P. officinalis,* or *P. suaveolens*), bearing

Hose-in-hose Primroses

GARDEN FLOWERS IN COLOR

Wanda, a richly colored hybrid of Primula Juliae, is a low-growing variety. The blooms are borne singly on stems a few inches high. This is a choice variety for a moist corner in the rock garden.

The showy blooms of Primula japonica are typical of the bog or candelabra Primroses. Established plants often produce three whorls of florets on a single spike.

its clusters of drooping flowers above the foliage in a most picturesque fashion. The so-called Polyanthus Primroses with their brilliant array of colors and accentuating eyes are hybrids of *P. acaulis* and *P. veris*. A delightful Asiatic species with flowers like *P. acaulis* is *P. Juliae*, which has given us the reddish purple variety Wanda.

Among the bog or candelabra type Primroses, perhaps the most commonly grown species is the showy *P. japonica* or Japanese Primrose. The gay whorls of florets, usually two or three on each spike, are borne on stems 18 to 24 inches tall during May and June. Rose, pink, red, terra-cotta, flesh, and white are among the hues available.

The Silverdust Primrose, *P. pulverulenta*, is so called because of the curious mealy white substance that covers the entire plant. Crimson and orange tints are dominant in these candelabra-like flowers, which often grow 2 feet or more in height.

The Bulley Primrose, *P. Bulleyana*, is unique for its buff, orange, and apricot tones. Several tiers of flowers grace the stems of this sturdy 18-inch species. Separate colors are offered, but the greatest surprises come from selected mixtures.

The Denticulata group of Primroses includes *P. denticulata cache-miriana*, with large heads of lavender flowers on 12 to 18-inch stems.

P. cortusoides, with its deep lavender blooms and conspicuous wavy foliage, is a compact plant seldom more than 9 inches tall. Then there is *P. Sieboldi*, a taller-growing species of vigorous habit. White, pink, and lavender-pink forms are offered.

Primulas thrive best in rich sandy loam. The bog species prefer a heavier soil than those requiring less moisture. Partial shade is desirable for all species, and the question of moisture is vital. Moist soil does not mean poorly drained soil, for poor drainage is deadly to Primulas in winter. So, too, is stagnant water. Plant the bog species on the edge of a stream or bog, or near a spring (artificial or natural). While the various species common to cottage gardens need less moisture, nevertheless they must never be allowed to dry out. Propagation is by seed or division. Obtain fresh seed and sow it in a coldframe in early spring to obtain blooming plants for the following year. Established clumps are easily divided, preferably after flowering.

Primula polyantha   Primula Auricula

GARDEN FLOWERS IN COLOR

PUSSY WILLOW

Each year while wintry blasts are still with us, the well-loved Pussy Willow, *Salix discolor*, sends forth its soft grayish catkins as a gentle reminder that spring is not far away. It is native to the northern and middle Atlantic States. For the most part, the attractive twigs which are taken indoors to use in arrangements are gathered from the wild, but plants can be grown in gardens where space permits. Although the Pussy Willow in its mature form develops into a tree 20 feet or more in height, the young plants of graceful whip-like growth can be included in the shrub border.

Usually found in low moist places and especially along streams, the Pussy Willow readily adapts itself to most garden soils. Plants can be set out in either spring or fall. Frequently the twigs which are taken indoors when the fluffy catkins develop, send out roots when placed in water. Cuttings of this sort are often the beginning of Pussy Willow trees seen in gardens.

GARDEN FLOWERS IN COLOR

Pyracantha coccinea

PYRACANTHA

Firethorn, the common name for Pyracantha, is actually the English translation of the Greek genus name. In addition to its evergreen foliage and its broad spreading growth, *Pyracantha coccinea* is noted for its large clusters of bright orange-red fruits borne in the fall. The plants are vigorous, often 12 feet or more in width and height, with thick rigid spiny stems. The fruits sometimes remain on the plants all winter but usually they are quickly devoured by the birds. The white blooms are borne in early spring.

In regions where the Pyracanthas can be grown, they are particularly desirable on the home grounds either as specimens or in shrub plantings. Where a broad spreading hedge is desired, Pyracantha can be used to good advantage. The variety *P. coccinea Lalandi*, often used for espalier effects against walls and chimneys, is especially decorative throughout the year. Although not hardy in the northeastern United States, *P. coccinea* can be grown successfully as far north as Long Island.

Plants obtained from nurserymen are generally small specimens from pots, since their deep rooting habit prevents large plants from being moved easily. Pyracantha can be set out in spring or fall. Provide a sunny location and mix a few shovelfuls of leaf-mold or peat with the soil when planting. Little pruning is required except to improve the form of the plant. Allow ample space for it to develop.

Pyrethrum, Pink Bouquet

PYRETHRUM

The name Pyrethrum has been associated with the colorful Painted Daisies for so long that it is commonly believed to be a correct botanical name. Actually, though, these showy hardy perennials are forms of *Chrysanthemum coccineum*. In late spring the daisy-like blooms, both single and double, in shades of white, pink, and red, make a bright splash in the home garden. The plants make mounds of finely cut foliage from which rise the 2-foot flower stems. In addition to selected strains there are many named varieties; some have beautifully crested centers, like Pink Bouquet. The flowers are particularly desirable for cutting because of their fine keeping qualities.

Pyrethrums grow best in full sun, and need fertile soil rich in organic matter. Plants can be set out in early spring or in the fall, and when established need to be reset every three years. Set them a foot apart; the improved forms require an abundance of moisture.

FLOWERING QUINCE

The Japanese or Flowering Quince is an old dooryard shrub commonly listed as *Cydonia japonica*, but now classified as *Chaenomeles lagenaria*. Mature specimens may reach 10 feet in height and often in width. The brilliant red flowers appear on spiny branches in April. Many improved varieties with blooms of pure white, pink, orange, and red have been introduced. This handsome shrub has attractive foliage and can be used to advantage in many parts of the garden. The fairsized greenish yellow fruits maturing in the fall are similar to the edible quinces and are often used to make fragrant pomanders.

Plants can be set out in spring or fall; they grow well in most soils and do best in full sun. Prune after flowering to improve their form.

GARDEN FLOWERS IN COLOR

RHODODENDRON

Although botanists make no generic distinction between Rhododendrons and azaleas, these two groups of closely related acid-soil plants are featured separately by the nurserymen who sell them. These showy evergreen shrubs are among the most attractive plants for permanent effects in the home garden, particularly in shaded areas.

One of the earliest to bloom is our native Carolina Rhododendron, *Rhododendron carolinianum*, which produces its rosy purple blooms during May and June. The plants seldom grow more than 6 feet tall and are easily distinguished by their small leaves and their compact habit.

From the mountainous regions of Virginia and Georgia we have the Mountain Rose Bay, *R. catawbiense*, a magnificent shrub reaching 15 feet or more in height, and often making as great a spread. This plant, characterized by clusters of large lilac-purple blooms, is the parent of many notable hybrid forms. In June and July, the Great

Carolina Rhododendron, R. carolinianum

GARDEN FLOWERS IN COLOR

Hybrid Rhododendrons

Laurel or Rose Bay, *R. maximum*, makes its appearance. Mature specimens may reach 20 feet or more in height. Unlike the hybrid Rhododendrons and the other species, its light pink blooms are often partially hidden by the foliage.

Many of the hybrid Rhododendrons offered by nurserymen have been developed from our native *R. catawbiense* and the tender Oriental species, *R. arboreum*. More than fifty outstanding named varieties in shades of pink, lavender, and red, as well as white, are found in the catalogs of the leading growers.

The Rhododendron is distinctly an acid-soil plant. As with all broad-leaved evergreens, the plants grow best in protected areas; windswept spots and southern exposures should be avoided. The roots of the Rhododendron prefer a moist but well-drained soil that is rich in organic matter. Neutral or sub-acid soils can be improved by the use of aluminum sulphate. Other sources of acidity include peat moss, pine needles, and oak-leaf mold. Plants can be set out in spring or early fall. Fall-planted specimens may need protection in addition to a mulch of oak leaves or pine needles. (For further cultural information, see the discussion under azaleas on page 38.)

ROSE

The Rose, christened the queen of flowers by Sappho more than 2500 years ago, is still the most beloved garden flower. In art and architecture, in history, in literature—even in modern advertising—everywhere we turn, there is admiring reference to the Rose. This is easy to understand when we consider that no flower has greater beauty of form, a more pleasing color range, or more delightful fragrance. Roses have been growing in gardens and in the wilds for thousands of years, sometimes under the loving care of a Rose enthusiast and at other times under entirely natural conditions. Modern plant hybridizers have improved Roses to such an extent that no garden is complete without their loveliness.

Rosa gallica

The Rose, the most adaptable of garden plants, can be used in numerous ways in gardens large or small. Where only a few plants can be grown, the bush Roses, including the Hybrid Teas, the Polyanthas, and the Floribundas, make delightful informal masses of color. In large gardens they can be planted to advantage in broad groups in the foreground of shrub borders; the foliage of evergreens and flowering shrubs makes an effective setting for the bright color of the blooms. The Rugosas, the species or wild Roses, and many of the Hardy Climbers which can be trained on posts are often used to compose a Rose planting or border. Large-flowered Climbers and the Trailing or Rambler Roses lend themselves to hedge use when simple wire supports are provided, or they can be planted to hold a slope against erosion. In selecting places for the informal planting of Roses, it is necessary to prepare the soil well, and to avoid locations where deep shade and tree roots interfere.

Hybrid Teas, Polyanthas, and Floribundas are the most widely planted kinds throughout the country. Their use in solid beds has been popular for generations but it is not necessary to have a large formal garden in order to enjoy these bush Roses. Beds 5 feet wide will provide space enough to accommodate three rows of plants; this is an ideal setup. When wider beds are planted, the problem of maintenance be-

Roses planted in an informal border

GARDEN FLOWERS IN COLOR

comes more difficult. Since Roses require considerable spraying, it is a good plan to have all beds and plantings easily accessible from all sides.

The various kinds of Climbing Roses trained on trellises, porches, pergolas, and posts require little care. In selecting varieties, ample space for their development must be provided since many are very rampant in their growth; others, known as Pillar Roses, seldom reach more than 8 feet in height.

An amazing number of Rose varieties and species are available to modern gardeners. Nearly 5,000 altogether are classified in "Modern Roses II," by J. Horace McFarland (published by the Macmillan Company in 1940). While the species or wild Roses often thrive with little or no care, the multitudes of named varieties sometimes have peculiar preferences as to soil and climate. So, in selecting Hybrid Teas, Climbing Roses, Polyanthas, and other improved forms, a beginner soon learns that some Roses are better suited to his garden than others. In order to distinguish various types, the classifications which follow are generally used in the catalogs of nurserymen.

The Tea Roses, though not always frost-hardy in the North, are old-time favorites in warm climates, particularly south of Washington, to the Gulf Coast and California. They are important because they are the foundation of the myriads of Hybrid Teas that are so widely grown all over the country. Many of the old Tea Roses have mild, tea-like fragrance, but their color range is limited.

Most widely planted of all are the Hybrid Teas. These were developed in England and in France by crossing the recurrent-blooming Tea Roses with the vigorous Hybrid Perpetuals which bloomed but once a year. The vigor and rich color derived from the Hybrid Perpetual, combined with the free-blooming habit of the Tea, have made the Hybrid Tea an indispensable garden Rose. Often referred to as

Hybrid Tea Roses of distinctive form and color

monthly or everblooming Roses, the Hybrid Teas are best characterized as a recurrent-blooming class which produces several crops of
flowers through the growing season. Actually during the hot summer
months the plants bloom but little. It is during their first bloom period
in June and in the cool autumn months that the Hybrid Teas are at
their best. They vary in height from 15 inches to 4 feet or more, according to the variety, the climate, and the soil in which they are grown.

Mention should be made here of the tree or standard forms of the
Hybrid Teas, usually referred to as Tree Roses. These are plants
grafted on a sturdy stock to provide a tall stem, and often used in formal plantings. They grow best in regions where the winters are mild.
In cold climates the plants are laid down in late autumn and heavily
mulched with soil and leaves.

Particularly outstanding for their hardiness, their upright vigorous
growth, and their large blooms, the Hybrid Perpetuals make their
burst of bloom in June, and occasionally some varieties also produce
flowers in autumn. Unlike the Hybrid Teas which bloom on new
wood, the Hybrid Perpetuals produce their flowers from growth made
the previous year. Those familiar with old-time gardens often recall
with pleasure the fine old specimen plants of the white Frau Karl
Druschki and the favorite red variety General Jacqueminot.

Another favorite group of Roses making a brilliant display are the
numerous Hardy Climbers, which are outstanding in color and fragrance. There are both large-flowered forms like Dr. W. Van Fleet
and Paul's Scarlet Climber and small, bunch-flowered varieties, commonly spoken of as Ramblers. They are often used to advantage on
trellises, fences, arbors, and pergolas, as well as on banks. Mention
should also be made of the Climbing Hybrid Teas. These are plants of
moderate growth, best treated as Pillar Roses. They are not as frostproof as the Hardy Climbers, and are best suited to warm climates.

Hybrid Teas are particularly attractive when the blooms are partially open

GARDEN FLOWERS IN COLOR

Irish Single Roses

Two groups of bush Roses that have attracted notable attention in the past twenty years are the Polyanthas and the Floribundas. Polyanthas may best be described as compact bushy plants varying from 1 to 2 feet in height, with blooms borne in clusters. The flowers of some varieties measure less than an inch across, and others are considerably larger. As a result of intensive hybridizing, the plants are noted for their free-flowering habit and may be appropriately called ever-blooming Roses, for there is always evidence of some bloom on the plants. To distinguish the small-flowered Polyanthas from the improved forms with large blooms—some measuring 3 inches or more in diameter—the name Floribunda was introduced. It is a most appropriate title for these large-flowered cluster Roses. Many outstanding varieties are available.

Of recent introduction are the miniature or Baby Roses, most of which are derived from *Rosa Rouletti*. In addition to the familiar pink form, there are white, yellow, and red varieties. The tiny blooms, less than an inch in diameter, are borne freely from mid-May until checked by hard frost. The plants, varying in height from a few inches to a foot, are useful for edgings and borders, and for rock gardens.

Because of their rugged growth, their attractive foliage, and fine blooms, the Rugosa Roses have been frequently planted as specimens and hedges. The 8 to 10-foot plants are wide spreading.

Many of the old-fashioned Roses like *R. gallica*, the Provence

GARDEN FLOWERS IN COLOR

© The Hybrid Tea Rose, Mary Margaret McBride

GARDEN FLOWERS IN COLOR

Austrian Copper, a Shrub Rose   The Miniature Rose, Pixie

or French Rose, *R. moschata*, the Musk Rose, *R. cinnamomea*, the
Cinnamon Rose, and *R. damascena*, the Damask Rose, may appropriately be considered as shrubs. Innumerable varieties were developed in the eighteenth and nineteenth centuries, particularly in
France and England. They are cherished today not only for their
beauty and fragrance, but for their rich associations in history, literature, and tradition.

The catalogs of some Rose specialists feature numerous groups of
Roses which, although not widely grown, are distinctive in many ways.
Outstanding among them are the charming Irish single varieties.
The old China, Bourbon, and Bengal Roses are mostly small plants
with double blooms, produced in abundance all season.

Several important factors are essential in planting Roses. A sunny
location suits them, but they can be grown successfully in light shade.
When the plants arrive—preferably dormant outdoor-grown ones—
get them into the ground promptly. If planting must be delayed, either
store them in a cool place in the package in which they arrived, or
dig a trench in a protected place and cover the roots with soil.

Roses need a well-drained soil, and grow best in a medium clay
loam. Heavy soils require drainage; Roses cannot endure "wet feet."

Spade the Rose-bed to a depth of 18 inches. If possible, put in
the bottom of the bed a generous layer of well-decomposed stable
manure, or some good commercial fertilizer mixed with peat moss,
or turned-under sod. Holes for individual plants are prepared in
the same way. Prepare the Rose-bed several weeks in advance, and
allow the soil to settle before the bushes are planted.

Keep the plants in a pail of water or thin mud before planting, to prevent the roots from drying out while the holes are being dug. Examine the plants carefully; cut away all broken branches and roots. Hybrid Teas, Polyanthas, and Floribundas are usually spaced 15 to 18 inches apart each way; the Hybrid Perpetuals need at least 2 feet each way. If planting in the fall, prune the canes back to about 12 inches; if in the spring, to 6 or 8 inches.

Dig the hole large enough to accommodate the roots easily. Long roots may be shortened. Set the plants deep enough so that the knobby bud is just beneath the surface of the soil. Firm the ground well around the roots with the full pressure of your feet. Fill the hole with water, and allow it to soak in before replacing the top soil. The stems need to be mounded up with 6 inches of earth until growth starts.

For protection over the winter fall-planted Roses need to have the soil hilled up around the stems to a height of at least 6 inches. A mulch of leaves or evergreen boughs can be applied after the ground has frozen hard. In severe climates most home gardeners find it wise to hill up established plants of Hybrid Teas, Polyanthas, and Floribundas, and to provide a mulch of leaves or evergreen boughs.

To prolong the spring planting period many growers sell pot-grown Roses during the late spring and early summer. These can be planted with ease whenever available and are usually very satisfactory once they are permanently established.

The easiest way to have good Roses is to keep them growing vigorously. An application of some good complete fertilizer can be given in

Polyantha Rose, Golden Salmon

© Floribunda Rose, Donald Prior

GARDEN FLOWERS IN COLOR

the spring and again before the plants come into bloom. Another feeding in midsummer will help to improve the size of the fall blooms, but no fertilizer should be used after August 1 in the eastern United States. There are many good commercial fertilizers available. Watering during long dry periods is sometimes necessary. Give the plants a thorough soaking, and avoid wetting the foliage.

Several kinds of insects and diseases sometimes find their way to Rose-beds. Black-spot and mildew, common diseases of many garden plants, often affect Rose foliage. Aphids and chewing insects also come into the picture. The pathologists and entomologists have been hard at work for some time on the matter of insects and diseases, and now spray kits containing stomach poison, contact insecticides, and dusting powders are available. All are easily applied, and complete instructions are always printed on the packages. If Roses are kept in vigorous condition and have been sprayed before the insects are likely to appear, there is little to worry about.

The lovely Hybrid Tea Rose, Katherine T. Marshall

GARDEN FLOWERS IN COLOR

Paul's Scarlet Climber, one of the finest of the Climbing Roses

Keeping dead flowers picked off, thorough watering during dry seasons, several feedings of fertilizer, and a sensible spraying program will keep Roses in good condition through the year.

Pruning Roses is simply a matter of common sense. After removing winter protection, cut away dead wood and shorten weak growth. Close pruning produces compact growth, while high pruning results in growth that is inclined to be lanky. In removing dead wood, cut back to a point just above the bud or eye, preferably one on the outer side of the stem. The purpose is to keep plants open in growth and not to allow stems to cross. Climbing Roses require little pruning in the spring except for the removal of dead wood. After the plants have finished blooming, shorten the growth on the older canes. Every few years old wood can be removed entirely, and new growth encouraged. Ramblers are best pruned after blooms have passed; cut out all wood that has produced flowers. The shrub Roses require only such pruning as you would give to any other flowering shrub. Polyanthas and Floribundas need only to have dead wood and weak canes removed. Pruning to improve the form of Rose plants merely requires the same skillful use of a pair of sharp shears.

Hybrid Salpiglossis

SALPIGLOSSIS

The dainty hybrids of *Salpiglossis sinuata* are aristocrats of the plant kingdom which came to us originally from South America. They are among the choicest of annuals. In its color range and its requirements, this flower—sometimes called Painted-tongue—is in a class apart. A well-grown bed of Salpiglossis is an achievement for any amateur to be proud of. Poised in loose clusters, the funnel-shaped blossoms with distinctive veinations are not unlike petunias in form; they stand erect on stems 2½ to 3 feet tall. Rich in blended tones of scarlet, maroon, purple, and golden yellow, these first-rate annuals are superb cut flowers. A dwarf strain less than 2 feet in height is also available to the home gardener.

Start the seed in a hotbed or coldframe, or in the open ground (in regions where the spring season comes early). Since the plants are sparse of foliage, they should be set 6 to 9 inches apart. A sunny location and rich soil is most favorable for them. The seedlings are apt to be weak and spindly in the young stage, and will benefit by applications of liquid manure. The young plants must be kept in active growth to prevent stunting, which is bound to produce unsatisfactory results. Transplant the seedlings as soon as they are large enough to be easily handled. It may be necessary to stake the tall-growing varieties if they are not grown in a sheltered location. Pinch back the young plants to make them branch. Salpiglossis grows best in sections where the summers are cool.

Scarlet Sage, Salvia splendens

SALVIA

The showy Scarlet Sage, *Salvia splendens*, and Garden Sage, *S. offici-nalis*, an old-time perennial herb used for flavoring, are perhaps the most commonly grown Sages in the home garden. However, there are many other outstanding species, some of them with extraordinary blue flowers which are particularly pleasing in hardy borders.

The annual Scarlet Sage, *S. splendens*, is planted everywhere. In addition to the common red-flowering form, there are pink, white, and purple kinds, varying in height from 2 to 3½ feet or more. The Mealy-cup Sage, *S. farinacea*, produces racemes of lavender flowers on 2-foot stems. Although a perennial, it is often grown as an annual.

Among the perennial Sages is *S. officinalis*, grown primarily for flavoring. One of the earliest to bloom is Meadow Sage, *S. pratensis*. But the most spectacular of all is the lovely old-time Clary, *S. Sclarea*, with large loose panicles of pinkish lavender flowers on 3-foot stems in late June. Another showy kind is the Violet Sage, *S. virgata nemorosa*, bearing spire-like violet flowers on 2-foot stems in July. In autumn we have the Azure Sage, *S. azurea*, and its improved forms. The plants, often 4 feet high, have somewhat sprawly stems and need to be staked.

The annual Sages require a long time to develop; seed is best started indoors or in a hotbed or coldframe. The perennial Sages grow well in most garden soils and prefer a sunny location. All of these can be grown from seed, but most gardeners prefer to obtain plants from nurserymen, to be set out in early spring or fall.

Annual Scabiosa

SCABIOSA

Mourning Bride, Sweet Scabious, and Pincushion-flower are familiar names particularly associated with the delightful annual species, *Scabiosa atropurpurea*. The perennial kinds should be more widely grown in gardens, for their lavender-blue and white blooms are especially attractive for flower arrangements.

The free-flowering habit, the showy blooms on long, slender stems 2 feet tall or more, and the wide variety of colors have made the annual Scabiosa a very desirable plant and cut flower. Lavender, several shades of pink, red, yellow, and white kinds are included.

The perennial species *S. caucasica* produces large flat lavender-blue blooms on 2-foot stems. During late summer and early fall *S. Fischeri*, a species of recent introduction, furnishes quantities of lavender-blue flowers. *S. japonica* is considered more rugged than *S. caucasica*, but it often acts like a biennial.

The perennial Scabiosas prefer full sun and rich well-drained soil. Good drainage is essential because the crowns rot easily in wet soils. They are usually transplanted in early spring or fall. Sow the seed of the annual kinds in a hotbed, a coldframe, or in the open ground after frost danger has passed, and set the plants 6 to 9 inches apart in full sun.

Hybrids of Scabiosa caucasica

GARDEN FLOWERS IN COLOR

241

SCILLA

These brave little bulbous plants often endure the hardships of wind, rain, and late snow to force their way into the spring landscape. The Siberian Squill, *Scilla sibirica*, growing 4 to 5 inches tall, blooms in early April. It is best planted in informal drifts in borders and rock gardens. The Spanish Bluebell, *S. campanulata* (*hispanica*), bears clusters of drooping bell-shaped flowers during May. The blue and white varieties, with an average height of 12 to 18 inches, are effective when massed with yellow azaleas. The English Bluebell, *S. nutans*, with 12-inch blooms of pink, white, and blue, appears in early May.

Scilla sibirica

Scilla bulbs are planted in the fall. Set *S. sibirica* 2 inches deep; the Campanulata sorts 4 to 5 inches deep, with the same distance between them. Full sun or partial shade suits them.

Scilla campanulata

GARDEN FLOWERS IN COLOR

SHASTA DAISY

The great white hardy daisy-like flowers which have been featured in catalogs of the leading growers in recent years are for the most part hybrids of *Chrysanthemum maximum*, the Pyrenees Daisy, and commonly called Shasta Daisy. The late Luther Burbank, who introduced many of the large-flowered kinds, maintained that he developed them from our common Field or Ox-eye Daisy, *C. Leucanthemum*. An amazing number of varieties are featured in many parts of the country. The large showy blooms, single, semi-double, or truly double with crested centers, are much prized for cutting as well as for the attractive display they make in summer gardens.

The plants vary in height from 15 inches to 3 feet. In selecting varieties of Shasta Daisies, it is wise to choose those that will provide a succession of bloom over a long period. Alaska is a dwarf-growing kind with large single blooms. The variety Favorite bears immense blooms with bright yellow centers on 3-foot stems in June and July. King Edward is useful, since it flowers later than Alaska. Then there is Mayfield Giant, noted for its free-blooming habit in midsummer, and Silver Star, whose claim to recognition lies in its prolonged blooming habit and its large single blooms. A free-blooming compact grower is Snowbank, which produces its single flowers over a long period. Phyllis Elliott and Chiffon have several rows of quilled petals, and Admiral Byrd has slightly frilled petals. The crested centers of Esther Reed and White Swan are among the latest developments made in Shasta hybrids.

The Shasta Daisy requires a sunny location and deep, well-drained soil that is rich in organic matter. Allow at least a foot of space between plants. Established groups should be reset every other year in order to keep them in a thrifty condition. New plants can be set out in the spring or fall. Many of the single forms of Shasta Daisies can be raised from seed, but the double kinds are propagated by root division. They need to be watered during dry spells, and plants grown in exposed areas benefit greatly by being mulched over the winter months.

Shasta Daisy, Esther Reed

SNAPDRAGON

Although they are perennials in their native habitat, the Snapdragons developed from *Antirrhinum majus* are treated as hardy annuals in the eastern United States, where they often self-sow. In areas where the climate is mild, the plants live over winter.

The types may be grouped according to height. Maximum or Super-Giant kinds often exceed 3 feet in height. The Majus types, averaging 2 to 2½ feet, are most suitable for the home garden, but both these kinds need staking. The Nanum Grandiflorum types, 12 to 18 inches tall, make effective masses in small areas and are best suited to the average garden. Among the novelties are the midget Antirrhinums, which are seldom more than 6 inches tall.

Seed is best started in a hotbed or a coldframe. Pinch the centers of the seedlings and set them in rich garden soil. Set the plants 6 to 15 inches apart, depending upon their ultimate height. Recently a rust disease almost put an end to these sturdy annuals, but rust-resistant strains are now available which are recommended for the home garden. Diseased plants should always be destroyed.

SNOWDROP

Snowdrops deserve a place in every garden. Like the crocuses, the scillas, and the winter aconites, these bulbous plants anticipate spring. Some old botanist named this dainty plant Galanthus, which in Greek means "milk flower." The small white blossoms of *Galanthus nivalis*, suspended from delicate stems seldom more than 6 inches long, remind one of a series of bells cracked by the frosty winter winds of February and early March. *G. Elwesi* is larger than the common kind.

Planted in groups, Snowdrops soon make intimate colonies. Along a shady walk or underneath shrubbery and trees they adapt themselves readily. Rich loam, to which some leaf-mold has been added, suits them well. Early September is the ideal planting time; set the bulbs 3 inches deep. This early-flowering bulb multiplies readily and can be depended upon to make a permanent showing in the garden.

The Common Snowdrop

GARDEN FLOWERS IN COLOR

Spiraea Vanhouttei

SPIRAEA

Perhaps the commonest shrub found in gardens throughout the United States is the ubiquitous Bridal Wreath, *Spiraea Vanhouttei*. There is hardly a home gardener who at some time or other has not planted some form of Spiraea. An amazing number of species and hybrids are cultivated by nurserymen. Most of them are plants of easy culture that make a brilliant display for the space they occupy, although some, like *S. Vanhouttei*, have been so widely planted that their blooms are somewhat tiresome in the landscape. The Spiraeas are free flowering in habit, and all have durable foliage which is attractive throughout the growing season.

S. arguta, flowering in early May, bears long spikes of single white blooms in great abundance on plants averaging 5 to 6 feet. Usually the plants are shapely in appearance. Although the species *S. Bumalda* is not much cultivated in gardens, the variety Anthony Waterer, with great flat clusters of bright crimson bloom on plants 3 to 4 feet tall, is commonly seen during June and July. So too is the hybrid form *S. Billiardi*, which grows 4 to 6 feet tall, producing pyramidal spikes of rosy pink bloom during July and August. *S. prunifolia plena*, sometimes referred to as the True Bridal Wreath, has showy spikes of double white bloom in late spring. *S. Vanhouttei*, the common Bridal Wreath, hardly needs to be described. The plants are often used as specimens or informal hedges, producing their showy white flowers in May and June. A recently introduced species, *S. trichocarpa*, blooms somewhat later but the flowers are not so white as the old familiar form. More upright in form than *S. arguta* is the attractive *S. Thunbergi*, with spikes of showy white flowers. The plants, of pleasing upright habit, average 5 feet in height and bloom in May.

Spiraeas are among the easiest shrubs to grow. They tolerate a wide variety of soils but do best in full sun. Plants can be set out in spring or fall. They require little care except the skillful use of the shears to keep them within bounds. Dead wood is easily removed in early spring, and pruning for improved form can be done immediately after flowering. Pruning to encourage new growth from the base of the plant helps to keep the Spiraeas vigorous.

Spiraea Thunbergi   Spiraea Billiardi

GARDEN FLOWERS IN COLOR

Ornithogalum umbellatum

STAR OF BETHLEHEM

Although native to the regions bordering the Mediterranean, the Star of Bethlehem, or Summer Snowflake, *Ornithogalum umbellatum*, has become naturalized in many parts of the eastern United States. This hardy bulbous plant multiplies rapidly and requires ample space in the shrub border. Its white flowers in late spring, borne in clusters on 6-inch stems, rise from grass-like foliage which disappears in midsummer.

Among the tender species which are very desirable for the window garden is the fragrant white *O. arabicum*. *O. maculatum* produces light orange blooms, and *O. splendens*, orange-red. The Chincherinchee, or Wonder Flower, *O. thyrsoides*, and its golden yellow variety *aureum*, are remarkable for their long-lasting flowers.

The common form, *O. umbellatum*, is planted 2 inches deep in the early fall. The winter-blooming kinds are planted in pots, put in a cool place until roots develop, and then set in a sunny window.

STAR OF TEXAS

An annual of recent introduction is the showy Star of Texas, classified as *Xanthisma texanum*. As its name suggests, it is a native of the state of Texas, where it grew and flourished unnoticed until a few years ago. Its claim to attention in gardens is its large yellow blooms and the fact that the plants grow readily in hot dry places. Very often the home flower garden suffers neglect during the hot days of midsummer, and sturdy drought-resistant annuals like Xanthisma are needed to provide color. The plants average 1½ to 2 feet in height, and bloom freely over a long period.

Sow the seed in the open ground, and thin the plants to stand 9 to 12 inches apart. Ordinary soil and full sun are the simple requirements for this new annual. By removing the seed pods frequently, the plants can be kept blooming long.

GARDEN FLOWERS IN COLOR

Ten Weeks Stock

STOCK

For garden use it is important to select the early-blooming varieties of Stock, *Mathiola incana*. A perennial in warm climates, it is treated as an annual in northern gardens. The Ten Weeks Stock, *M. incana annua*, comes into flower quickly (in approximately ten weeks, as the name implies) and averages 15 inches in height. Lavender, purple, pink, white, soft yellow, and dark red are representative of the colors offered. A strain known as Cut-and-come-again is grown for its recurrent bloom. *M. bicornis*, the Night-scented Stock, valued for its fragrance rather than for its single lilac flowers, blooms in the evening.

Start the seed in a hotbed, a coldframe, or in the open ground, and transplant the seedlings as soon as they have produced four to six leaves. Young plants allowed to become rootbound in pots or flats often fail to bloom. Stocks grow best in a cool, moist temperature where the soil is rich in available plant food. Water the plants freely, especially during dry spells, and grow them in full sun.

STRAWFLOWER

Most familiar of all the Everlastings or Strawflowers is the genus Helichrysum. (The common Everlasting is discussed on page 108.) The name Helichrysum, derived from the Greek, means "sun gold," in reference to the rich yellow centers of the papery flowers. This sturdy Australian annual, often reaching a height of 2½ feet or more, provides a colorful mass when planted in beds or with other annuals. Red, rose-pink, yellow, violet, and white varieties are obtainable in separate colors. Recently a strain of dwarf hybrids, averaging about 15 inches in height, has been introduced. Strawflowers and many of the other Everlastings, combined with dried grasses, are often used for winter decorations in cemeteries as well as in the home.

Plant the seed in a hotbed, a coldframe, or in the open ground. Set the seedlings 15 inches apart, in a sunny location. When growing Helichrysums in quantity, the plants are usually set in rows. For winter bouquets cut the flowers before they have expanded fully, remove the foliage, and hang the blooms in a dark place with their heads down until dry. Even the tiny buds will open, and they are more attractive than the larger flowers.

Helianthus, Coronation

SUNFLOWER

Both the annual and the perennial Sunflowers are among the most vigorous of summer garden flowers. The giant annual forms which often grow 8 feet or more have a beauty all their own, particularly when grown as specimens in the vegetable garden. Most seedsmen list the Cut-and-come-again strains, hybrids of *Helianthus cucumerifolius*. These vary from 2 to 4 feet in height.

Among the hardy kinds is *H. orgyalis*, with small flowers in loose clusters resembling those of coreopsis. The showy 6-foot plants bloom in late summer. Another tall-growing, late-flowering species is *H. angustifolius*, with single yellow blooms on 5-foot stems. A double-flowered perennial form of recent introduction known as Soleil d'Or makes a shrubby mass about 3 feet tall, with warm yellow, double dahlia-like blooms. Coronation is one of the finest of all the Sunflowers, with golden yellow crested blooms on 4-foot stems. Lodden Gold, a sturdy, full double variety, is also available.

Seed of the annual Sunflowers can be sown in a hotbed, a coldframe, or in the open. The plants can be expected to thrive in any sunny location and require little attention. The hardy kinds can be set out in spring or fall. Divide the plants every three years.

SWAN RIVER DAISY

The Swan River Daisy, *Brachycome iberidifolia,* is a pleasing annual from Australia. It is sometimes referred to as the annual cineraria, because the flowers closely resemble those of the familiar cineraria grown by florists.

Its tiny daisy-like blossoms are borne on slender stems useful for miniature bouquets. The available colors are purple, blue, pale lilac, rose, and white. Some have interesting zonal markings in contrasting colors which add to their attractiveness. In the rock garden, as edging plants, or in masses, these 12-inch plants are most effective.

For an early start sow the seed in a hotbed or a coldframe; it can be planted in the open ground when all danger of frost has passed. To create a solid mass of bloom, set the plants 4 to 6 inches apart. It is hardly advisable to set them in single rows, even for borders; they are much more effective in double rows for wide edgings. Pinch back the young plants and set them in full sun to develop sturdy growth. Most annuals benefit greatly from applications of liquid fertilizer, which can be applied a week or ten days after the plants have been set in their permanent places and again just before the plants come into bloom. This practice is advisable in growing the Swan River Daisy.

Blooms of the Swan River Daisy

GARDEN FLOWERS IN COLOR

A favorite
color in
Sweet Peas

SWEET PEA

Sweet Peas, varieties of *Lathyrus odoratus*, are not equally successful in all parts of the United States. These delightfully fragrant annual vines need a cool temperature, for they tend to weaken and wither in extreme heat. In many parts of New England and in the Northwest they grow well through the summer months, but in the warmer sections of the country they are best in the spring.

Most seedsmen list summer and winter-flowering kinds. The winter-flowering sorts, while especially adapted for forcing, are often grown in gardens because they bloom several weeks earlier than the summer-flowering types. Blue, lavender, cerise, crimson, purple, salmon, orange, white, and many variations of pink are found among the numerous named varieties.

Sweet Peas require more effort to obtain good results than do most annuals. If possible, dig a trench in the fall, spading it to a depth of

GARDEN FLOWERS IN COLOR

1½ to 2 feet, and a width of a foot. (Some gardeners have satisfactory results with trenches a foot deep.) Fill in with old manure to a depth of 3 inches; then fill the trench with rich loam. Sweet Peas thrive best in fertile soil that is moist but well drained. Sow the seed as early as possible in the spring, covering to a depth of 2 inches, and thin the seedlings to stand 6 inches apart. To hasten germination, the seed may be nicked with a sharp file or soaked in water overnight. Some gardeners treat or inoculate the seed with special nitrogen-fixing bacteria to insure better growth.

There are several other methods of starting the seed. It may be sown in the late fall before the ground freezes. Cover the seed with soil to a depth of 2 inches and mulch the seed bed well after the ground has frozen hard. (In the South seed is sown from November to February.) Many gardeners start their seed indoors in flats during February or early March, then transplant the seedlings to pots, and place them in a coldframe until it is warm enough to set the plants in their permanent places. When the seedlings have reached 6 inches in height, they need supports because the plants climb by means of tendrils. Brushwood or chicken wire at least 4 feet high may be used. Occasional applications of liquid manure, ample amounts of water, and a mulch of stable manure, peat moss, or grass clippings during dry spells are important in maintaining vigorous plants for a long blooming period. Spraying to eradicate pests is sometimes necessary.

GARDEN FLOWERS IN COLOR

255

The blooms of Sweet Sultan

SWEET SULTAN

The fluffy Sweet Sultan is a member of the cornflower or bachelors-button family, and is known to botanists as *Centaurea imperialis*. The loosely arranged thistle-like blooms are obtainable in many colors, and are particularly delightful for summer flower arrangements. Although of easy culture, they are not commonly seen in the home garden. The plants, which vary in height from 1½ to 2½ feet, produce sweet-scented blooms which measure several inches in diameter. They come into flower quickly, and home gardeners will do well to make several plantings to provide a succession of bloom. White, pink, purple, lilac, lavender, red, and yellow are the dominant colors listed in most seed catalogs. The Sweet Sultan grows well in full sun, and most ordinary garden soils suit it.

For an early start, seed can be sown in a hotbed or a coldframe, but care must be taken to transplant the seedlings as soon as they are large enough to be handled because they are not easily moved in warm weather. Most gardeners will find it practical to start their seed in the open ground as soon as the soil can be prepared. Sow it sparsely, and thin the young plants to stand 9 to 12 inches apart. The bloom season can be greatly prolonged by removing all dead flowers.

Showy heads of Sweet William

SWEET WILLIAM

This fragrant perennial, with its colorful, long-lasting blooms, has been a garden favorite for centuries. Of its many picturesque common names, Sweet William is the one that we usually associate with *Dianthus barbatus*. Although generally spoken of as a hardy perennial, it is best treated as a biennial. Typical varieties average 12 to 18 inches in height, but recently new alpine forms seldom more than 5 or 6 inches tall have been introduced. Pure colors in shades of pink and red, as well as pure white, are listed by seedsmen, but the greatest surprise is found in a packet of mixed seed. The strain Holborn Glory is noted for its distinctive auricula-eyed blooms. Sweet William can be used to advantage with Canterbury bells, foxglove, delphinium, and early summer-flowering plants; the dwarf alpine strain makes a superb edging.

Few plants are easier to grow than Sweet William. Seed is usually sown in July or early August. When the seedlings are large enough to handle, space them 3 or 4 inches apart. The young plants can be set out in their permanent location in the fall, or can be grown in a place by themselves for transplanting in the early spring. Although the plants are amazingly hardy, they often need a winter mulch in exposed areas. This attractive biennial frequently self-sows.

GARDEN FLOWERS IN COLOR

TIGRIDIA

Shellflower and Tiger-flower are common names for the Tigridia, a bulbous plant from Mexico. Many elaborately tinted hybrids have been developed from the species *Tigridia Pavonia*, including combinations of pink, white, lilac, yellow, scarlet, and orange, blotched and spotted with shades of crimson and maroon. Usually the stems are 2 to 2½ feet tall and do not require staking.

Since the stems are rather stiff and the foliage sparse, Tigridias are most effective when planted in shrub borders or with vigorous-growing perennials like peonies. Groups of them may be massed with pleasing effect in front of white phlox. To further enhance their beauty, they should have the benefit of a low foreground planting.

The bulbs or corms are set out in late spring, 4 inches deep and 6 inches apart. Tigridias grow best in full sun. As with other tender bulbous plants, they must be lifted in late fall.

Tigridia hybrids

GARDEN FLOWERS IN COLOR

Tithonia, Fireball

TITHONIA

Tithonia is useful for backgrounds and for planting where temporary screens are needed. As brilliant as the pottery of its native land is the sturdy tall-growing Mexican Sunflower, *Tithonia rotundifolia*. No doubt it had a place in the gardens of the ancient Inca civilization, since it is known as the Golden Flower of the Incas.

Although it is hardly a plant for a small garden, since it often grows 12 feet or more in height, especially during wet summers, this annual is an admirable cut flower. The large, coarse foliage resembles that of a fig or mulberry tree, and the showy flowers of brilliant vermilion are like single dahlias, and often measure 3 to 4 inches across. The variety Fireball, a dazzling shade of orange-scarlet, is found in the lists of many seedsmen.

Start the seed early in a greenhouse, a hotbed, or a coldframe, for the plants require a long period to develop. In areas where the growing season is long, seed can be planted in the open ground. Set the plants 3 to 4 feet apart in full sun, and hope for maturity before frost. An abundance of moisture or too much available plant food seems to stimulate growth of foliage rather than flowers.

TRITOMA

Kniphofia (Tritoma) Galpini

The Tritoma hybrids are fleshy-rooted perennials of unusual beauty. These showy members of the lily family, often referred to as Torch-lily, Red-hot-poker, and Flame-flower, are species of Kniphofia. The brilliant blooms, which appear in midsummer on sturdy stems 1½ to 4 feet tall or more, are colorful exclamation points in the hardy garden.

Varieties of high merit are available, among them the Pfitzeri hybrids, averaging 3 to 4 feet. Autumn Tints is a striking combination of red and gold, as is Flaming Torch, a predominantly red flower shaded yellow. Well-chosen names, which are self descriptive, have been attached to the forms known as Old Ivory, Golden Thoughts, Sulphur Spire, Orange Glow, Salmon Beauty, and Tower of Gold. Royal Standard is a spectacular bicolor form of chrome-yellow and scarlet.

The species *Kniphofia Pfitzeri* (*K. Uvaria grandis*) is valued for its free-flowering habit and its showy spikes of orange-scarlet shading to rich salmon-rose. Seedlings of this variety tend to vary in color. Among the smaller kinds is the species *K. Galpini*, with orange-saffron blooms on slender 2-foot stems. Its graceful spikes of flowers, only 4 to 6 inches long, are borne in profusion from July until October.

Tritomas are not hardy where the winters are severe. As snow seems to be very detrimental to them, in the cold climate of New England it is hardly wise to rely on a heavy mulch to protect the roots. It is far better to store them over winter in boxes, with some soil. South of Philadelphia they usually prove hardy under a protective mulch. Divide or transplant the fleshy rootstalks in early spring. Set the crowns about an inch deep, with a foot or more between plants. Rich soil in full sun is necessary to get the best results.

Pfitzer
Hybrid
Tritomas

GARDEN FLOWERS IN COLOR

Trollius, Sussex Queen

TROLLIUS

The Trollius or Globe-flower is an attractive hardy perennial which flowers during May and June. Some of the species are native in Siberia, and some in western China. Gardeners often speak of them as Giant Buttercups, since they are related to our native kinds.

The most familiar forms are orange and yellow varieties of *Trollius europaeus*. The plants vary in height from 18 to 24 inches, and sometimes send forth a few blossoms in early fall. From Siberia we have the showy species, *T. Ledebouri*. It is taller than *T. europaeus*, averaging 24 to 30 inches in height, with showy orange cups on tall stems. The variety Sussex Queen is outstanding, for it extends the blooming period of the Trollius. A dwarf species, *T. pumilus*, is sometimes grown in rock gardens.

The Trollius, like the Primula, prefers rich, moist soil. It grows well in sun or shade, but shady places are preferable where the summers are hot and dry. New plants are easily grown by division after the blooming season or in early fall. Experienced gardeners will find it interesting to grow the plants from seed, which needs to be sown in early June to produce plants for bloom the following year.

TUBEROSE

The fragrant Tuberose, *Polianthes tuberosa*, is a summer-flowering tuber reminiscent of old-time gardens. This member of the amaryllis family, a native of Mexico, has long been cherished for its fragrance and white beauty. Like the flowering tobacco, *Nicotiana affinis*, the fragrance of the Tuberose is most penetrating in the evening air.

The large double Tuberose known in commerce today as The Pearl, and the single variety Mexican Everblooming, are both worth growing. The Tuberoses are often associated in the garden with heliotrope and scented geraniums; their tall stems and sparse foliage make them suitable for interplanting. Since the penetrating fragrance is objectionable to some people, they should not be planted too near windows or porches.

Tuberoses grow well in full sun or light shade. For early flowering, start the tubers in pots indoors. A succession of bloom may be enjoyed over a long period by planting them at two-week intervals. They can be set out as soon as frost danger has passed. Set the roots at least 2 inches deep, in clusters of three or more, preferably in rich soil. A long growing season is required in order to produce large roots of blooming size; hence most home gardeners find it practical to buy new roots each year.

Tuberose, The Pearl

May-flowering Tulips planted in color groups make an attractive border, especially when combined with pansies and the hardy blue phlox. The Tulip is a showy flower in the garden, as well as a most useful cut flower. A dozen each of eight or ten varieties in separate colors provide great pleasure in the small home garden, and the bulbs will produce bloom for several years.

GARDEN FLOWERS IN COLOR

TULIP

Darwin Tulip

The Tulips we grow in our gardens have a fascinating history. The name Tulip is from *tauleban* or *toliban*, the ancient Persian name for "turban," and refers to the shape of an inverted flower. More than three hundred years ago they became favorite flowers in Holland, and the work of improvement begun at that time has been steadily carried on by the Dutch growers who raised large quantities of bulbs for exporting. They are also grown commercially in other parts of Europe and in America.

One of the strangest periods in modern history was that of the so-called "Tulip mania" in Holland, which occurred early in the seventeenth century. By 1634, Tulips had become so popular there that people were neglecting their affairs to gamble in them. Bulbs of the "broken" or striped types brought fabulous prices; one variety, of which there were only two bulbs, sold for 5,500 florins (about $3,080). Curious stories have been passed on to us about the enormous amounts of goods that were exchanged for a single bulb.

By selecting varieties from the various groups, including the species or wild forms, the Single Early, the Mendel, the Triumph, the Cottage, Darwin, and Breeder, it is possible to enjoy Tulips for nearly two months. Often they are planted in solid beds, but they are equally effective in groups of a dozen or more in perennial and shrub plantings. Pansies, violas, forget-me-nots, and English daisies interplanted with them make delightful combinations; these can be replaced with annuals for summer bloom.

The Darwin group, originally a selection from the Breeders, comprises a vigorous family with large shapely flowers in a wide range of self-colors. The long strong stems, varying from 2 to 3 feet, make the Darwins desirable cut flowers interesting in all stages of development, even when the blooms are fully expanded. They bloom in May with the Breeder and the Cottage groups, and varieties of all three classes are often interplanted. There are hundreds of Darwin varieties in commerce, and it is an easy matter to obtain favorite colors.

The Mendel and Triumph Tulips are usually grouped together in catalogs. Mendel Tulips resulted from crosses of Darwin and the Duc Van Thol group of Single Earlies; they include a few delightful varieties resembling the Darwins in size but with somewhat shorter stems.

More varied is the ever-increasing list of Triumph Tulips, which resulted from crosses between the Single Early and the Cottage, Darwin, and Breeder groups.

The Breeders are the descendants of the old Dutch Tulips, and until quite recently included only the "art" shades—the combinations of rich brown, bronze, deep orange, and purple; but the color range has been widened considerably. Many of the dusky-colored varieties are

A bed of Darwin Tulips in a dooryard garden

GARDEN FLOWERS IN COLOR

A group of May-flowering Tulips

favorites with amateurs, who enjoy the subdued beauty of the intense colors. The flowers of the Breeders are quite large, usually egg-shaped, and are produced on heavy stems of about the same length as the Darwins. In the heat of the day they open up, showing their attractive centers, but they close again as evening approaches.

The Cottage group was originally composed of the bright-colored, slender-flowered types collected from cottage gardens in the British Isles, where they had been grown for generations. Now, this class includes crosses of these with Breeders and Darwins, and most catalogs list the so-called lily-flowered varieties with distinctive pointed petals in this group. Cottage Tulips bloom at the same time as the Breeders and Darwins, and include fine yellows, brilliant reds, clear pinks, and the whitest of whites, as well as a wide range of shades and tints. Their stems are slender, but quite strong enough to hold the flowers upright.

The Parrot, or Dragon Tulips, are so called from the fancied resemblance of the opening flower to a parrot's or dragon's head. Their flowers are very large, with deeply slashed petals, oddly twisted and feathered, and always with green shades mingled with their brilliant colors. As cut flowers, the Parrots have unusual decorative possibilities, and blooming after the Single Early Tulips, they provide cut-flower material at an opportune time.

There are two groups in the Double Tulips. The early sorts are used by florists in great quantities for forcing for late winter and early spring sale, and are sometimes planted in gardens; the late double varieties are now being intro-

"Broken" Tulip

duced to gardens. The Double Early Tulips succeed the Single Early sorts, while the Late Doubles come with the May-flowering classes.

Single Early Tulips are forced by florists, since they can readily be brought into bloom in midwinter under glass. Where early spring weather is mild, these are delightful in the garden.

Among the species Tulips are many fascinating garden subjects. Not all of them are permanent, but most species are unusually beautiful and well worth growing. One of the most extraordinary is the Turkish Tulip, *Tulipa acuminata* (*T. cornuta* or *T. stenopetala*), 12 to 18 inches tall, with narrow petals of light yellow with red lines. *T. australis* (*T. Celsiana*) bears yellow flowers tinged reddish bronze on the outside, on stems 12 inches tall. The dainty Lady Tulip, *T. Clusiana*, is about the same height; it produces graceful white flowers striped cherry-red on the outside. Clumps in the rock garden or border are particularly effective in early spring before the hybrid forms make their display. Set the bulbs 9 inches deep.

Several brilliant scarlet Tulips have come to us from western Asia. The gay *T. Eichleri* bears large flowers of crimson-scarlet with light reverse markings, above a glistening black base. The most striking of all the brilliant red kinds is *T. Fosteriana* from Turkestan, with immense blooms accentuated with yellow or maroon at the base, on stems less than a foot high. Its variety Red Emperor (Mme. Lefeber) grows 18 inches tall, with huge flowers 9 to 10 inches in diameter of truly gorgeous brilliant scarlet coloring, produced in April or early May. Another interesting red Tulip is *T. Greigi*, with 6-inch flowers of

Lily-flowered Tulip

Parrot Tulip

Single Early Tulip

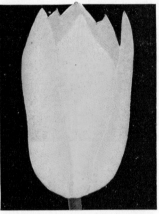

Cottage Tulip

Breeder Tulip

Triumph Tulip

GARDEN FLOWERS IN COLOR

Late-flowering Double Tulips

orange-scarlet on 10-inch stems. The blooms resemble some of the other red species but the foliage has irregular purplish brown spots. Much lower—only 6 inches tall—is *T. Hageri*, a rock-garden favorite from Greece, with 3-inch flowers of mahogany-red, colored buff and orange on the reverse side.

T. Kaufmanniana, the Waterlily Tulip, is one of the choicest of all. The cream-colored flower, heavily marked with carmine, opens in waterlily form. Among the first Tulips to bloom, it appears in April on stems less than a foot tall. *T. Marjoletti* is a late-flowering species of straw-yellow, with the petal edges feathered rosy carmine. *T. praestans* bears several orange-scarlet flowers on a single stem seldom more than a foot tall. *T. sylvestris* (*T. florentina*) is a late sort with slender bright yellow flowers on 15-inch stems.

Well-drained soil and a sunny location are the simple requirements for Tulips. An application of bonemeal when the soil is being prepared will provide slowly available plant food for the bulbs. Some gardeners dig in well-decomposed stable manure, but this is not always easy to obtain. In heavy soils or where drainage is doubtful, the

The Lady Tulip

bulbs are best set on a handful of coarse sand and covered with at least 4 to 5 inches of clean soil. Some growers plant them 6 inches deep or more. The sand will keep the base of the bulb dry but allow the roots to search for moisture. The easiest way to plant a solid bed is to remove 6 inches of soil, spot a handful of sand where each bulb is to go, set the bulbs on the sand, and replace the soil. Tulips may be left in the ground as long as they keep healthy and bloom well. Some gardeners take them up as soon as the foliage dies down in early summer, clean and dry them, and store in a cool cellar, to replant again in late fall, but this is often a difficult task and is not really necessary.

Tulips are sometimes affected by the Tulip fire (*Botrytis galanthina*), which appears on the foliage as a burnt spot and gradually destroys the entire leaf. This is a fungous disease spread through carelessness and unsanitary conditions. Spraying with Bordeaux, removing and destroying plants found to be diseased, and planting the bulbs in a new location or at least in new soil each year, are preventive measures.

The mosaic disease affecting Tulips forces self-colored flowers to "break," or become striped and blotched. The chief objection to broken Tulips is that the mosaic disease is often transmitted to other plants such as lilies.

The Waterlily Tulip

Annual Verbena

VERBENA

Although generally thought of as a perennial, *Verbena hortensis* is treated as a hardy annual. There are numerous named sorts in a variety of colors. These large-flowered, fragrant Verbenas are useful in beds and borders as well as porch boxes. The plants are somewhat sprawly in habit, averaging 12 to 15 inches in height; there are also dwarf varieties, 6 inches tall. Many of the perennial species are seen in rock gardens.

The seed of the annual Verbenas can be sown in a hotbed, a coldframe, or in the open. Set the plants in a sunny location, spacing them 12 to 15 inches apart. Choice varieties are often carried over winter in a coldframe, greenhouse, or window garden, and plants are propagated by cuttings. Perennial kinds are set out in spring or fall.

VERONICA

Many species of this desirable perennial, mostly from Asia Minor and Europe, have been introduced to American gardens. Some are low and procumbent, others dwarf and compact, and still others are tall species of notable landscape value.

One of the most cheerful lavender-blue flowers for the rock garden in April and early May is the dainty *Veronica filiformis*. The somewhat rounded leaves make a low-growing mat of foliage which is usually concealed by the tiny saucer-like flowers a few inches high. *V. gentianoides* has sturdy flowers of rich steel-blue on 9 to 18-inch stems in May and June.

Another outstanding May-flowering species is *V. repens*, with clusters of pale blue flowers. *V. rupestris*, the Rock Speedwell, and its varieties, with evergreen foliage and prostrate growth, are a joy in the June garden. The showy blue flower spikes terminate 15-inch stems.

The silvery foliage and spikes of deep blue flowers of *V. incana*, the Woolly Speedwell, on stems 12 to 15 inches tall, are often seen in gardens during June and July. A pink form is also available.

V. spicata, the most commonly cultivated species, grows 2 feet or more in height, and blooms profusely during July and August. A recent hybrid known as Blue Spire is much darker in color than *V. spicata*. Most spectacular of all are the rich blue-violet spikes of *V. longifolia subsessilis*. This sturdy form is one of the outstanding perennials in late summer gardens.

Ordinary soil and a sunny location suit Veronicas best. They are easily propagated by root division in spring or fall; some species are grown from seed. The clumps need division every few years to retain their vigor.

Veronica, Blue Spire

The showy fruits of the Viburnums are borne in loose clusters

VIBURNUM

A truly important group of shrubs are the Viburnums, many of which are native to various parts of the United States. Some assume the height of trees, and others are dwarf, compact growers. The Viburnums are outstanding for their vigor, their hardiness, and their showy fruits and flowers; some have richly colored foliage in autumn, and others provide delightfully fragrant blooms.

Among the tall kinds averaging 10 feet or more are *Viburnum Opulus*, the European Cranberry-bush, with flat heads of white bloom in May. In late summer the drooping clusters of red fruits appear, and as the season progresses the foliage assumes rich autumn tints. Also desirable is our native Cranberry-bush, which is similar in many ways to *V. Opulus*. Most spectacular of all are the forms of *V. tomentosum*, the Double-file Viburnum. This species is outstanding for its broad horizontal branching habit, its rich autumn foliage, and its great flat clusters of white bloom, followed by reddish fruits turning black. The Japanese Snowball, *V. tomentosum sterile*, produces great snowball-like white flowers in late May. The Common Snowball, *V. Opulus roseum*, is less desirable because of its susceptibility to aphids.

Several Viburnums averaging 6 to 8 feet or more are offered by nurserymen. The Withe-rod, *V. cassinoides*, bears its white flowers in June and July, followed by pink to bluish black fruits and rich red foliage in autumn. A dense-growing, round-headed shrub is *V. dilatatum*, the Linden Viburnum, with white blooms, notable clusters of red fruits which remain on the plants a long time, and foliage of subdued fall coloring. The Leather-leaf Viburnum, *V. rhytidophyllum*, is noted primarily for its dark shining foliage, which is partially evergreen in most climates. Seldom seen but very worthwhile is the Tea Viburnum, *V. theiferum*, a stately plant of upright habit, with somewhat drooping leaves. The flowers are white, and the loose clusters of orangered fruits are particularly attractive with the richly colored foliage.

In many home gardens space is limited and only a few shrubs can be grown, but among them should be *V. Carlesi* or the somewhat taller hybrid, *V. Burkwoodi*. A compact, round-headed shrub seldom more than 5 or 6 feet tall, *V. Carlesi*, sometimes called the Korean Spice Viburnum, produces its waxy white tubular blooms in rounded clusters. The flowers of this extremely hardy shrub scent the air with a sweet and pungent fragrance. *V. Burkwoodi* blooms a week or ten days later; it is somewhat taller, with slightly larger blooms, and the glossy foliage is partially evergreen in mild climates.

Viburnums are shrubs of easy culture, flourishing in full sun or light shade. Ordinary soil conditions suit them; they can be planted in spring or fall. They are seldom seriously attacked by insects and diseases, and require little care except pruning to improve their appearance and check their rampant growth.

Viburnum tomentosum sterile

Viburnum Burkwoodi

GARDEN FLOWERS IN COLOR

VIOLA

A favorite flower in the festivals of ancient Rome, the Violet has long been the symbol of humility. The diversified forms and colors of the many species and hybrids now included in the genus Viola were unknown a century ago. On the other hand, the old favorites of by-gone days return periodically to favor. Such is the case with the Johnny-jump-up or Heartsease. (See Pansy, page 200.) In addition to these diminutive Violas, there are the many hybrid forms of Pansies— the bedding Violas or Tufted Pansies, the innumerable native species, and the hybrids of the fragrant *Viola odorata*, the Florist's Violet.

Little comment is necessary regarding *V. tricolor hortensis,* the

Viola, Floraire

GARDEN FLOWERS IN COLOR

Violet, Royal Robe

Johnny-jump-up. Once it is established in a garden, it jumps about to suit itself. For the most part, the plants are hardy annuals or biennials rather than true perennials; because they self-sow readily they are commonly but incorrectly referred to as perennials.

Those plants we think of as Tufted Pansies or Violas are for the most part hybrids of *V. cornuta* and *V. tricolor hortensis*. With the exception of the very satisfactory hybrid Jersey Gem, many of them are not reliably hardy perennials, and are best treated as biennials. Viola Apricot is noted for its bright coloring, and Arkwright Ruby for its crimson and mahogany tones. Blue Perfection and *V. cornuta*, both in the lavender-blue range, together with *V. cornuta alba*, are widely grown. A popular English variety with large mauve-blue flowers accentuated with white near the center is the dainty Maggie Mott. Snowdrop is of compact form, with large white flowers. The variety

GARDEN FLOWERS IN COLOR

Violet, Rosina

Violet, Marie Louise

Violet, Frey's Fragrant

Violet, Snow Queen

Jersey Gem, the most satisfactory hybrid, gave rise to many varieties —Jersey Belle, Jersey Jewel, Royal Gem, and several others. An outstanding small-flowered variety from Switzerland is the lovely Floraire, which blooms abundantly.

Many species are useful in the garden for masses or as ground covers. Among these the dainty Birds-foot Violet, *V. pedata*, and its bicolor form are distinctive. Turning to the species *V. odorata*, one is reminded of the fragrance of such single hybrids as the deep purple Prince of Wales and the rich coloring of Royal Robe. Rosina is usually described as rosy pink—a small, free-flowering form which blooms in late fall as well as in early spring. Two delightful companions are the varieties Snow Queen and Frey's Fragrant. The double Russian form is cherished both for its unique flowers and for its fragrance. A variety called Marie Louise is listed in some nursery catalogs.

Violas are easily grown. *V. tricolor hortensis* is readily raised from seed. (See Pansies for cultural instructions.) Jersey Gem and similar sorts are usually propagated by division in late summer. If the plants are divided every other year, they retain their form and vigor. After the divisions have been set out, they may require shading and watering for several days. The native species may be grown from seed or division, and the forms of *V. odorata* are best propagated by division. To keep the various kinds of Tufted Pansies in vigorous condition, keep the seed pods removed and shear back the plants in midsummer before applying some easily handled fertilizer. Rich well-drained loam and partial shade suit these plants best.

VIRGINIA BLUEBELLS

When *Mertensia virginica* blooms in early spring, every garden enthusiast who sees it growing in the wild desires a woodland garden. In large masses or in combination with daffodils, Mertensia makes a striking picture. The glaucous foliage is profuse, and the sturdy stems, 1½ to 2 feet tall, support great clusters of bell-like flowers which vary from pale blue to noticeable rose-pink shades. The foliage disappears in midsummer; hence it is important to mark the location of the dormant roots so as not to disturb them later in the season.

Often the tradesmen classify the roots with miscellaneous bulbs because they are offered in the fall. Rich loam suits them best, and they can be planted in full sun or in partial shade. Set them 3 to 4 inches deep and group the roots in broad irregular masses. The Mertensia is no plant for formal treatment but looks best when grown like other wildflowers. Plants can be raised from seed sown in early summer.

Mertensia virginica

Siberian Wallflower

WALLFLOWER

The true Wallflowers of English gardens are perennials classified as *Cheiranthus Cheiri*, but they are seldom seen in America. They grow best in cool climates, where they produce spikes of single fragrant blooms in shades of yellow, orange, and red-brown on plants 2 feet or more in height. The showy orange and yellow Siberian Wallflowers flourishing in spring gardens are listed as *Cheiranthus Allioni*, but are really forms of *Erysimum asperum*.

Usually treated as biennials, the Siberian Wallflowers produce delightfully fragrant flowers on stems averaging 12 to 18 inches in height. They are often combined with spring-flowering bulbs, pansies, violas, forget-me-nots, and English daisies, and make a brilliant display during May and June.

Seed of the Siberian Wallflowers is sown in July or early August, and the young plants transplanted as soon as they are large enough to be handled. In mild climates they can be set in their permanent places in the fall. Where winters are severe, they are carried over in a well-drained area or in a coldframe, to be set out in early spring. Like most biennials, Siberian Wallflowers can be expected to live over winter in hardy borders if a mulch is provided after the ground has frozen.

WATERLILY

The loveliest of all water plants for the home garden are the Water-lilies, species and varieties of the genus Nymphaea. Usually they are divided into two broad groups, the hardy kinds and the tropical or tender forms. The blooms of the hardy kinds rest on the foliage on the surface of the water, whereas the tender or tropical kinds bear their blooms on erect stems several inches above the water. Shades of pink, white, red, blue, purple, and yellow are the dominant colors offered by specialists. In addition to the attractive blooms, there is the added charm of the picturesque foliage, which makes interesting patterns on the surface of the pools in which the plants are grown.

Waterlilies need full sun and a generous supply of rich soil. They are usually grown in concrete pools in the home garden, where they are planted in tubs or crates. In large pools a layer of soil at least 8 inches deep is sometimes provided instead of individual containers. Some gardeners grow them in old wash-tubs. The hardy kinds can ordinarily be successfully carried over winter by carefully covering the pool with boards and mulching with leaves. The tropical kinds are difficult to keep over winter; they are generally replanted each spring after all danger of frost has passed. Most specialists provide detailed cultural directions with all roots that they sell. If goldfish are maintained in the Lily pool, mosquitoes can be avoided.

The showy blooms of hybrid Waterlilies

GARDEN FLOWERS IN COLOR

Weigela, Bristol Ruby

WEIGELA

Like the mock-oranges, the lilacs, and other hardy shrubs, the Weigelas are frequently seen in gardens. In some nursery catalogs they are listed under the name Diervilla, which is actually the genus name of a related group of plants. The hardy, easily grown Weigelas make an attractive appearance during their flowering period in May and June; in addition, their foliage is pleasing throughout the year.

The most commonly grown form is *Weigela florida (rosea)*, with rose-pink flowers borne in great profusion on large spreading plants often reaching 8 to 10 feet each way. The hybridizers have introduced many improved forms of upright habit averaging 5 to 7 feet in height, in shades of red, pink, and white. The old variety Eva Rathke has been replaced by the rich red-flowering Bristol Ruby. Among the worthwhile varieties offered by nurserymen are Avalanche, a white kind; Richesse, silvery pink; Othello, rose-colored; Girondin, deep pink; and Feerie, a combination of clear pink and rose.

Weigelas do best in full sun and can be planted in spring or fall. Prune flowering canes immediately after they bloom.

WISTERIA

Among the showiest of hardy flowering vines, the Wisterias are widely planted in gardens. The best-known kinds are the blue and white forms of the Chinese Wisteria, *Wisteria sinensis*, which climbs vigorously by means of twining stems. Tree and semi-prostrate forms are sometimes seen as specimens in gardens. Much more spectacular are the improved forms of the Japanese Wisteria, *W. floribunda*. Among these are the Multijuga forms, with racemes of bloom 2 feet or more in length, in shades of lavender, purple, and white.

In many old gardens there are established plants of Wisteria which grow with little care except pruning to keep them within bounds. Oftentimes amateur gardeners complain that their plants do not bloom, but reliable dealers sell grafted plants which usually flower.

Plants can be set out in spring or fall. Wisteria is amazingly hardy, and grows well in most garden soils. Best pruning time is generally midsummer, and a fertilizer is best applied in late fall. Some growers recommend severe pruning for plants that fail to bloom. Branches of the current season's growth can be cut back to three or four buds, and root pruning with a sharp spade is advised to induce flowering.

Chinese Wisteria, Wisteria sinensis

GARDEN FLOWERS IN COLOR

YUCCA

Best described as a striking accent plant, the stately flower spikes of Adams-needle (or Adams-needle-and-thread), *Yucca filamentosa*, remind one of a carillon of miniature bells. It is native from North Carolina to Florida and as far west as Mississippi, but is hardy in gardens throughout the eastern United States. Many species are found in the desert areas in the warmer parts of the country. Plantings of Yucca are often seen in public parks and show gardens.

Hardly a plant for small gardens, this hardy perennial is definitely architectural in form, and may be used as an accentuating mass in formal gardens or with shrubs or perennials. It is often used at intervals in formal plantings for its distinctive year-round beauty. The vigorous growth of the Plume-poppy, *Bocconia cordata*, makes a splendid background for it. During July and August the tall sturdy spikes of white bell-shaped flowers, often 4 to 6 feet or more in height, add interest to the garden. The stiff evergreen foliage, sword-like in form, with a sharp spine at the end of each leaf, makes a stately appearance in the garden. A form with variegated foliage is listed by some nurserymen.

Yucca filamentosa

Other interesting species which are native to the South and Southwest include *Y. aloifolia*, *Y. gloriosa*, and *Y. glauca*. The common names Spanish Bayonet or Dagger, and Bear Grass, are generally used in referring to these plants. All are picturesque plants of unusual beauty.

Full sun and well-drained soil are the simple requirements for Yucca. Plants can be set out in spring or fall, allowing 3 feet between them. The flower stalk should be removed after the bloom has passed, to encourage the development of offsets, which after several years produce a flowering plant. Some growers start their plants from seed, but it takes several years to get mature plants.

GARDEN FLOWERS IN COLOR

Crown o'Gold Hybrid Zinnias

ZINNIA

Zinnias, together with asters, marigolds, and petunias, are among the most useful and free-flowering annuals for the home garden. The name Youth-and-Old-Age has been applied to them because one often sees partly faded flowers on the same plant with half-developed ones.

A sufficiently large number of hybrids of varying sizes, forms, heights, and colors is available today to make an entire garden of Zinnias. Perhaps the most striking are the Giant Dahlia-flowered Zinnias, the blooms of which sometimes exceed 6 inches in diameter and 3 inches in depth. Shades of scarlet, rose, orange, yellow, white, and lavender are offered in separate colors. Well-developed plants usually grow 3 feet tall. The so-called California Giants are distin-

GARDEN FLOWERS IN COLOR

Fantasy Zinnias

guished for their large size, and as they are flatter in form than the Dahlia-flowered types they are often preferred for cutting.

Then there are the Dwarf Double-flowering kinds, known as the Cut-and-come-again type, with flowers averaging about 2 inches in diameter, borne on plants 18 inches tall. These provide an abundance of bloom and are often used where tall edging plants are needed.

Lilliput or Pompon Zinnias are very useful for cutting; they bloom profusely over a long period, producing double flowers an inch or more in diameter. Fifteen inches is usually the limit of their height. In addition to selected colors there are several strains including one noted for its pastel colors. The Button Zinnia Red Riding Hood is decidedly miniature, with its half-inch flowers borne on 12-inch plants. Among the dwarf Zinnias, the Tom Thumb mixture is distinguished for its 4 to 6-inch plants.

Crown o'Gold is a new form of Zinnia—a variation of the giant-flowered type. Its claim to distinction is the golden yellow touch at the base of each petal of the large flowers.

Fantasy Zinnias are hybrids of the Quilled and Crested types. They produce medium-sized flowers with twisted petals on stems 2 to 3 feet tall, and are available in a variety of colors.

Zinnia linearis is a recent Mexican contribution to American gardens. It grows 9 to 12 inches tall and has a tendency to semi-prostrate growth. The single orange-yellow flowers have dark centers. It has great possibilities as a border plant, and blooms profusely from midsummer until frost.

Mexican Zinnias (*Z. Haageana*), measuring an inch or more in diameter, are valued for their rich mahogany shades and for the unique bicolor forms that occur in many of the recent hybrid mixtures. The plants are compact in form, and average 15 inches in height.

Zinnia Haageana

GARDEN FLOWERS IN COLOR

Lilliput Zinnias

Picotee Zinnias are vigorous-growing plants with medium-sized flowers. Delicate picotee edgings mark the tips of the petals.

Although the Quilled or Cactus Zinnias are by no means new to many garden lovers, excellent improved strains of these varieties have been offered by seedsmen in recent years.

The new Scabious-flowered Zinnias have crowned centers circumscribed by one or two rows of ray petals, and resemble the annual scabiosa. The plants grow about 2 feet tall.

Zinnias are so easily raised from seed that they are often among the first plants which beginners grow. Start the seed in a coldframe or in the open ground after frost danger has passed, and transplant the seedlings before they become spindly. When planting Zinnias in beds and borders, provide ample space for the development of the seedlings; usually the distance between plants should equal one-half of the height of the strain being grown. Although not particular as to soil, they thrive in rich loam, and full sun suits them best. Applications of liquid manure will improve the size of the blooms.

Cultural Practices
in the Garden

In the pages that follow suggestions are made for the conditioning of soils, the planting and care of annuals, the growing of perennials, flowering bulbs, trees, shrubs, and vines. These chapters are addressed primarily to the beginner, and no attempt has been made to treat any of the subjects exhaustively. Soil, climatic conditions, and other factors have a direct bearing on the growing of plants in the home garden. Personal experience teaches the gardener more than can be contained in any single volume, or for that matter in a whole shelf of books.

SOILS

Although well-prepared soil is requisite for growing good garden flowers, satisfactory results can be expected from the most ordinary ground. Soil is the result of the disintegration of rock through climatic action and other natural factors. In addition, the remains of plants and animals contribute to its fertility and texture.

The ideal soil for most garden flowers is a fertile crumbly loam that is rich in organic matter or humus, as it is commonly called. When soil is judged by color only, the amateur may conclude that a rich dark color indicates fertility, but such is not always the case. In most home gardens soils are not ideal. They may be composed of a large amount of gravel, sand, clay, or ashes; in many cases they fall into the classification of sandy loam, silty loam, or clay loam.

SANDY SOILS

Soils containing a large amount of sand are usually light in texture and do not long retain moisture or plant food. Because they are of loose texture, they warm up quickly in the spring and can be dug for planting sooner than heavy soils. For the most part, it is easy to improve sandy soils by adding humus in the form of peat moss, leafmold, compost material, or stable manure. A green-manure crop can be sown in the late fall to be dug under in early spring.

CLAY SOILS

Clay soils are heavy, and may retain so much moisture as to become water-logged. Slow to absorb heat in the spring, they are slow to dry out, and therefore cannot readily be prepared for early planting. During dry weather clay soils tend to form a hard crust, especially if not cultivated frequently. Fall digging and the addition of sifted hard-coal ashes and humus in its various forms, as referred to under sandy soils, are the usual means of making clay soils loose.

SOURCES OF HUMUS

Humus is the organic matter that every home gardener strives to add to his soil. Its purpose is to retain moisture, to improve the texture of the soil, to promote beneficial bacterial action, and to retain the soluble plant foods which are essential for growth. In addition, humus permits easy root penetration for plants. The following sources of humus will provide easy means for soil improvement.

Stable Manure. Experienced gardeners know that well-decomposed stable manure is not so valuable for its food value as it is for the amount of organic matter or humus that it contributes to the soil. Unfortunately, in most suburban areas it is extremely scarce and costly. Whenever available it is well worth using. If it must be obtained fresh, it can be scattered on the ground in late fall to be dug under in the spring, or it can be piled up in a corner of the garden and allowed to decompose for later use. Better still, layers of fresh manure can be used in the compost pile, as explained later.

Peat Moss. Peat moss is widely used in gardens as a mulch as well as a source of humus. It is easily applied and greatly improves the texture of soils, while also increasing their water-holding capacity. When obtained in tightly packed bales it should be thoroughly saturated with water before it is dug into the soil or used as a mulch. Peat moss is usually acid in its reaction and makes an excellent mulch for acid-soil plants. On the other hand, if used in great quantities it may prove toxic to some plants that need an alkaline soil.

Compost Pile. The most convenient source of humus for the average home gardener is a compost pile. Compost is merely decayed vegetable matter of various kinds, including entire plants, leaves of trees and shrubs, trimmings of vegetables and fruits, and when obtainable layers of stable manure. A compost pile may be made in a bed below the level of the soil, or it may be stacked up in some convenient place where it is out of sight. The ideal way to build a compost pile is to alternate layers of soil several inches thick with layers of various kinds of vegetable matter and stable manure. Commercial preparations which aid in the decomposition of vegetable matter can be used to good advantage; one of the best known is Adco. An occasional thorough watering of the compost heap also aids in decomposition; turn the pile over and restack it occasionally as a further aid to decomposition. As the pile is being developed, a pound or two of commercial fertilizer can be scattered on the top of each layer to add to the fertility of the humus. To provide good drainage, build the pile so that it is somewhat wider at the base than at the top.

Green Manures. Green manures are not as widely planted in the home garden as they should be. Many people who build new homes on made or filled land often have to work for several years toward soil conditioning and fertilization. This effort would be lessened if more attention were given to the preparation of the soil before plants were set out. Green-manure crops provide a most satisfactory and inexpensive way in which to condition soils. They not only add humus when they are dug under, but many of the legumes provide additional needed nitrogen. Where a winter crop can be planted, winter rye is worthwhile. It can be sown any time until the ground freezes and will make additional growth very early in the spring, when it can be dug under. The legume crops such as clover, vetch, soybeans, and alfalfa are especially valuable because they provide desirable nitrogen-fixing bacteria for the soil.

SOIL TESTING

Soils often vary greatly even in the small area of an average garden. Most home gardeners think of two kinds of soil—acid or sour, and alkaline or sweet; soils which are neither decidedly acid nor alkaline are spoken of as neutral. The degree of acidity or alkalinity in soil is determined by a system known as pH. Soil reactions as revealed by simple chemical tests are expressed by numbers. For example, neutral soil has a reading of pH 7. Soil tests showing indications higher than 7 are on the alkaline or sweet side; those lower than 7 are on the acid or sour side. Soil tests may reveal an extreme condition on either side of the neutral scale, in which case a toxic situation develops and plant growth is not satisfactory. Many home gardeners have learned the advantage of soil testing. Some who have become students of soils, purchase testing kits and carry on their own soil analysis, but most people find it advisable to have tests made by competent analysts at the various county and state experiment stations.

THE USES OF LIME

Lime is valuable not only because it corrects acidity in the soil but also because it improves the soil texture, aids in liberation of plant foods, hastens the decomposition of organic matter, and provides calcium. (Lime is not itself a fertilizer.) Several kinds of lime are used in gardens. The two most common are ground limestone and hydrated lime. Ground limestone is slower acting but lasts longer than hydrated lime, which is usually best for quick reactions. When using

GARDEN FLOWERS IN COLOR

lime the gardener should remember not to dig it in at the same time commercial fertilizers or stable manure are added to the soil. This precaution is taken to prevent the rapid loss of the precious nitrogen through the liberation of ammonia when these substances are put together. In applying lime, simply scatter it over the surface of the soil and dig it in to a depth of 3 to 4 inches. The amount of lime to use depends primarily upon the needs of your soil, which are most accurately determined by a soil test. Too much lime can be detrimental.

ACID SOIL

Many of our native plants, as well as the choice hybrid azaleas, rhododendrons, and other broad-leaved evergreens and some deciduous plants, require an acid soil. While most garden soils need little preparation to make them suitable, many gardeners find it necessary to increase the soil acidity when they desire to grow acid-loving plants. Acidity in the soil can be increased by the use of acid leafmold (easily made from oak leaves), hardwood sawdust, sulphur, and such fertilizers as ammonium phosphate, ammonium sulphate, and urea. Many home gardeners use aluminum sulphate, which is merely scattered on the ground and watered in. A soil test will readily determine the necessary amounts of these materials to use.

COMMERCIAL FERTILIZER

Many kinds of commercial fertilizers are offered by dealers, and these are generally the chief source of plant food for the home garden. A "complete" fertilizer includes nitrogen, phosphorus, potash, and other elements. Usually the packages present formulas which indicate the proportions of the various elements used. For example, the formula 4-12-4 means that it contains 4 parts nitrogen, 12 parts phosphorus, and 4 parts potash.

Sometimes soil tests reveal a need for an abundance of nitrogen, or phosphorus, or potash. Nitrogen stimulates vegetative growth, and if too much is used an over-abundance of foliage will be produced at the expense of blooms. Phosphorus is essential to root development and the production of roots and seeds. Potassium has a balancing influence and is essential to natural plant development; its presence in the soil increases resistance to plant diseases. These three elements may be obtained separately in various concentrated forms but they should not be used carelessly, lest they damage the plants.

Commercial fertilizers are usually dug in when the soil is being prepared in spring or fall. Additional applications may be made at any time during the year, but they are particularly effective when water is applied immediately afterward. Some gardeners find liquid manure an easy stimulant to plants in midsummer.

GROWING ANNUALS FROM SEED

Among the annuals there are three distinct groups. Tender annuals will not bloom outdoors in sections where the summers are short unless they have been started in a greenhouse, hotbed, or cold-frame. Half-hardy annuals can endure little lowering of temperature, and, like tender annuals, must not be set out until all danger of frost is past. Hardy annuals, like bachelors-button and annual larkspur, may be sown directly in the open ground; oftentimes better results are obtained when the seed is planted in the fall. Certain tender perennials like snapdragons and *Salvia farinacea*, which bloom the first year from seed, are treated as annuals because they are best adapted as such in regions where winters are severe.

It is hardly necessary to say that only the best seed should be used. Seedsmen generally have given close attention to the improvement of particular strains and varieties of annuals, with the result that gardeners can now obtain seeds of superior quality.

Seed sown indoors in a sunny window may be planted either in seed-pans or in flats. Small flats about the size of a cigar-box or shallow clay pots of varying sizes are very convenient for the average gardener. Whenever possible it is better to get new pots; if old ones are used, scour them to destroy any fungous spores that may be lodged in the porous clay. For the same reason, clean all flats well.

SOIL PREPARATION

Drainage is the first consideration. Bore holes in the bottom of the wooden flats, or leave spaces between the boards when constructing the seed-boxes. Use a layer of gravel, cinders, or pieces of broken flower-pots above the outlets in pots. Well-sifted soil, composed of equal parts of loam, sand, and leaf-mold, is the most satisfactory medium for starting seed. No fertilizer should be used.

SEED SOWING

Having provided for drainage, fill the receptacle with the soil-mixture, and tamp lightly but firmly. A space of approximately a half-inch between the level of the soil and the top of the flat allows for watering. To conserve space and facilitate transplanting, sow seed in rows. However, very fine seeds should be mixed with sand, and, if sown in small quantities, may be scattered broadcast. Sieve sand or finely screened soil to merely cover the seed. Large seeds are generally covered to a depth of three times their diameter; small seeds are given only enough covering to keep them moist or, better still, are merely pressed into the soil. In any event, make the surface of the seed-pan or flat level, to allow for uniform watering.

GARDEN FLOWERS IN COLOR

WATERING

Watering is of vital importance. A piece of moist burlap, placed over the seed-flat, will prevent seed from being washed away. Even if this measure is not taken, water should always be applied through a fine spray nozzle. Sprinkling-cans with fine spray nozzles are easily obtained; for very small seed use an atomizer. Some gardeners prefer to set seed-pans in water, allowing the water to seep in through the drainage-holes until the surface of the soil is moist.

Not infrequently during rainy spells, damping-off occurs in hotbeds, coldframes, and greenhouses. The thread-like fungus causing the disease spreads rapidly over the soil, and makes the seedlings wilt. High humidity seems to encourage its development; hence watering should be done in the morning when air is allowed to circulate freely in hot-beds and coldframes. An organic mercury compound known as Semesan may be used to check this fungus. (See page 307.)

TRANSPLANTING

Many gardeners allow seedlings to develop eight or more leaves before transplanting, with the result that spindly growth is produced. Unless the seedlings are too small to handle conveniently, they should be transplanted when the first pair of true leaves has developed. (In growing annuals which resent transplanting, use individual clay, fiber, or paper pots.) Pinching out the tops of the main stems helps to develop strong root systems and bushy plants.

A border of annuals and perennials in a suburban garden

GARDEN FLOWERS IN COLOR

In a limited way coldframes and hotbeds take the place of a greenhouse in a small garden. Many amateurs find them indispensable for getting seeds off to an early start. Seed can be sown in hotbeds six to eight weeks before it can be safely planted in the open ground, and in coldframes about a month before. Coldframes also provide a convenient place to harden off seedlings that were started indoors, in a greenhouse, or in a hotbed. In late spring and early summer both hotbeds and coldframes are ideal places for the sowing of perennials and biennials. In areas where winters are usually severe, the home gardener can make good use of his hotbed or coldframe as a place to winter over such perennials as chrysanthemums, as well as seedling perennials that may not be large enough to set out in the open ground in the autumn.

A coldframe is an unheated, bottomless, wooden or concrete frame with a removable glass top made of window sash, used to protect seedling plants from cold weather. A hotbed is of similar but deeper construction, so that it may be filled with steaming fresh stable manure and later covered with several inches of soil to provide a good starting ground for young plants. When the heat of the manure is exhausted, the bed can be used as a coldframe.

If you have a window sash on hand, you can make your own coldframe or hotbed; the sash can serve as the top and you can build a frame for it. A frame 6 x 6 feet, requiring two 3 x 6 sashes, is practical for small gardens. Place the frame in a sheltered spot with a southern exposure where it will get full sun. The sash needs a pitch of at least 4 inches in a southerly direction. The building details are simple. The sides and ends, if made of wood, should be an inch thick, and sunk into the ground to a depth of 6 inches. The north side of most frames is usually 12 to 15 inches high, with the south side approximately 4 inches shorter. For more permanent construction use heavier lumber, or concrete about 2½ inches thick. Before sowing seed in a coldframe, provide for a mixture of 4 to 6 inches of well-prepared soil composed of one-third leaf-mold, one-third garden soil, and one-third sand.

To prepare a hotbed, dig out about 2 feet of soil and fill the trench with 1½ feet of fresh stable manure. It is best to order the manure at least a week before you plan to use it. After it has been piled it should be thoroughly soaked, to cause it to steam. Three or four days later it can be repiled, and in another few days it is ready for use. Tamp the manure firmly before covering it with 4 to 6 inches of well-prepared soil. Use the formula suggested above for preparing soil for a coldframe. The sash can be put on and the frame allowed to stand for several days until the soil temperature has dropped to about 75 or 80 degrees. In extremely cold climates, manure can be piled around the sides in order to retain the inside heat. In recent years electrically heated hotbeds have been offered by seedsmen, and they are worthwhile for those who care to make the investment.

Sowing Seed Outdoors

In planting annuals where they are to grow and bloom, one should realize that well-prepared, fertilized soil usually gives best results. Preparation should take place several weeks before planting; fresh manure needs to be dug in during the fall. To be sure, some annuals grow well in poor soil, or rather are hastened into bloom with scant fertility. However, plant food, either chemical or fibrous, is generally essential in preparing the annual garden, and applications of liquid manure at intervals throughout the season will prove helpful.

Maintenance

Perhaps the most neglected part of maintenance is the job of staking. Some plants by the very nature of their growth demand this attention, while others are greatly improved and give the garden a tidy appearance if stakes are used. Do not wait until wind and rain have laid low your choice annuals; stake your plants while they are straight and easy to handle.

Annuals respond readily to moisture. It is far better to water the garden thoroughly once a week than to give the surface of the ground a sprinkling every day. In areas where water is at a premium, the garden must rely on nature, cultivation, and the use of mulches. Lawn clippings, peat moss, decomposed stable manure, buckwheat hulls, and ground tobacco stems are useful mulches for both annuals and perennials. They help to conserve moisture and are not unsightly in the garden.

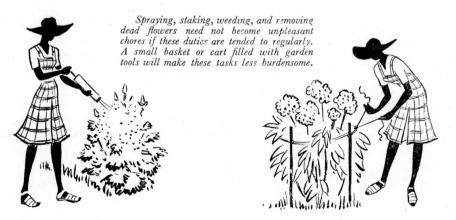

Spraying, staking, weeding, and removing dead flowers need not become unpleasant chores if these duties are tended to regularly. A small basket or cart filled with garden tools will make these tasks less burdensome.

GARDEN FLOWERS IN COLOR

HARDY PERENNIALS

All over America perennials have their place in sun and shade. They provide not only color and fragrance in the garden, but also an abundance of cut flowers for the home. In modest dooryards, in spacious gardens, and in city parks, perennials are an important part of the landscape. In contrast to annuals with a life cycle of one year from seed to seed, perennials live on for several years or longer, depending mostly on the care they get.

Many of the hardy perennials we grow today are native to our own country, and many more have been introduced from abroad. All are adaptable in some way to American gardens. We soon learn to know those that flourish in part shade, in full sun, in wet places, or in hot, dry areas. With this knowledge at hand it is possible to find plants to fit almost any situation.

Modern gardens are usually rather small in size. As a result we are challenged to make the most of the ground that is ours. Think of perennials as a part of your outdoor living-room—the plant materials which help to complement its color scheme, furniture, and decoration.

PLANNING THE PERENNIAL BORDER

Perennials are an indispensable part of every garden, however small. In the gardens of our grandmothers, peonies, iris, day-lilies, delphiniums, phlox, chrysanthemums, and a few other old favorites were the backbone of the perennial border. Today hybridizers have given us day-lilies that will bloom over five months, phlox in an amazing variety of colors, iris and peonies greatly improved in size, color, and form, and chrysanthemums of arctic hardiness and unlimited color range—to mention only a few. And in the past few years we have learned to grow many other new and desirable hardy perennials.

SIZE AND LOCATION

First of all, there is the question of size and location. If your garden is formal, the border will be bounded by straight lines. If it is to be informal, it is an easy matter to determine the curves by laying down the garden hose and moving it around until you find lines that are harmonious with the surrounding landscape.

Naturally the length of the border will be determined by the space you have at hand. As far as depth is concerned, a border 8 to 9 feet wide will provide a continuous display of color all summer. However, by using plants of moderate size attractive plantings can be developed in a narrower space. Provide for access from both sides for easy garden maintenance and air circulation. Plant diseases often breed in densely planted parts of the garden.

GARDEN FLOWERS IN COLOR

Perennial borders need some sort of background—a hedge, a shrub border, a trellis, a fence, or a wall. If a shrub border or hedge is used as a setting, allow several feet of space between the border and the background so that the shrub roots will not take all the plant food away from the border. This space also provides easy access for maintenance. Perennials, like most other plants, prefer full sun and well-drained fertile soil. A well-prepared perennial bed ought to produce good results for at least four years.

Choosing the Plants

If you are making a new perennial border or remaking an old one, you will undoubtedly have some plants in your garden that can be used. Perhaps they will need to be divided (frequent dividing every two or three years keeps them in healthy condition). In selecting material for your border it is far better to mass varieties in groups of three, five, or more than to use single plants of different varieties, for single specimens in a border usually produce a spotty and uninteresting effect. In planning your border do not neglect plants with foliage that will be striking even when they are not in bloom.

Color and Arrangement

It is quite certain that you will not always achieve the perfect color scheme the first time, but then half the fun of gardening comes with moving plants about until you find the most harmonious grouping and the location they like best. A simple rule for arrangement is tall plants for the background, low ones for the foreground or edges, and plants of medium height for the middle ground. However, the ordinary tier or bleacher effect will not give the most interesting results. Strong accent plants in the middle ground—for example, a clump of day-lilies at regular or irregular intervals, a group of delphiniums, or some showy coneflowers—will add distinction to your border.

Continuous Bloom

The ideal to strive for is an abundance of color throughout the entire border from spring until late fall. Try to group plants that bloom at one time. Flowering bulbs will provide additional color in spring; when these have faded, annuals can be set in their places. As you read the garden books and magazines and walk in your neighbors' gardens you will get many original ideas for plant combinations. See the chapter "Color in the Garden" for suggestions on grouping and arrangement. Continuous bloom can best be accomplished by the careful selection of sturdy perennials which are noted for their free-flowering habit as well as their hardiness.

GARDEN FLOWERS IN COLOR

A simple plan showing arrangement of irregular masses
for pleasing color effects

MAKING THE PLAN

After you have gathered together your list of plants, choosing the colors and varieties you like best, you can work out your plan on paper. Determine a convenient scale for easy plotting. If you like to dabble in color, use colored crayons to help visualize the effects. Remember to group your plants irregularly, and not to set them too close together. Allow space equal to approximately half their mature height between plants. For example, chrysanthemums reach a height of 2 to 3 feet; space them 12 to 15 inches apart.

PLANNING A ROCK GARDEN

Perennials have an important place in every well-planned rock garden. For the most part the hardy plants that naturally grow in rocky areas are low and compact in form. By nature, their roots prefer the protection and the moisture coming from close contact with stone. Many of them can endure hot, dry conditions easily and in fact seem to thrive on them. The sedums, the hen-and-chickens (sempervivums), creeping phlox, and the rock-roses (helianthemums) are but a few of these sturdy plants. There are also many alpines introduced from the mountain sections of our own country and from Europe that are well adapted to American rock gardens. Any list of rock plants is likely to be representative of mountain regions all over the world.

WALL GARDENS

Wherever dry walls can be utilized they add color and a pleasing note of interest to the garden. Usually they are made where there is a change of level. A wall garden of well-placed native stone provides a setting for many uncommon rock plants.

Many garden enthusiasts who enjoy miniature plants but have no place for a rock garden, find a desirable outlet by building a wall garden which lends year-round beauty. Even when there is little bloom in a wall garden, a pleasing picture is made by the distinctive foliage of tiny plants against the varied texture of the stones.

Perennials for the Wild Garden

Most of the native plants popular for naturalizing are perennials. Then there are many native shrubs which can be used for background effects to make a setting for your wild garden. Ferns and other low-growing perennials can be introduced effectively under shrubs and trees to serve as ground covers.

Fortunate is the home-owner who has a wooded spot on his grounds where wildflowers can be naturalized. By giving a little thought to the special requirements of the rarer wildings—that is, their particular needs as to light, soil moisture, and drainage—it is not difficult to create conditions under which they will grow as they do in the fields. However, many delightful wildflower gardens have been created even in city backyards.

Perennials in the Shrub Border

In spring, shrub borders are usually gay with color but as summer approaches they lack it. Here is just the place for some sturdy perennials. In small gardens with limited space, shrubs and perennials can be combined effectively in a double-purpose border, where each can supplement the other.

In selecting perennials for your shrub border choose rugged types that grow vigorously and require little care—hemerocallis, peonies, Oriental poppies, and coneflowers are good examples. To add further interest use gray or variegated-foliaged plants either for borders or in broad masses. In summer, clumps of white flowers will give the border a cool aspect.

A picket fence makes a pleasing background for a perennial border

Plants of all kinds naturally respond to care. Spraying, staking, weeding, and transplanting need not be a chore if they are done systematically. Here are some practical suggestions for keeping your garden in good order.

Staking. Stake tall-growing plants like delphinium before the wind has a chance to blow them over. Perennials that produce large heavy blooms also need support. In tying them up, try to partially conceal the stakes and the raffia that you use. After one group of plants has bloomed, dead flowers can be removed and the same stakes used for flowers coming later in the season. Good garden maintenance is akin to good housekeeping.

Keeping Plants Clean. Dead flowers are unsightly in a perennial garden and when allowed to form seed, detract from the strength of the plant. Cut off the dead flowers regularly. You will be well repaid by bloom on side shoots.

Weeding. Usually when perennials are set fairly close together, there is little chance for weeds to get much of a headway. Either dig the weeds out by the roots or don't weed at all, since you will just have to do the job over again.

Fertilizing. If your perennial border was well fertilized when planted, it will require no more fertilizer the first year. As plants increase in size many of the heavy feeders will benefit from occasional applications of bonemeal or some good commercial fertilizer. A mulch of well-decomposed cow manure can be applied in autumn.

Winter Protection. Perennials in exposed places sometimes need protection to prevent damage from winter sun and wind, which causes plants to heave and burn badly. Your holiday greens, or straw, salt marsh hay, or cran mulch are ideal for this purpose. Beware of using any material that mats easily, for it will cause the plants to rot.

Sanitation. The old adage, an ounce of prevention is worth a pound of cure, is as true in gardening as in anything else. After frost has discolored the foliage of your perennials, cut them back to the ground. Burn these dead leaves to eradicate any insects or diseases which might otherwise be carried over in the garden all winter.

Transplanting. Sometimes perennials need to be moved about for better color effects or because of soil conditions. They can be moved any time when the soil is workable, many when they are in full bloom if simple precautions are taken. Naturally, if a plant in full growth is dug without any soil around its roots, it will wilt badly and probably die. But it is an easy matter to take a plant with a ball of earth, usually after a rain, and transplant it from one place to another. If the sun is hot, provide shade for several days.

Dividing Plants. Most perennials need to be divided every three years. Rapid-growing kinds like hardy asters may require division every other year, and perennials like the chrysanthemum often need to be reset annually. Dividing can be done in early spring and fall. Spring-blooming plants are best reset in the fall, and autumn-blooming plants are usually divided in early spring after growth has started. Some species of perennials produce thick fibrous roots which must be cut with a sharp knife in order to make successful divisions; others are easily separated. When dividing, dig the plants, shake the soil off the roots, and make clean divisions, using a sharp knife if necessary. Plants having intertwining roots may require the use of a small ax. Before resetting the divisions, remove all decayed growth and broken roots.

Growing Perennials from Seed. Many hardy perennials are easily raised from seed. Most seedsmen offer a wide selection of varieties and selected strains which are worth trying. For example, a mixed packet of hardy chrysanthemum seed is bound to provide a great many surprises. Columbines, pyrethrum, the numerous forms of campanula, delphinium, and many other hardy perennials are readily grown from seed in the home garden. Collectors of rare and unusual plants who often find it difficult to obtain new species have learned to grow their own plants from seed. Perennial seed needs to be sown in late May or early June, in order to obtain plants large enough to set in the open garden in the fall. In areas where winters are unusually severe it is often best to carry the plants over winter in a hotbed or coldframe, or to provide a protective mulch. For instructions on sowing seed, see page 293.

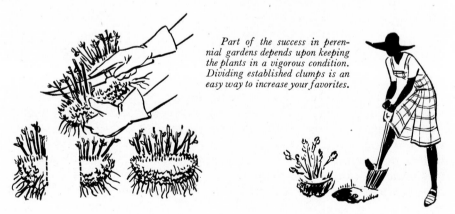

Part of the success in perennial gardens depends upon keeping the plants in a vigorous condition. Dividing established clumps is an easy way to increase your favorites.

GARDEN FLOWERS IN COLOR

FLOWERING BULBS

To most home gardeners the term flowering bulbs usually brings to mind the spring-blooming kinds like crocuses, snowdrops, hyacinths, narcissus, and tulips. These are outstanding and make a brilliant show in the spring garden, but a word must be said for the wide variety of summer-flowering kinds. These include basket-flower, Mexican shellflower, lilies, tuberous-rooted begonias, summer-flowering oxalis, gladiolus, dahlias, calla lilies, and many others.

Definitions

The word bulb is often loosely used. Actually some of the so-called bulbous plants are not true bulbs but are more correctly known as corms. Still others are tubers, tuberous rootstocks, and rhizomes. A true bulb is an underground bud composed either of a rosette of scales which overlap, as with a lily bulb, or of a series of completely enveloped coats or tunics, as one finds in a narcissus bulb. Within a true bulb is contained in miniature form the stem, the leaves, and the flower bud, all of which develop from the food stored within the bulb.

A corm is similar to a bulb in many ways but is of solid structure, showing no evidence of scales or concentric layers. The crocus and the gladiolus are typical examples of the corm.

A rhizome or rootstock may be compared to a side or lateral branch, known as a stolon; it creeps on the ground, eventually develops roots, and forms a new plant. When the stolon turns underground it becomes a rhizome of starchy structure, providing for food storage as well as reproduction. The German or bearded iris is a typical example of a rhizome.

A tuber might well be considered an enlarged rhizome or underground stem containing food for the development of stems, leaves, and flowers. Oxalis is a true tuber. Dahlia roots are often spoken of as tubers but are botanically classified as tuberous roots.

Spring-flowering Bulbs

Spring-flowering bulbs bloom when the growing year has just begun its cycle. They appear at a time when all plant growth is fresh, and make a fine display near flowering trees and early-blooming perennials. Usually when crocuses and snowdrops are in bloom, winter winds are harsh, and the pleasure the flowers bring is primarily one of anticipation. It is to the hyacinths and daffodils of various kinds that we must turn for our first group of flowering bulbs that can be combined with early-flowering perennials. The many forms of May-flowering tulips, the late-flowering scillas, and the bulbous iris finish the spring pageant of color.

Dahlias and gladiolus are widely planted by specialists who enjoy collecting numerous varieties for their distinctive coloring or size. Where space permits they can be used to advantage in the home garden either in rows by themselves or in conjunction with other plants. Often they can be used to make summer borders colorful. The small-flowered dahlias are particularly desirable for this purpose, and so too are clusters of gladiolus set in groups of a dozen or more. During the summer months when perennial borders are somewhat sparse in color, the showy tigridias, the montbretias, the ismenes, and numerous other kinds produce both a show in the garden and flowers for cutting.

LILIES

Of all the summer-flowering bulbs none are lovelier than the lilies. Although lily diseases are sometimes a problem, there are many lilies that can be grown easily in the home garden. A careful selection of varieties will provide bloom for several months. Like other flowering bulbs, lilies can be planted with hardy perennials or in the foreground of the shrub border.

CULTURAL SUGGESTIONS

Information on growing various bulbs has been given in the paragraphs devoted to each specific kind in the main text of this book. However, a few general statements are in order. All bulbs must be grown in well-drained soils. If the ground is heavy and inclined to be unusually retentive of moisture, provisions for drainage should be made. The use of liberal amounts of sand around bulbs is one means of insuring drainage. Where large beds are being prepared, it may be necessary to put in a layer of several inches of stones and cinders.

Most gardeners find it practical to mark the place carefully where various bulbs are planted. This is true not only for spring-flowering bulbs but for summer and autumn-flowering kinds as well. Many people have made the mistake of digging up an area where bulbs previously grew, only to discover after removing the soil that they have damaged something precious.

Bulb foliage must be allowed to die down naturally after the bloom has passed. When cutting the flowers of bulbous plants, some foliage should always be allowed to remain, in order to provide for the development of the new bulb. This requirement is just as essential for the tiny crocus as it is for the 10-foot lily. Some authorities recommend that lilies never be cut, unless one is willing to replace the bulbs frequently. Tall-growing lilies very often need to be staked; this work should be done before the plants have been damaged by wind or rain.

FLOWERING SHRUBS, TREES, AND VINES

The garden would hardly be complete without a few flowering shrubs, trees, and vines. These are the woody plants which we use in foundation plantings, for borders, hedges, and screens, or as specimens on the lawn. Among the flowering shrubs and trees which attain a fair size there are many which may well be a focal point in the garden. For example, a fine magnolia or a flowering dogwood, a flowering cherry, or a wisteria vine may be planted to terminate a path or a vista. Groups of flowering bulbs, low-growing shrubs, and perennials are often used in conjunction with a specimen shrub or tree to make an effective picture. Flowering vines have many uses in the garden. They can be trained on fences or walls or planted near arbors, pergolas, and porches to provide shade and to soften architectural lines.

PLANTING SUGGESTIONS

Most flowering shrubs, trees, and vines can be planted in spring or fall. Large plants should be moved with a ball of earth covered with burlap; these are sold by nurserymen as balled and burlapped specimens. They usually cost more money but they are well worth it, for they are saved some of the shock of transplanting. Small plants are generally shipped with bare roots. Where large specimens are moved from one part of the garden to another it is always wise to dig the plant with as much soil as possible; care must be taken not to destroy the tiny fibrous roots. Although spring and fall are the best times to move woody plants, most of them can be transplanted at any time of the year if proper precautions are taken to lift them carefully and provide a copious amount of water. Shading may also be necessary during hot weather. In addition, when plants are moved in full foliage it is advisable to remove some of the branches and foliage in order to prevent the loss of too much moisture. Broad-leaved evergreens that are set out in the fall should be planted as long as possible before freezing, so that the plants have some chance to become established. Where the winters are severe it is always best to provide a protective mulch, to prevent the damage caused by alternate thawing and freezing. In exposed areas broad-leaved evergreens may need an additional protection of evergreen boughs or pieces of canvas or burlap stretched on frames.

When setting out woody plants of any kind, care must be taken to dig a hole large enough to accommodate the roots or the ball of earth without crowding. If the soil is of poor quality, the hole should be sufficiently large to provide for the addition of new soil near the roots. A commercial fertilizer can be dug in, provided it does not come in contact with the roots. Several shovelfuls of compost or peat moss placed in the hole before the plant is set in, will provide humus—an ideal growing medium for the fibrous roots. When the plant has been set in place, the soil should be firmly tamped around it to eliminate air pockets. When the hole is half filled give the plant a thorough soaking and allow the water to settle before putting back the remainder of the soil. The surface of the soil around newly set plants should be slightly depressed in order to allow for additional watering.

PRUNING

Most woody plants require little care except careful pruning. Some shrubs bear their bloom on new growth. With others which produce flowers on growth of the previous season, care must be taken not to remove blossom buds. Accordingly, pruning of most shrubs is best done immediately after the flowering season. Spring pruning is often necessary for the removal of dead wood. Throughout the season pruning shears are in active use to improve the form of the various shrubs. The home gardener can best be guided in pruning by studying the natural habit of the plant; all effort should be directed to retain that natural form. Unfortunately many spring-flowering shrubs like the forsythia are often distorted into ugly globes and mounds by well-intentioned gardeners. This type of pruning detracts greatly from the natural beauty of the shrub.

Many shrubs like the lilacs, rhododendrons, and mountain-laurel produce somewhat unattractive seed pods. These should be cut off not only for the sake of appearance but also to encourage the development of new flower buds for the following year. Plants of many kinds which are allowed to form seed cannot be expected to flower as well the next season.

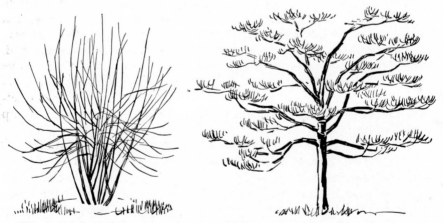

The branches of shrubs and trees add interest to the winter landscape

GARDEN FLOWERS IN COLOR

INSECTS AND DISEASES

Insects and diseases seem to be a necessary evil in the home garden, but most of them can be repelled or controlled if sprays and dusts are applied with some degree of regularity and persistence. For example, amateur gardeners learned long ago that periodic spraying of roses is the best insurance against the pests which attack them. But insecticides and fungicides are not the only means of combatting insects and diseases; several other factors are worth considering. Plants kept in a vigorous condition are better able to withstand the attacks of insects and the ravages of diseases. Many garden pests live over winter in the soil, in the remains of plants and in the weeds that often border gardens. One of the best ways to eradicate many pests is to eliminate the host that carries them over winter. Too much cannot be said about sanitation in the garden, which includes the cleaning up in late fall of all foliage and stems of plants and weeds as well. Hand-picking and immediate destruction of insects is a most practical means of eradicating them. A can of kerosene oil is a handy means of collecting the various kinds of beetles.

Kinds of Insects

Insects commonly found in gardens are divided into two classes: the chewing insects, which attack foliage, flowers, and stems, and the sucking insects, which suck the juices from the plants. The chewing insects include caterpillars, borers, and beetles. Most of the sucking insects are much smaller and less easy to detect; this group includes aphids of various kinds, thrips, white fly, the tarnished plant bug, the scale insects, and the leafhoppers.

Common Plant Diseases

Plant diseases manifest themselves usually in the form of spots on leaves and stems, and a general unhealthy appearance of the plant. Often there are parasitic growths on the plants which cause them to be distorted in form. Generally speaking, plant diseases are caused by fungi (low forms of plant life which are parasitic), bacteria, and viruses. Some are more difficult to combat than others, but many can be held in check and successfully eliminated by the persistent use of a fungicide and the persistent practice of sanitation. It is seldom advisable to attempt to treat plants that have been permitted to become badly diseased; the most practical solution is to destroy them.

A common disease of seedling plants, especially in damp humid weather, is known as damping-off. It occurs in greenhouses, hotbeds, coldframes, and even in the open ground. The tiny seedlings decay at the soil level, and fall over. Damping-off is best controlled by disinfecting the seed before planting; zinc or red copper oxide, or any of the commercially prepared materials like Semesan can be used. Some gardeners sterilize their soil before sowing seed by treating it with steam or tear gas; it can also be sterilized by placing it in containers in the kitchen range at baking temperature for at least one hour. Water all seedlings early in the day, and avoid watering during cloudy weather, except where absolutely necessary.

Methods of Control

Dusters and sprayers are an indispensable part of every home gardener's equipment. They are obtainable in various sizes, and will do service over a long period if carefully cleaned after each use. Many home gardeners find dusting materials easy to use. A simple duster can be made by attaching a cheesecloth bag to a stick; after the bag has been filled with dusting material, it can be held over the plants and tapped lightly with a stick. However, the most thorough applications of dusting material are made with a pressure duster. The attachments supplied with these dusters make it possible to force the insecticide under the foliage and through the entire plant. Dusts are best applied when there is little wind; they are more effective if used when the foliage is a little wet, either in early morning or late evening. Spraying requires more time because solutions must be diluted in water before being used, but it is often the only means of controlling particular insects and diseases. Sprayers should be cleaned out and washed thoroughly after each spraying, since many of the spray materials are corrosive.

INSECTICIDES

The most familiar spray materials for combatting chewing insects are such stomach poisons as arsenate of lead and Paris green. These are strong poisons harmful to men and animals and should be kept out of reach of children. In recent years these have been mostly replaced in the home garden by rotenone, pyrethrum, and various compounds in which these materials are included. These preparations are effective against both chewing and sucking insects and are non-poisonous to men and animals. Nicotine sulphate, a contact insecticide, commonly referred to under such trade names as Black-leaf 40, has long been used to control the various sucking insects. Contact insecticides react on the soft bodies of insects and destroy them. All of the insecticides mentioned are obtainable in both liquid and dry form for use in sprayers or dusters. When preparing materials for spraying it is good practice to use common laundry soap, liquid soap, or soap flakes to make the spray material stick to the foliage. All prepared insecticides contain directions for use, which should be followed carefully; otherwise tender foliage may be badly damaged.

FUNGICIDES

Bordeaux mixture (composed of copper sulphate and hydrated lime) and dusting sulphur are the most commonly used fungicides in the home garden. Both are inexpensive and easy to obtain. Bordeaux mixture can be prepared at home by dissolving 1 pound of copper sulphate in 1 gallon of water (use a tightly corked glass jug); in a separate jug dissolve 1½ pounds of fresh hydrated lime in 1 gallon of water. Shake well each time before using. These two solutions can be made up early in the season and used as needed. A quart of each solution is enough to make 3 gallons of spray.

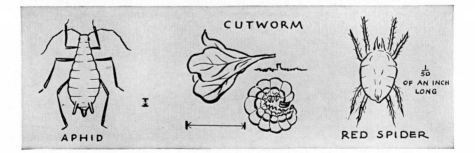

CUTWORM

APHID

RED SPIDER

1/50 OF AN INCH LONG

GARDEN FLOWERS IN COLOR

Many insects commonly associated with vegetable crops also attack flowering plants, and some pests and diseases are common to almost all kinds of growing crops. In areas where the Japanese beetle is a problem, it takes but little time to discover that this annoying pest finds its way not only to flowering plants but to fruit and shade trees, as well as to numerous crops in the vegetable garden. In the pages that follow, insects and diseases are discussed primarily in relation to those plants on which they are commonly found.

Ageratum. The plants are subject to attack by white fly, which can be eradicated by using pressure to force a nicotine sulphate solution under the leaves and through the entire plant. Leaf-eating insects can be controlled with a stomach poison or rotenone.

Flowering Almond. Borers are sometimes troublesome. Their ravages are easily discovered when the leaves and ends of the branches wilt. Cut away wilted twigs, search out the offender, and destroy it. If the damage is discovered in time, a sharp knife can be used to cut out the borer, or if it has made considerable progress a wire can be forced up into the stem until the pest has been killed. San Jose scale may attack the stems; spray with a dormant miscible oil spray in late winter or early spring before the flower buds unfold.

Althea. This summer-flowering shrub and the related hollyhocks and mallows are often seriously attacked by Japanese beetles, since they bloom at the height of the Japanese beetle season. Handpicking is about the best way to eradicate the beetles on the open blooms; as a repellent, spray the foliage with a stomach poison.

Alyssum. Flea beetles may do considerable damage to young plants of the annual kinds, especially when grown near vegetables. Spray or dust with a contact insecticide.

Anemone. The fall-blooming kinds are sometimes attacked by blister beetles in late summer and early autumn. Hand-picking or dusting with rotenone will check them. Be sure to wear gloves if you pick them by hand, for these beetles blister the skin. Several diseases are apt to be prevalent. Crown rot which affects the stems of the plants at the surface of the soil usually does permanent damage. Destroy infected plants.

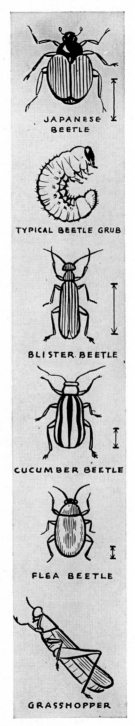

JAPANESE BEETLE

TYPICAL BEETLE GRUB

BLISTER BEETLE

CUCUMBER BEETLE

FLEA BEETLE

GRASSHOPPER

GARDEN FLOWERS IN COLOR

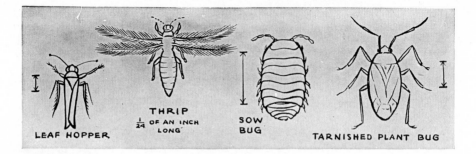

THRIP
1/24 OF AN INCH LONG

SOW BUG

LEAF HOPPER

TARNISHED PLANT BUG

Aster. Several insects and diseases are known to attack Asters, especially the China kinds. Stem borers may destroy young plants. Blister beetles are often annoying, and can easily be controlled by dusting with rotenone. When China Asters are grown in the same bed for several years, the plants are inclined to be attacked by tiny root aphids which cause the plants to wilt and die. This can be checked by digging tobacco dust into the soil and by destroying ant hills that may appear. Leafhoppers known to spread fungous diseases are sometimes troublesome. These are best repelled by an insecticide. Pests on Asters have become such a problem that many commercial growers now raise their plants in cloth houses.

Several diseases including the rot, the wilt, and the yellows have been serious on Asters in recent years. Wilt-resistant strains have been developed, and these are to be recommended to all home gardeners. Infected plants are best destroyed immediately, since diseases are spread quickly by insects, wind, and other means.

Azalea. A small lace bug which sucks the juice from the leaves is sometimes found on the plants in both adult and partially mature stages. It may be controlled with a nicotine and soap solution. Some years in early summer a small white fly appears; get rid of it with a summer oil spray. When leaf galls or blisters are found on the foliage, they should be removed and burned, together with all infected parts.

Calendula. These plants are subject to attacks of aphids, especially in hot weather. Treat with nicotine or rotenone. Several leaf-eating insects are likely to be found on the leaves; spray with any convenient stomach poison or use rotenone.

Camellia. Several scale insects are to be found on the stems and leaves. A miscible oil preparation can be used to eliminate them. Any of the leaf insects can be destroyed by the use of a stomach poison.

Campanula. In wet seasons evidence of decay is occasionally found at the base of the stems. Remove all infected parts, and water the crowns of the plants with a solution of Semesan, used two teaspoonfuls to a gallon of water. Badly infected plants should be removed and burned.

Carnation. The tiny red spider (actually not a spider but a tiny mite) can be controlled by the use of a vigorous spray of water or an application of lime sulphur. Thrips can be checked by nicotine. All leaf-eating insects can be destroyed by the use of a stomach poison.

Flowering Cherry. Watch for tent caterpillars, and destroy all nests at once. Use a stomach poison for leaf-eating insects. See Flowering Almond.

Chrysanthemum. Nematodes sometimes appear during dry summer weather, causing brownish blotches on the lower leaves. When severe infestation is present, the plant will lose a considerable amount of its foliage, or the leaves that remain will have a scorched appearance. Remove all infected foliage and burn it. A formaldehyde treatment is recommended, but this is not always practical in the home garden. A mulch of tobacco dust a half-inch thick has been found satisfactory in areas where infestation has been serious. Aphids may appear at almost any time during the growing season; spray with nicotine or rotenone. The Chrysanthemum midge which causes small swellings appearing like pin heads on the leaf surfaces can be controlled by a solution of nicotine and soap. Red spider appearing on the underside of the leaf can be detected by a gray webby mass. These insects are extremely tiny and often very persistent. Spray with a solution of nicotine and soap. The tarnished plant bug, a yellow and brown insect a quarter-inch in length, sometimes does considerable damage to plants. Hand-picking and spraying with nicotine are the recommended treatments. Several leaf-eating and stem-eating insects, including caterpillars, snails, slugs, and cutworms, can be routed by the use of a stomach poison. Mildew is common on many Chrysanthemums. It can be controlled by dusting with sulphur or using any fungicide. Rust leaf-spot and leaf-drop are other diseases that can be checked with a convenient fungicide.

Clematis. Well-established plants are often attacked by a fungus which causes most of the foliage and stems to wilt badly; eventually they turn brown and die. The fungus develops near the base of the stems just above the surface. All infected growth should be removed at once. Dust the crown with sulphur or Semesan to stop the spread of the disease. Since the collar of the Clematis is an especially weak point, the stems should be tied to a stake so that they cannot be bruised. Mildew can be checked with sulphur. The ravages of rodents are best controlled by the use of a stomach poison; a protective collar of wire set an inch below the ground and extending several inches above the soil, affords protection. The Clematis borer sometimes attacks the plants at soil level. If the plants wilt suddenly the cause may be a borer rather than the wilt referred to above. Examine all plants carefully to determine the source of the trouble and use the proper treatment.

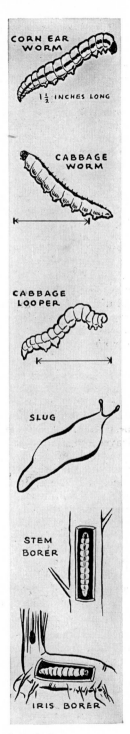

CORN EAR WORM

1½ INCHES LONG

CABBAGE WORM

CABBAGE LOOPER

SLUG

STEM BORER

IRIS BORER

GARDEN FLOWERS IN COLOR

Columbine. A leaf miner which causes conspicuous white markings in the leaves often attacks the plants. Destroy all affected parts and spray with a nicotine solution. Cultivate around the plants in early spring to destroy the eggs. Crown rot and a destructive borer are other pests; all infected plants should be eliminated.

Flowering Crab. Fire blight, causing die-back, blackening, and wilting of twigs is sometimes present in early summer. Remove and destroy all infected parts as soon as discovered. Borers may be troublesome also. (See reference under Flowering Almond.) Scale insects on the stems can be controlled with a dormant oil spray in early spring. Woolly aphids are eliminated with nicotine and soap.

Dahlia. Leaf-eating insects can be controlled with any stomach poison. The tarnished plant bug often damages the foliage; immature forms or nymphs can be checked with an insecticide. Destruction of all weeds in nearby areas is another good practice to stop the spread of this pest. Borers of several kinds may do considerable damage. Their presence is easily detected by the wilting of foliage or stems. If they are discovered in time, the stalk can be slit with a sharp knife and the borer removed. Among the other things which affect Dahlias are mildew, best controlled by a sulphur dust or a fungicide; leaf-spot, causing discoloration of foliage, is best avoided by destroying all diseased parts and burning all refuse in the fall. Wilt and soft rot can be checked by planting only healthy tubers and by rotating crops where the diseases are prevalent. A disease referred to as stunt can best be avoided by keeping the plants growing vigorously and by destroying all diseased ones.

Delphinium. Delphiniums are unfortunately subject to several annoying pests and diseases. Thrips sometimes attack the new foliage in spring, causing distorted leaves and buds which sometimes become blackened as the plants attempt to grow. Spraying with an insecticide is the best way to check these minute insects. The cyclamen mite is perhaps the most destructive of all pests that attack the Delphinium. It causes the distorting and twisting of the leaves and stems and the blackening of affected parts. Even when the plants grow to a fair size, the buds fail to open and remain tightly clustered in black misshapen masses. If the pest has not attained too much headway, it can be checked by dusting with sulphur or a fungicide. The red spider sometimes affects Delphiniums. It often passes unseen until one notices tiny webs on the underside of the leaves and the lack of color in the foliage. Use the treatment recommended for cyclamen mite. Black rot affects the crown of the plants at the surface of the soil, causing the lower leaves to turn yellow, and eventually affecting the entire plant. All badly diseased plants should be destroyed and the soil removed. Bacterial leaf-spot, which brings sticky black areas on the upper surface of the leaves, needs the same treatment as crown rot. Spray new growth with Bordeaux mixture. Bacterial mildew can also be checked with lime sulphur or Bordeaux mixture.

Dogwood. Borers may cause considerable damage to established Dogwood trees and sometimes to newly planted specimens. Examine plants in spring and fall. See reference under Flowering Almond.

Euonymus. Many species of Euonymus, especially the evergreen forms, are subject to a scale insect, known as Euonymus scale, which sucks juice from the stems and foliage. Use a miscible oil spray in early spring before new growth starts and again in late summer. Follow instructions on the spray package.

Gladiolus. The most troublesome pest is a tiny grayish black insect known as the thrip. It is often difficult to detect because it hides in the leaf sheaths and sucks juices from both leaves and flowers. Evidence of its damage is in the form of grayish blotches which eventually turn brown. Most prevalent in warm, dry weather, this pest is carried over in the corm. It is best to destroy badly infected corms. Some gardeners treat the corms after they are dug in the fall with an ounce of naphthalene flakes for each one hundred corms. These are placed in tightly covered containers, together with the naphthalene flakes, for three or four weeks at a temperature of about 65 degrees. All remains of foliage and flowers should be burned in the fall; rotation of crops is also desirable. During the growing season the plants can be sprayed with a solution containing 2 ounces of tartar emetic and 8 ounces of brown sugar. Apply when the plants are 6 inches high and repeat weekly for six weeks. Among the diseases which sometimes attack the Gladiolus are the scab diseases which cause ugly colored spots at the base of the foliage, and sunken areas on the corm. In bad cases of infection, it is best to destroy diseased corms and start over again with new ones.

Gourds. The squash bug and the cucumber beetle often attack Gourd plants. Both can be repelled by using tobacco dust or rotenone. Handpicking wherever possible will help to eliminate these pests. The cucumber beetle should be checked as soon as possible because it may also do considerable damage by spreading bacterial wilt which kills the vines.

Hawthorn. For fire-blight damage, borers, aphids, scale insects, and other pests see reference under Flowering Crab.

Iris. Leaf-spot, soft rot, crown rot, and borers are the most serious pests that attack the Iris, particularly the Germanica kinds. Leaf-spot causes water-soaked areas and brown spots on the foliage. It is best controlled by removing all diseased parts and destroying the remaining foliage in late fall. Soft rot affects the base of the leaves and the rhizomes, and results in a most unpleasant odor when deterioration sets in. This condition is usually associated with the ravages of the Iris borer. In most instances it is advisable to dig up the rhizomes and destroy them. If the borer is just beginning to make headway and the rot has not advanced to a

RUST ON HOLLYHOCK

CROWN ROT OF DELPHINIUM

PHLOX MILDEW

BOTRYTIS BLIGHT ON PEONY

LILY MOSAIC

(SEEDLINGS) DAMPING OFF

GARDEN FLOWERS IN COLOR

serious stage, infected parts of the rhizomes can be cut out and treated with a pink solution of potassium permanganate. Some gardeners sprinkle copper salt or dusting sulphur over the rhizomes. By digging in lime and super-phosphate the soft rot can be kept in check.

Larkspur. See Delphinium.

Lilac. Among the insect pests which attack the Lilacs is a borer sometimes found in the stems. As soon as evidence is discovered, the borer can be re-moved by inserting a long wire into the cavity; in some cases the damage may be so great that the stem will need to be removed. Most annoying of all is the oystershell scale, a tiny insect which appears along the stems, resembling a miniature oyster shell. Lilacs which are badly infected with this disease may die if the trouble is not eradicated. A dormant oil spray is the usual recom-mendation, to be applied according to instructions on the package, before the plant sends out new foliage in the spring. A spray composed of a quarter-pound fish-oil soap, a quarter-ounce Black-leaf 40, and a gallon of water makes an effective spray to kill the young scale in early June. Foliage is injured by the Lilac leaf miner to the point of becoming skeletonized; spray with a nico-tine-soap solution. Powdery mildew commonly seen on Lilac foliage is best checked by spraying with any sulphur fungicide. Bacterial blight, which makes young growth turn black and die, should be removed and burned.

Lily. Because of several serious diseases, some species of Lilies are difficult to grow in home gardens. The mosaic disease, caused by a virus, is easily recognized by light and dark mottling on the leaves, as well as by twisted and distorted stems and blooms. The disease is transmitted by the melon aphis, but oddly enough not through seeds; hence the easiest way to avoid mosaic is to grow your Lilies from seed. All infected plants should be de-stroyed. Botrytis blight is caused by a fungus, and makes round or oval spots on the leaves; it often appears in damp weather. As the weather gets warmer the spots dry out, leaving transparent areas on the leaves. Botrytis can be eradicated by frequent sprayings of Bordeaux mixture. All infected parts of plants need to be removed and burned. Basal stem rot is caused by bruising the bulbs, which often occurs in shipping and handling. Before planting, decayed parts of Lily bulbs should always be cut off, even though it may re-quire the removal of one or more complete rows of scales. Several other diseases including rust and brown tip are sometimes noticed. Sanitation in the way of removing all infected parts is good garden practice. Aphis found on Lilies are controlled by any convenient insecticide; chewing insects that destroy stems and flowers, by a stomach poison.

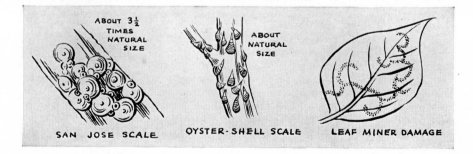

ABOUT 3½ TIMES NATURAL SIZE   ABOUT NATURAL SIZE

SAN JOSE SCALE   OYSTER-SHELL SCALE   LEAF MINER DAMAGE

Lupine. Both annual and perennial kinds are subject to the same diseases that affect Delphiniums, discussed on page 312.

Magnolia. Plants are affected by a large round scale insect which appears on the stems. As with other scale insects, a spray of miscible oil is used before the buds break in the spring.

Marigold. Aphids may be troublesome, but these are easily checked with an insecticide. Leaf-eating insects often found on stems, foliage, and flowers can be controlled with any effective stomach poison. Occasionally plants present a sickly appearance, with yellowish leaves. These should be removed and destroyed.

Morning-glory. As with many annuals, aphids and leaf-eating insects are often troublesome. These are controlled with the usual insecticides.

Narcissus. Plants are affected by several insects, but these are seldom if ever serious in the home garden. Diseases of the foliage and bulbs are sometimes due to poor drainage. Home gardeners usually find it advisable to destroy all infected plants and replant bulbs in new soil.

Pansy. Aphids and leaf-eating insects are occasionally troublesome, but these are controlled by the usual insecticides. In damp weather the plants may rot at the soil level because of an excess of moisture. Badly infected plants should be removed at once. Spraying with a fungicide usually helps to check this condition.

Peony. Contrary to popular notions, the ants often found on Peony plants, especially before the blooms open, are simply eating the sweet substance excreted from the buds, and do no damage to the flowers or plants. Leaf-eating insects, particularly rose bugs, eat Peony blooms and often do considerable damage. The best way to check them is by hand-picking or by covering the plants with cheesecloth before the buds open. Other leaf-eating insects that sometimes destroy the stems and leaves are best killed with a stomach poison. Botrytis blight is common in wet weather and may appear on the young shoots in early spring or on mature plants, affecting the leaf stems, buds, and crown of the plant. Destroy all infected parts and remove and burn all Peony foliage in the late fall. Spraying with Bordeaux mixture or any other convenient fungicide helps to check the disease. The stems are

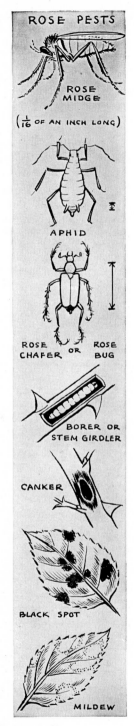

ROSE PESTS

ROSE MIDGE

($\frac{1}{16}$ OF AN INCH LONG)

APHID

ROSE CHAFER OR ROSE BUG

BORER OR STEM GIRDLER

CANKER

BLACK SPOT

MILDEW

GARDEN FLOWERS IN COLOR

sometimes infected by a scale insect which can be controlled by spraying with fish-oil soap and nicotine sulphate.

Phlox. Several diseases are common to the hardy Phlox. Leaf-spot, which appears on the lower leaves first, may spread and defoliate the plants to a serious extent. Powdery mildew, in the form of grayish masses on the leaves, is another pest. Both these diseases can be controlled by the use of a fungicide, but spraying should be done every ten days beginning when the plants are a few inches high. All refuse should be cleaned up in the fall and the stems cut off level with the ground. Stunted plants with badly curled leaves are usually infected with nematodes at the root. Red spider, causing gray masses on the undersides of the leaves, can be eradicated with an insecticide. Leaf-eating insects of various kinds are checked by a stomach poison.

Primrose. Slugs and snails often prey on the young growth in the spring and on the mature foliage in the summer months. Most of the damage is done at night. They can be sought out with a searchlight and destroyed. Sometimes gardeners surround the crowns of their plants with coarse ashes; others scatter lime around them, or poison bait (composed of a stomach poison, cereal, and a sweet sticky material like molasses). Aphids, flea beetles, and red spider are often found on the undersides of the leaves; use an insecticide.

Rhododendron. See Azalea.

Rose. Several insects and diseases are known to attack the Rose. Aphids are often found on young growth in the spring and at other times during the year. These are controlled by frequent spraying with nicotine sulphate or any other insecticide. Japanese beetles, Rose chafers or Rose bugs, and several other beetles feed upon the foliage and blooms. Numerous chewing insects, including caterpillars, are sometimes found on the foliage. All of these pests are best combatted by the use of a stomach poison. Stem borers are checked by removing the infected stems.

The commonest of all Rose diseases is black-spot, which causes black and yellow marks on the foliage; the leaf eventually turns yellow and drops off. In serious cases, an entire plant may be defoliated. Spray with Bordeaux mixture or any convenient fungicide as foliage develops. Massey dust, containing nine parts dusting sulphur and one part lead arsenate, has been found most successful in combatting this disease, if so applied as to reach both sides of the leaves. Mildew on the foliage can be checked in the same way. Brown canker, which makes oval spots on the canes, is usually noticed early in the season. When pruning, all infected parts should be removed. A dormant spray of lime sulphur early in the season, followed by dusting sulphur during the summer months, is an effective means of combatting this disease. Crown gall, which produces growths at the crowns of the plants and on the roots, weakens and stunts the plant growth. All diseased plants should be removed.

Sweet Pea. Several diseases affecting the leaves and roots are best checked by rotating crops. All infected parts should be destroyed. Aphids appearing on the leaves and stems can be controlled with an insecticide.

Tulip. The Tulip mosaic, which forces solid-colored Tulips to "break" and become striped in appearance, seems to have no serious effect on the plants, but this disease is often transmitted to other bulbous plants where it does serious damage. Botrytis blight causes gray spots on leaves and blooms. Destroy all infected parts.

Index

Abelia, 18
Acidity, 292
Aconitum spp., 185
Acroclinium, 108
Adams-needle, 284
Adams-needle-and-thread, 284
Ageratum, 19; Hardy A., 106
Agrostemma Coronaria, 175
Alkanet, 23
Almond, Flowering, 20
Althea, 21; *A. rosea*, 138
Alum-root, 81
Alyssum, 22
Anchusa, 23
Anemone, 24–26
Annuals, culture of, 293–296
Antirrhinum majus, 244
Aquilegia spp., 77, 78
Armeria, 26
Aster, 27–30
Astilbe, 31
Avens, 121
Azalea, 32–38
Azaleamum, 65

Bachelors-button, 39
Balloon-flower, 40
Balsam, 40
Barrenwort, 104
Basket-flower, 39, 149
Basket-of-gold, 22
Bear Grass, 284
Beauty-bush, 41
Bee-balm, 184
Begonia, 42, 43
Bellflower, 52
Bellis perennis, 102
Bergamot, 184
Bishops-hat, 104
Black-eyed Susan, 79
Blanket-flower, 117
Blazing Star, 157
Bleeding-heart, 44
Bluebell, 242
Bluebells of Scotland, 52
Blue-bottle, 39
Boneset, 106
Brachycome iberidifolia, 253
Bridal Wreath, 246, 247

Brunnera macrophylla, 23
Buddleia Davidi, 45
Bugloss, 23
Bulbs, culture of, 303, 304
Bull Bay, 177
Bunchberry, 99
Burning-bush, 105
Buttercup, Giant, 262
Butterfly-bush, 45

Caladium, 101
Calendula, 46, 47
Calico-bush, 154
California-poppy, 216
Calla Lily, 48
Calliopsis, 49
Callistephus, 27
Calluna vulgaris, 130
Camellia, 50, 51
Campanula, 52–54
Candytuft, 55
Canna, 56
Canterbury Bells, 52
Cape-marigold, 57
Cardinal-climber, 89
Cardinal-flower, 172
Carnation, 58
Carthamus tinctorius, 88
Castor-bean, 59
Catananche, 60
Catchfly, German, 175
Celosia spp., 76
Centaurea spp., 39, 256
Chaenomeles lagenaria, 225
Checkered-lily, 114
Cheiranthus spp., 280
Cherry, Flowering, 60, 61
Chincherinchee, 248
Chinese Lantern, 62
Chinese Sacred-lily, 193
Chionodoxa spp., 125
Christmas-rose, 16
Chrysanthemum, 63–69, 243
Cineraria, Annual, 253
Clary, 239
Clematis, 70–73
Cleome, 74
Cobea, 75
Cockscomb, 76
Coldframes, 295, 296
Colocasia esculenta, 101
Color in the garden, 9–16

Columbine, 77, 78
Compost, 290, 291
Coneflower, 79, 80
Conoclinium, 106
Convallaria majalis, 171
Coral-bells, 81
Coreopsis, 49, 82
Cornelian-cherry, 99
Cornflower, 39
Corn-marigold, 66
Cornus spp., 99
Cosmos, 83, 84
Cowslip, 219
Crab, Flowering, 84, 85
Cranberry-bush, European, 274
Crape-myrtle, 86
Crataegus spp., 129
Crocus, 87, 88
Crown Imperial, 114
Cucumber-tree, 177
Culture, garden, 289–316
Cup-and-saucer-vine, 75
Cupids-dart, 60
Cydonia japonica, 225
Cypress-vine, 89

Daffodil, 190
Dahlia, 90–92
Daisy, Crown, 66; English D., 102; Field D., 243; Michaelmas D., 28; Northland D., 64; Ox-eye D., 243; Painted D., 66; Pyrenees D., 243; Shasta D., 243; Swan River D., 253
Damping-off, 294, 307
Daphne, 93
Dasheen, 101
Day-lily, 133
Delphinium, 94–96, 152, 153
Deutzia, 97
Dianthus spp., 58, 214, 257
Dicentra spp., 44
Digitalis spp., 113
Dimorphotheca spp., 57
Diseases, control of, 307–316
Dividing plants, 302
Dogwood, 98, 99
Doronicum, 100
Dusting, 308
Dutchmans-breeches, 44

GARDEN FLOWERS IN COLOR

ACKNOWLEDGMENTS

IN planning and writing this book I have had the valuable assistance of many of my associates at the Mount Pleasant Press, as well as the comments and criticisms of friends and neighbors who enjoy gardening as a hobby. I am particularly indebted to Dr. J. Horace McFarland and to Miss Catherine E. Meikle for their helpful criticisms and suggestions in editing the manuscript. I am also indebted to Dr. Thomas L. Guyton of the Pennsylvania Department of Agriculture for his assistance in preparing the chapter on insects and diseases.

Grateful appreciation is extended to the following seedsmen and nurserymen who have made possible many of the color plates used in this book: Stumpp & Walter Company, New York, New York; Jackson & Perkins Company, Newark, New York; Bobbink & Atkins, East Rutherford, New Jersey; Greenbrier Farms, Inc., Norfolk, Virginia; Bristol Nurseries, Inc., Bristol, Connecticut; James I. George & Son, Fairport, New York; Carroll Gardens, Westminster, Maryland; Farr Nursery Company, Weiser Park, Pennsylvania; Pitzonka's Pansy Farm, Bristol, Pennsylvania; Conard-Pyle Company, West Grove, Pennsylvania. The cooperation of A. B. Morse Company, St. Joseph, Michigan; Sweeney, Straub & Dimm, Portland, Oregon, and Dr. Joseph E. Harned, Oakland, Maryland, is also gratefully acknowledged.
                                    DANIEL J. FOLEY